ACTING FOR FILM

ACTING FOR FILM

TRUTH 24 TIMES A SECOND

Mel Churcher

First published in Great Britain in 2003 by

Virgin Books Ltd
Thames Wharf Studios
Rainville Road
London W6 9HA

A catalogue record for this book is available from the
British Library

ISBN 0 7535 0723 4

Typesetting by Phoenix Photosetting, Chatham, Kent
Printed and bound in Great Britain by
Antony Rowe Ltd., Chippenham, Wiltshire

CONTENTS

ACKNOWLEDGEMENTS AND PICTURE CREDITS

I am deeply indebted to the many theatre and film practitioners with whom I have worked in my career. Particular thanks are due to the late Kate Fleming, Harold Lang and to my many colleagues including Cicely Berry, Nina Finburgh, Vanessa Ewan, Clare Davidson, Dinah Harris and Luc Besson.

I am especially grateful to all the wonderful actors I have worked with both privately and professionally, on films, in theatre, at the Actors Centre and at so many drama colleges over the years.

Grateful thanks to everyone who so generously shared their technical expertise and anecdotes including: Jean Bourne, Thea Carr, David Connell, Mel Corrie, Brian Cox, Denis Crossan, Matthew Desorgher, Peter Elliott, Paul Engelen, Peter Gleaves, David Harris, Maureen Hibbert, Niven Howie, Dave Humphries, Stefan Lange, Sharon Levinson, Karen Lindsay-Stewart, Sarah Longmuir, Sarah Monzani, Chris Munro, Ian Munro, Annie Penn, John Rodda, Brigitte Shmouker, Phil Smith, Lucinda Syson, Scott Thomas, Mike Westgate, Jeff Wexler and Jason White.

Thanks to: the executors of the Robert Donat estate for permission to quote from Robert Donat's essay on film acting; Lillian Ross and Simon & Schuster Adult Publishing Group for permission to quote from *The Player* by Lillian Ross and Helen Ross (copyright © 1990 by Lillian Ross and Helen Ross); A & C Black for permission for the quote from *Fight Direction for Stage and Screen* by William Hobbs; Faber & Faber Ltd and Judy Daish Associates Ltd for permission to reproduce an extract from *Victory* from *Collected Screenplays 2* by Harold Pinter © Harold Pinter 2000 © 1990 Fortress Films. Faber & Faber Ltd and Grove/Atlantic Inc. for the speech from *Reservoir Dogs* by Quentin Tarantino © Quentin Tarantino 1994; Methuen Publishing Ltd for the quotes from *Stanislavski's Legacy* by Constantin Stanislavski (edited and translated by Elizabeth Reynolds Hapgood); Penguin for the quote from *The Go-Between* by LP Hartley; Prion for permission to quote from the foreword to *Directors A-Z* by Geoff Andrew; Thames and Hudson for the quote from *Duse: A Biography* by William Weaver, © 1984 Thames and Hudson Ltd, London; and Wordsworth Editions Ltd for permission to quote from

The Wordsworth Dictionary of Film Quotations, ed. Tony Crawley. Every effort has been made to trace and acknowledge all copyright owners. If any right has been omitted, on notification to the publishers, this will be rectified in subsequent editions.

Thanks go to my wonderful and patient editor Kirstie Addis and Virgin Books. To Philip Wilson for driving me on, Masha Vlassova for her invaluable help on film workshops, John Donat for his kind help and Chris and Ben Roose for their valuable support.

PICTURE CREDITS
Scene stills on pages 166–167 are:

Top left – *Jackie Brown*, 1997 (d. Quentin Tarantino). Samuel L Jackson, Pam Grier (Kobal Collection).

Bottom left – *Alfie*, 1966 (d. Lewis Gilbert). Michael Caine, Shelley Winters (JS Library).

Top right – *The French Connection*, 1971 (d. William Friedkin). Gene Hackman (JS Library).

Bottom right – *Saturday Night Fever*, 1977 (d. John Badham). John Travolta (JS Library).

PART ONE
MAKING A START

INTRO

Training for film in Europe is like looking for a black hole. You know it's out there somewhere but you can't find it. Drama schools may offer a few token classes, with access to a small studio, but most are geared to theatre. The Actors Centre in the UK provides classes for professional actors and some television companies, like Sky, fund short summer workshops in camera techniques. But, for the most part, it is assumed that any acting training will apply to film as well as to theatre.

Well, to some extent it does, but film has very specific needs. Those skills are gradually assimilated by actors who work a lot on film, but for the actor getting his or her first break, it can be a baptism of fire and a wasted opportunity. You need to know how to adjust your training to make it work for you on screen.

Some film actors may not have done any formal theatre training at all. Instead of coming through a theatrical apprenticeship, they have been cast for a particular quality that the director needs. They may have been models, singers or just have fallen magically into film.

This book will show you how to break down a script from scratch and offers practical help with acting – tried and tested – whatever your background. It may serve to highlight areas where further work would be useful. There is also help for directors who want to make their dealings with actors as effective as possible, both in scripted films and when using improvisational techniques.

You need enormous stamina to be an actor – especially on film where the hours will be long, often tedious and sometimes uncomfortable. You need perseverance to get work, a discipline to keep yourself ready for it and an ability to rehearse on your own so that you are ready to make every second of screen time count. You need a stroke of luck for the first break and talent to make more follow.

Many books and teachers will tell you that you have to know your type – that you will be stereotypically cast because you have to work within your own physicality. But fashions in movies change – one year it's gangsters, the next it's period drama. A flexible actor can move between genres and many fine actors manage to escape typecasting. And even if an actor plays roles that are similar, or capitalises on a particular persona, each character will be subtly different. In the end you may

3

come to realise that you are cast in some parts more readily than others, but you need to keep stretching yourself and working in many ways on many different roles. You cannot put a ceiling on your imagination and aspirations.

The work and exercises outlined in 'The Art' section can be used for any medium, but I have chosen exercises I've found especially useful for film where you will be doing your preparatory research and character work in isolation off the set. You will find 'Quick-Tip' sections throughout the book so that you can return to them later to refresh your memory of the work.

'The Craft' section is specifically about film techniques on set that will make a real difference to your presence on screen. There are tips from top film professionals to show you how to make the most of their expertise on set. Though primarily aimed at cinema, these can be applied to any screen acting.

All films mentioned are listed at the back of the book. The word actor is used throughout for both men and women. To quote Sigourney Weaver, 'I'm an *actor*. An *actress* is someone who wears boa feathers.'

DEAR READER ...

Actors coming into films arrive from many different routes. There are also people from other disciplines in the film world for whom an understanding of the acting process is invaluable. Here are some specific thoughts for some of them:

TO THE DIRECTOR:

It helps to understand how an actor works towards a role so that you can couch your instructions in helpful language. Of course every situation is different and the old adage, 'louder and faster', can sometimes be the only possible request and can bring magical results. But as the Coen brothers remark in their foreword to *Directors A–Z*, 'Comments like, "Could we try it a little less fakey?" or "You call that acting?" or "Why did you keep making that stupid face?" must be edited'!

Generally, the most useful way of guiding an actor is through objectives and actions – in other words, what do you want and how do you get it.

I don't for a moment think that you should permanently censor what you want to say. Sometimes a 'feeling' request like, 'be more upset', can give you exactly the effect you need. There is a danger, though, that asking for external results will take the actor away from a truthful response. You need to be sure that they're not 'playing' the emotion but the action.

Actors' problems tend to fall into two camps – in the first are those performers who are not rooted in truth and are too disconnected from themselves to find any inner life. These actors tend to rely on external generalised gestures and tip towards large performances where they 'signal' or show the audience what to think.

More common these days are the actors in the second group, who want to be really truthful but are scared to react freely in case it looks 'ham' and so end up being smaller than life. They still end up looking as if they are 'acting' because the energy never flows outwards, the voice is often breathy and tense, and reactions are muted.

The first group need help with character building and finding connections with their own lives – 'this is you as if such and such were the situation'. If you have time (and I know that's a real problem during shooting), take the actor aside and see if there are any parallels in their own lives, or if they know someone specific on whom they can base their character. Being specific is the key, rather than playing generalised characteristics that lead to caricature.

Do they know everything about the role they are playing? Ask them to jot down the background of the character and how he or she got to this point, however small the part. Yes, I believe it is important (though it has become a joke) for the actor playing Lady Macbeth to know how many children she has – if any. How else can she do the speech about ripping the child from her womb? Encourage the actor to talk about the character in the first person.

If the script mentions a place or person – can they see it? What is the environment, what do they feel, smell, see in this place? If they're playing drunk, for example – how exactly is it affecting them? Are they trying to hide it? To achieve something in spite of it? When we are drunk we attempt to appear sober. What exactly do they want from the other character at any given moment? How do they get it?

Slow the actors down sometimes, by getting them to whisper the lines slowly and then speak them out loud without changing energy or emphasis. Or try cutting out pauses. Changes to tempo and rhythm are very helpful when the actor has learnt by rote, or has done them too often and the lines aren't making sense any more.

The second, timid group need different support. Encourage them to make their choices braver, to make their needs stronger, more important. Not to love someone a bit but to crave them with every fibre of their being; not to feel a little interested but to need to know more than anything in the world; not to *quite* want something but to drive to get it with every ounce of mental strength. Then tell them they can bury those needs, cover them up and act as the script demands. But those strong drives will ensure the energy of the scene will stay powerful. Sometimes it helps to give them a mental scale from one to ten. If they are reacting at around level three, ask for level nine.

Ask them to improvise and then go back to the script without changing energy. A really extreme exercise that gets great results is to get them to tell you the lines in nonsense language – gibberish. They will be 'bigger' and use more movement. Then ask them to repeat it normally without losing energy. Or, if the scene has action that doesn't seem urgent enough, try doing it without words and then putting them back in. These actors need reassurance that when they feel themselves using more energy, they are not becoming untruthful. As they are already grounded in an inner reality, just upping the stakes may do the trick.

The main difference between viewing the script as an actor and as a director is the focus. The director has the whole story in view and sees clearly how the many roles balance and interact. The director's job is to tell the story of the movie. The actor sees the world of the film through the character's eyes. The actor's job is to tell the story of the character. Ask any actor the plot and you will hear the story from his or her POV: 'There's this princess who's been sent to sleep for a hundred years ...' 'There's this prince who's looking for a wife ...' 'There's this witch who really likes spinning ...' Only very experienced actors in very small roles will see their characters as functionaries to the plot.

A director divides up the text in terms of the movement of the story. These 'units' become scenes and are then broken down again into shots that tell the story. These shots do not always match the actor's viewpoint and you may need to help the actor see how the character interlocks into the story as a whole. Reactions that feel right to the actor may not fit into your scheme of things, so sharing your wider vision can be helpful. Taking the time to do this, even with an actor in a small role and especially with extras, may prove invaluable in the end.

Some actors feel it is their right to watch playback during shooting. It can be helpful, especially if the set-up is tricky or the actor is in an uncomfortable position and needs to know that it looks natural on screen. It can work well for newcomers to give them confidence. It can also be time-wasting or damaging. (I have observed that British actors, perhaps because of their training, often don't want to watch playback as much as Hollywood actors.)

This is where *your* needs and sensitivity come into play. Whether actors watch playback or go to rushes should ultimately be your decision (although in practice, really big stars do want to work in the way they're used to). Seeing yourself on screen is a powerful experience that is bound to change the performance in some way – either for better or worse.

All actors, no matter how experienced, are nervous of not filling the role to their own high standards and are in need of support. It's very hard, when time is short and the actors are fine, to tell them they're doing well. The more comfortable that you make them feel, though, the better they'll perform and the braver they'll become.

There is no better way of understanding how actors function and how vulnerable they are, than acting yourself. When directors work as if they were actors, they find the experience really revealing. So, apart from a few asides, the rest of this book is written as if to the actor.

The only instruction Michael Curtiz ever gave to James Cagney was,

'Don't do it the way I showed you. Do it the way I mean.' So be an actor and try out all the exercises. The more you know about how actors need to function, the more chance you stand of getting them to do it the way you mean.

TO THE FILM ACTOR

So you've been at the cliff face already. Perhaps there was more that you wanted from the work or something that didn't completely satisfy you.

You know all about the problems of working those long hours, doing scenes out of order and meshing your vision of the role with the director's. How did you keep that vision alive, take after take? Did your tensions get in the way? Were you pleased with the results? Now you want to go further, take on bigger challenges or increase your range of roles. Good actors are never satisfied, so you will be on that quest for the rest of your career. When you're not, it'll be time to retire!

I hope this book offers some things that will be new to you and new ways of thinking about things that aren't.

As well as continuing to work on film at every good opportunity you get, I also urge you to do theatre or theatre workshops of every sort: improvisations, classical theatre, physical theatre, comedy, tragedy, mask work, clowning and high comedy. By exploring every different kind of reality, you will feel more confident at finding the peculiar super-reality needed by film. And you will open yourself up to new choices and instincts.

TO THE THEATRE ACTOR

You already know how to act, how to approach a role and how to find an imaginative reality. You may be reading this book out of general interest to see if there are some extra tips you can pick up or because you haven't done much film work and are wondering what differences there are.

Theatre actors sometimes have trouble relating the work they do on stage to acting for the camera. In theatre you play to a thousand eyes. In film you are seen by one – the camera. Imagine a triangle: for theatre, the apex of the triangle is pointing at the stage and the wide end is the audience – you radiate outwards towards them. For film, the triangle is reversed. All the interaction is happening along the wide end – between the actors. The energy from that interaction is gathered to the single point of the apex, which is the camera. The camera does the work for you. On screen you never play to an audience – you don't even play to the camera. The camera observes you.

As a play gets closer to opening night, the director starts standing at the back of the stalls – he or she retreats from the actors to get the wider picture. In a film, the director does it in reverse. First he shoots in long shot, then mid-shot and finally in close-up. He advances on the actor to get the closest, most intimate view.

The camera will pick up the slightest hint of showing the audience what you are thinking. It really is like being under a microscope. This shouldn't frighten you – as long as you really know what you want and drive that need, you will appear real.

Your performance doesn't need to be held in or made smaller, as long as you are carrying out your objectives and these may be enormous. There is an exercise used by Stanislavski for theatre actors: start with your own imagination and belief in the circumstances, then widen your circle of concentration to include your fellow actors, then to include the whole stage and finally increase the circle to include the audience. For a tight film close-up, rewind that circle right back to its beginning. There is no audience, no wider circle, only that enormous concentration held at its centre – your thought.

The important thing is to make sure that you're simply talking to the people in the scene as you would in life, without worrying about being heard by anyone else. Instead of playing *to* an audience, you are recorded *by* a camera. Because it has become second nature for you to talk to the person sharing the stage and, at the same time, to open that reality out to an audience, it is hard at first to give yourself permission to cut out any sense of playing to a watcher or listener. To trust that the smallest flicker of thought will be seen.

Thanks to the wonders of modern technology and the marvellous sound department, you need never raise your voice in close-up. The people close to you on set may not even hear you, but the ones with headphones will! For long or wide shots, you may need to give more volume, but again, it will be only the volume that you'd need in life. You may find this enormously liberating.

The other really big difference from theatre is that you do only short moments of the role, which you have to repeat again and again, and these moments are usually completely out of order. So it is hard to get a sense of the through line and to experience the character's life as a continuous journey. Instead, it is a continual experience of single moments. Which can be exciting as well as challenging.

What might come hardest is the boredom. Unless you have a really large role, you will find the pace desperately slow and often be called for whole days and do nothing. Try to get on to the set for a while. Watch the whole circus in operation and see how it all works. Bring a good book. Stay relaxed and prepare for your role.

Most actors enjoy working in different media. Film is likely to reward you more financially but I think you'll find it emotionally rewarding too. I hope your career will enable you to work in both film and theatre. Ralph Fiennes has said he finds theatre more actor-friendly but film can show things in a human face in a way that theatre isn't able to. The great actor, Robert Donat, wrote, 'Of this I am quite certain. I am a better actor for my film experience. Two qualities – concentration and sincerity – are even more necessary on the screen than on the stage, and one's work cannot fail to be the richer for the exercise.'

TO THE SINGER

You are already working as an actor! A lot of singers, especially opera singers, are very shy about acting. And yet in a song or an aria you are acting out the thoughts and needs of the character – singing it in just the same way as an actor uses spoken text. Speak your songs aloud and you will see what I mean.

Songs (Sondheim excepted!) do not use a lot of subtext. That is, they say what they mean, unlike most film scripts. You may need to work a little to find out what your character means underneath what they say and trust that thought, letting the words take care of themselves.

I often ask actors to work the other way and sing the text. This gives them a freedom and allows them to feel the weight of the words. So you're already starting with an advantage. Sing your text and explore it emotionally as you do so. Now whisper it and keep the thoughts and feelings that you found. Now speak it keeping the same interior connection with the words.

If you're a soprano, tenor or counter-tenor, you may speak with your larynx still slightly in the singing position. This will have the effect of taking your pitch up a little and making you sound a little 'poetic'. Make sure you're acting in a normal speaking voice and get some help from a spoken voice teacher if you find it difficult to access a stronger voice or your lower range.

You are already using the emotional energy needed for performance and simply need to refocus it.

TO THE DANCER

You have enormous commitment, self-discipline and energy. You have an inner vision that releases itself into the outside world through your body. Many actors would envy you that release and freedom of movement. But text may daunt you.

The impulse that leads to a movement is exactly the same impulse that leads to words. Start by finding a dance for your character and then add sounds to go with the dance that make you feel like the character. (You don't have to be naturalistic.) Add words to the dance – these might be chanted or sung or whispered. Distil the dance into some key movements – these can still be surreal – and couple them with some key words. (These are the character's 'Psychological Gestures'.) Now bury these movements within you. Stand still and speak normally, but let the internal dance infuse your words. This exercise can be a wonderful way for an actor to work, breaking patterns and releasing new character possibilities.

Because you may have very strong abdominal muscles, especially if you are a ballet dancer, it could be hard to release these muscles to breathe deeply. This will increase nervousness, lead to neck and face tension and take your voice pitch higher. So it would pay dividends to work on relaxation, breathing and voice.

Capitalise on your innate grace, feeling for rhythm, posture, poise and energy.

TO THE PRESENTER

Being comfortable with microphones and cameras will be a great asset. But if you do only one kind of presenting – for example, a music programme, a children's programme, or advertising – you will be using just one aspect of your persona. It is easy to become used to certain energy or intonation patterns, so work on lots of different material to widen your choices.

If you have been presenting a news-based or current affairs programme, you have had to find an objectivity and detachment from your own feelings about the material. You've been used to communicating facts. You may have been using an auto-cue, where there is no time to absorb the text in any depth but only to present it with clarity. So it would be helpful to work on material that engages you emotionally – plays and poetry.

The big difference between presenting and acting is that you need to inhabit a fully rounded character who springs from you but is not you – who must feel like you but who takes choices you might not take – who reacts as you do not normally react – who uses words that are not yours and yet are the only ones possible in that situation.

Film is also 'fourth wall'. That is, the camera is prying into a private world – you are not interacting with the viewer. Therefore you won't look into the camera lens. Camera and audience no longer exist for you, only the imaginary world you are in and the characters who inhabit it. You no longer have to consciously please or interest the viewer, only believe in the given situation and engage with it.

TO THE MODEL

If you are a model, you will already have a rapport with the camera. You're comfortable sharing your thoughts and feelings with the lens. You've also been surviving in a tough, competitive world. So the round of interviews and auditions, meetings and screen tests won't be new to you.

But you may never have needed to use text or had to enter the world of another character. You'll benefit from an organised approach to the acting process to help you find your character and deal with the dialogue.

Instead of relating directly to the camera, it will observe you as you interact with other characters and exist in an imagined reality. Instead of capturing a fleeting moment, you may be sustaining a part throughout the film, so you will need to know your character as well as you know yourself. This means knowing exactly what is the same and what is different between you and your role and how to use the 'magic if' – 'if I were a drug dealer', 'if I were a doctor', 'if I lived in 1900' and so on.

Don't be frightened of text. After all, you speak all the time in life to get what you want and to negotiate the complicated conventions of society. Improvise your text in your own words. Then, when it feels real, change to the given words. Keep moving between improvisation and script until they feel the same.

TO THE BEGINNER

Getting your first film role or screen test is thrilling and terrifying. The excitement you feel will transform itself into energy and magic. Sometimes, though, nerves stop you making the most of your opportunity. If energy is unfocused, it won't serve you.

When the first take is over, how do you find the way to do the next twenty? How do you prepare a role without an organised rehearsal? How do you keep the logic of that role when you shoot completely out of order? I hope the sections that follow will help to answer some of these questions and more.

Take every opportunity you can to get used to every part of the filming process. Do television, commercials, student films and go to workshops. The more you work in front of the camera, the more you can forget it and concentrate on exploring your character's relationships and desires.

TO THE ACTING TEACHER

I'm sure you will have come across some of these thoughts and exercises before but perhaps these are presented differently or have a different focus or interpretation. And there will be fresh ones.

This book has come out of a direct involvement in the process of film-making, in working with many skilled film directors and fine actors and in helping prepare roles and scripts for real parts in real films. And I have seen these exercises make a tangible difference.

Sometimes they have released potential talent into fine performances, and the work has provided insecure performers with confidence and support.

Most importantly, in an industry where most actors have little power in the final product, thorough preparation has given them a sense of having some control over their own destinies.

For, after all, isn't that why we do our work? To become facilitators and enablers. Not to go on helping the actors we work with for ever, but to open up ways for them not to need us any more. To take over the work themselves.

ACTING IS CHILD'S PLAY

Dictionaries define acting as 'play' and 'freedom of movement' as well as 'performing'. When we enter a darkened auditorium, we join in complicity with the cast. We agree to suspend disbelief and believe in the make-believe, and in return we hope to be entertained, uplifted or enlightened. So a performance is a shared game – the great French teacher, Jacques Lecoq, called it *le jeu*.

But it's a serious game that requires total belief and commitment from the actor in the moment of playing. When my son was seven, he had a cardboard box in the garden that was his spaceship. He believed in it utterly and I humoured him as he added bits and pieces to it every day. Eventually it was time for lift-off and he was inconsolable when he didn't soar above the house in his cardboard box. Your belief in *le jeu* must be as total as when you were seven.

You remember how engrossed you were in the world of miniature cars, your dolls, your train set or an upturned table that took you across dangerous oceans. The game of tag or hide and seek that got too real and your heart raced as you tried to avoid what felt like certain death. The exhilaration of sneaking out of the house after dark that could turn to terror in a moment as the shadows moved.

This is what Stanislavski called the 'magic if': if . . . you were a racing driver, a parent, an explorer, a wanted criminal or an escaped convict. And in the same way that you were able to leave your magic world instantly when your mother called you to orange juice and cakes from the back door, so you can move between the parallel worlds of the reality of your imagination and the actuality of your surroundings. It is what allows you to notice the aeroplane going over, remember the continuity, hit your mark – all without losing a heartbeat of the character. It is what lets you play Hannibal the Cannibal or Hamlet the Prince day after day without going insane. It's what actors call 'flying'.

Acting is not about having 'a bag of tricks' but about learning to remove the protective blocks that inhibit our natural responses. And then combining that childlike instinct with an adult sensibility and focus. It is about trusting the simplicity of an inner truth. Rod Steiger said that 'all artists have one quality that is priceless – eternal childhood'.

There is a moment early in most actors' training when they realise the make-believe must be for real. The body of your dead lover lies at your feet and you are saying the lines beautifully, movingly – even crying a little. And the director says, 'I don't believe you.' And you think, 'But I'm acting really well.' And the director says, 'But he's your lover for God's sake – and he's dead. How does that make you feel?' And you feel a little fear, a little excitement and you think, 'But I can't possibly do it for real ... if that really were my lover, and he was dead, oh my God!' And you suddenly realise you've got to go all the way in belief. In that moment you have to give yourself up to it totally – even though it's a game. It's an amazing moment – a breakthrough. And your work will never be the same again.

Or maybe you really do feel it and yet a similar conversation still happens. You know you've just done exactly what the director is now asking you to do. You're feeling it but we're not reading it. Maybe you're thinking about feeling it. Acting is about communicating. Film acting in close-up can be more private, more internalised than stage acting but the very term 'acting' means the energy goes outwards into action. That action might only be a thought but it is still action and we will see it in your eyes. You can never go dead for a second on screen.

How to act on film: commit to complete belief (or make-belief) in the situation; know what you want; act to get it. Or: think hard; really listen; keep breathing; speak and move when you need to. 'That's all, folks.' It sounds easy but it's an engrossing lifetime's work. Acting is doing – action, reaction and interaction. No book can make up for the experience of getting out there and acting but it can point you in the right direction. It can help you ask the right questions even if it can't provide all the answers. Acting is something you used to do as a child. Now you just have to go back to that innocence – that belief.

THE PLAYING FIELD

Unfortunately your inner child has to operate in a hard adult world. Apart from an elite band in Los Angeles and maybe in India, very few actors in the world can make their livings entirely by doing films. (Indeed, very few can make a living entirely by acting!) For most actors, a film part is a rare and prized opportunity. All the more reason, then, to be prepared when you do have the chance to work on a movie.

In the last few years, there has been a surge of American-funded film productions made in Canada, Australia, Britain, France and Ireland. This is partly to do with tax concessions and partly to do with the wealth of technical knowledge available at a good price in these countries. British film crews, for example, are judged to be amongst the finest in the world and yet earn much less than their American counterparts.

Britain has also been enjoying more international success recently from home-grown films such as *Four Weddings and a Funeral*, *The Full Monty* and *Billy Elliot*. The studios at Pinewood, Shepperton and Bray, which had been half empty and in danger of closing through the bleak years of the 1970s and 80s, are now so full that other stages and studios are hurriedly being built or converted. If it had not been for the perseverance of dedicated film-makers, the great mansion house studios would have been converted to luxury hotels long ago, for the film business in Britain had all but disappeared. World events have knocked things back in the short term, but in the last few years it has been busier than ever. Film production expenditure in the UK rose from £98 million in 1992 to £750 million in 2000. That's more than a 750 per cent increase. Figures released from the Cinema Advertising Association in summer 2002 showed UK box office takings to have been the highest on record since the bumper summer of 1972. All of which is very good news for actors.

It's not only the home-grown produce that's providing jobs for European actors. American-funded films made in Europe tend to use local actors as well as the Hollywood 'money'. (The 'money' is the title given to stars whose names are so appealing that the film is financed in the hope that the box office will reflect that appeal – and their salaries reflect that nomenclature!) British themes have become so fashionable lately that Hollywood stars (such as Cate Blanchett in *Charlotte Gray* and *Elizabeth*, Gwyneth Paltrow and Ben Affleck in *Shakespeare in Love*,

Angelina Jolie in *Lara Croft: Tomb Raider*, Jodie Foster in *Anna and the King* and Johnny Depp in *Neverland*) are queuing up to do British accents in movies and British actors are getting cast in all the supporting roles.

And it is not just Britain that has been enjoying this growth in film opportunities. More European directors than ever are being given American money to make English language films with international casts. European films have always had – and still have – a reputation for fine acting. This may be because in Continental Europe there has been a strong 'art house' tradition to filmmaking. In France, cinema is known as 'the seventh art'.

Owing in no small part to the Oscar-winning success of Sam Mendes' *American Beauty*, the emerging British directors who have come from a theatre tradition are gaining a new respect in Hollywood. And in America and Europe, many actors – like Kevin Costner, Clint Eastwood, Warren Beatty, George Clooney, Jodie Foster and Kenneth Branagh - have been moving over to directing.

A talent that these theatre and performance-based directors share is an ability to deal with actors and acting. They take the concept of theatre rehearsal with its depth of focus on character and text into their preparation for the screen. Of course, some film directors who don't rehearse still have a natural affinity with actors and know what makes them tick. But it sometimes comes as a surprise to first-time film actors to discover that not all film directors have this skill. These directors often don't come from a background that has provided this knowledge. They have been editors or writers or directors of photography and their skills are about movie-making not directing actors. They can make them look wonderful and they can edit out the fluffs but they can't cure acting problems. Or they are often just too busy.

Peter Ustinov once said, 'The film director is rather like a cabinet minister: it's a vague profession. Anybody who sets out to be a film director must start somewhere else.' There are so many elements to making a film and a director may become very successful by casting competent actors and then being brilliant at the action sequences or the visual elements of storytelling. The director Lindsay Anderson, whose prophetic film *If . . .* is being rediscovered by a new generation of film-goers, said that casting was 90 per cent of directing. You could say that good casting is part of the brilliance, but if it lets the director down they don't all know how to help: their skills lie in directing the film, not the actors.

A director often relies on actors being able to get themselves out of trouble and the notes that they give may actually hinder rather than help. An experienced actor learns how to interpret those notes to make them work. Which is what you need to do.

PLAYING BY THE RULES

However talented you are, it is hard, though not impossible, to break into films without an agent. Leading roles are usually cast from a shortlist known to the casting director personally or by repute. Or the director and producers will ask for someone specific. Actors for supporting roles are sometimes suggested by agents regularly used by the casting director. Sometimes the casting department will browse through *Spotlight*, where all British actors have an entry, and if you look really right you could get a call – with or without an agent. But this is unlikely to happen if you are in a mainstream casting category where every agent will have dozens of actors on their books who could play the role.

You can write around the casting agents directly and if your picture lands on the desk at precisely the right moment, especially if you have distinctive looks or peculiar skills, it could happen. But it's rare.

Getting an agent is hard. They need to see you in something. It doesn't have to be a film, but some are better than others at journeying to see you in a far-flung fringe show. If you go to an accredited drama school, then agents will attend the final showcases and you may get one that way. It's worth doing student films and low-budget movies to get yourself a show reel. You can pay to have one made, but if you can get clips from actual productions it looks better.

A good agent is like gold dust but an average agent is going to greatly increase your chances of work. Casting directors and producers much prefer negotiating through an agent. There are co-operative agencies run by groups of actors who put in a certain amount of time and money to keep them operational. It takes a lot of time and effort but at least you will feel you are doing something concrete about getting work.

Agents don't all get you work as actively as you'd like, but they make it more possible for you to seek work yourself and they handle the negotiations when you get it. You should pay only around 10–15 per cent of your fee to your agent (although some charge more for certain types of work) and in theory they should pay for themselves by getting you better money than you'd get for yourself. Never join an agency that asks for money up front.

In America some actors have a manager as well as an agent, whereas in Britain the role of personal manager and agent is usually combined. In

Hollywood, the agent is very powerful and may put together a 'package' of the director, the star and the supporting actors.

CULTURAL DIVERSITY

Channel 4 has started a cultural diversity database and both the Actors Centre and Women in Film have recently held workshops and seminars exploring neutral casting for roles. This means that unless the plot demands specific casting, a character can be of any race. Often this doesn't happen simply because it has not occurred to the writer, director or producer to cast the part like this. Britain lags behind America in using neutral casting and in having ethnic role models who are big box-office stars. (The year 2002 was a great Oscar night for black actors when two African-Americans, Halle Berry and Denzel Washington, won Best Actor awards.)

More actors from Africa, the Caribbean, Asia and the Far East, as well as many for whom English is a second language, are entering drama schools in Britain and this is increasing the available pool of talent for film-makers to use. The situation is improving but more are needed.

Directors in the West, however, remain predominantly white. As do writers, producers, casting directors and film crews. Only when all these areas contain a mix of ethnicity will true integrated casting become a reality and challenging roles be created for all actors.

WOMEN IN FILM

Most films offer fewer parts for women and leading roles tend to be younger than those written for men. Things are changing gradually and female heroines like those in *Thelma & Louise*, *First Wives Club*, *Nine to Five*, *Run Lola Run* and the *Alien* quartet can now be the protagonists driving the action rather than just passive supporters. European films in particular, like *Under the Sand* with Charlotte Rampling or *La Pianiste* with Isabelle Huppert, offer stronger roles for women and deal more with older women.

Female directors are still in the minority. The more women writers and directors work in film, the better roles women will find. The organisation, Women in Film, offers support and workshops for women already working in the industry.

TO WALK ON OR NOT TO WALK ON

There are many agencies that you can join to do extra or walk-on work. In Britain you will find these listed in *Contacts*, the reference book published by Spotlight. But should you?

The positive aspect is that a little extra work will make you familiar with a film set and put you at ease when you get a role. The director Blake Edwards first worked as a film extra, and distinguished French actor Simone Signoret learnt her craft by starting as an extra and watching others. Avoid television, where you run the risk of someone's computer listing you as a walk-on, but you could consider some background work on a commercial or film. You can do it under a pseudonym but you won't want to do it for long.

The negative aspect is that the work is boring, soul-destroying and you mustn't get known to casting people as an 'extra'. It's also badly paid. It's certainly no route to acting work.

Stand-ins and runners are often trying to break into acting or directing and again, if you're offered a short spell, by all means take it. But see it as a totally different area to your job as an actor.

If you are offered a named part, even if there are no lines or very little dialogue, you will be treated in all respects as an actor. It's a very status-ridden industry – extras even eat in different tents on location!

WORKING IN THEATRE

I really recommend that every film actor does theatre work as well. Tom Hanks said in an interview that film is a director's medium, television is a producer's medium and theatre is an actor's medium. And indeed, a lot of Hollywood actors are coming over to London or going to New York to do theatre.

Theatre gives you the luxury of time to develop characters in depth and experiment with brave choices. And if you do other non-naturalistic styles from different periods and genres, you will find there are different kinds of reality. This will not interfere with your film work but give you a new insight into it.

Because of the long rehearsal period, there is not the pressure, as there is in film, to find the 'right' performance instantly. There is continual interaction with the other characters and the relaxation and shared responsibility of teamwork in performance. In film, preparation is done in isolation. Theatre rehearsal allows the freedom for exploration and growth.

A theatre performance allows you to make your own mistakes. You become your own director and editor, albeit guided by the original rehearsals. You repeat each night, but not in little snippets as in film, but through the whole linear development of the character so that you emerge with more knowledge for the next night's journey – when it will all happen again as if for the first time.

And you get instant feedback from the audience, something theatre actors always miss in film. This living immediacy, depth of characterisation and wholeness of performance will give you more confidence for the fragmentation of film.

Theatre is like exploring the universe through a telescope and film is like examining the atom through a microscope! But the macro and micro worlds illuminate each other.

THE BIG SCREEN

So often books and acting classes lump film and television together as if they were one and the same, whereas each presents a unique challenge to the actor. As well as some technical differences, which we'll explore in a minute, the main divergence is one of style. Yes, of course there are overlaps and many television dramas contain fine, subtle acting and excellent cinematography. Nevertheless, when you roam around your television dials in the evening, can't you usually tell whether you're watching something made for cinema or television? (And incidentally, I bet you can always tell a documentary and that you're watching a 'real' person and not an actor. But that's another story.)

I think it's worth exploring the differences, as most European actors work more in television than film and drama students often base their acting aspirations on television role models. So when they come to film they may be unprepared.

Some of this difference in style is really a difference of money. Feature films have the budget to allow the director to make sure each take is visually perfect and contains the best performances possible. That means each scene is shot from different angles and each angle is done in many 'takes'. Just to give you an idea: a television soap is made on video in one or two days and a drama might take a week. A more ambitious mini-series done on film could have a six-week schedule but a film destined for the big screen will normally shoot from between ten to thirty weeks or longer, depending on the budget. Television talks budget in terms of thousands – sometimes hundreds of thousands – but film in millions – sometimes hundreds of millions.

A TV film would expect to make from four to five minutes of screen time in a day's shooting to keep within budget, whereas a feature film would only be looking for between one and two minutes at best. That means, every minute of film you see on screen has taken a day to shoot. Visitors to sets arrive in eager anticipation and are bored to death after the first hour. 'It's so slow,' they say. You need stamina to make a movie. But the more time you have, the more of a perfectionist you can be.

Stanley Kubrick, the extreme perfectionist, whose films are classics and who used to shoot a lot less than a minute a day, would say that time was the director's most precious commodity. For the actor it can be a marathon of waiting.

Although we see a lot of feature films on television, either re-edited in 'scan and pan' (where someone decides which bit to fit into the television screen) or in their original 'letterbox' format, they are designed to be seen in a cinema – in the dark – with each close-up of the human face blown up to fifty times its normal size. If that isn't going to affect style I don't know what is. That face is going to be scrutinised for truthfulness as if under a microscope. The smallest twitch, tension or desire to 'show' us the emotion is going to be magnified in a way that television will never do. That is until every home has a projector playing the TV in the dark on to a giant screen. Even then I think we will accept different styles from television and film because of the way the two genres have developed and what we expect from them.

We feel a lot more intimate with TV personalities. With all their human imperfections, they have been sharing our homes – sometimes as a kind of wallpaper – for a long time now. When close-ups are used in television, they are viewed more or less in proportion to the size of a real human head. Television actors often report that people come up to them in the street thinking that they are friends and, because they share our homes with us, in a way they are.

Lately television has started to do more and more 'docu-soaps' using real people, who in turn become personalities, thus blurring the line even more between them and us. Hence we accept all sorts of imperfections and habits from actors on television that we wouldn't expect to see in film acting.

Television scripts are wordier than those used in film. The smaller screen gives us less visual detail to feast our eyes on and to give us clues and we watch in a lit room, so television drama has a stronger emphasis on dialogue than films. It comes to us in a direct line from radio where producers were thrilled by being able to add pictures to their words. Indeed, many people only half watch television whilst doing other tasks, so they need to listen to the story as well. You don't want to miss the plot line while you pour your cup of tea.

When television drama first appeared, it took over some of the style of theatre. At first, it began as outside broadcasts of stage performances. Some of this theatrical connection lingers and situation comedies are often still filmed in front of live audiences with stand-up comedians 'warming up' the house.

Television dramas used to be rehearsed for several weeks in a church hall like a stage production and then moved to the studio for a rehearsal day. They were filmed the next day using four cameras, with the director choosing the shots as he (they almost always were 'he' then) went along. Initially it wasn't recorded but went out live, which was pretty nerve-wracking to actors. Unlike theatre, you had to remember all the white marks to hit as well as the dialogue and rehearsal time was short. Inevitably nothing seemed to transfer smoothly from the church hall to the recording studios, moves were changed at short notice, lines were fluffed – and it went out to a huge audience by theatre standards.

Camera plots looked like battlefield maps as the enormous cameras had to weave around the actors without seeing each other or the microphone booms (a telescopic pole with the microphone on the end of it). Very experienced actors in long-running series like *Z Cars* amused themselves and terrified newcomers by playing chicken. They'd see by the red light on the camera whether they were being recorded or not and when the camera wasn't on them, they'd pull faces at poor colleagues who were trying not to 'corpse', jumping back into character in time for their shot.

There was a feeling amongst actors that it wasn't as important as theatre – that they could fake it. Indeed, to show that you were a real professional you had somehow to appear to 'turn on' the acting at just the right moment and then switch it off just as quickly. 'I've got no real work, I'm just slumming it in television,' actors would say to each other. And as there was no training for camera work, actors adapted as best they could.

As video got more technically advanced, some editing was possible and shows were recorded rather than going out live but there were still only fifteen minutes allowed for retakes of fluffed lines at the end of the day. So television became a hybrid between theatre and film, with the problems of each but none of the solutions. Without the rehearsal time of theatre or the ability to keep doing retakes like film, actors opted for short cuts and clichés to get by. Editing was intrinsically part of shooting and any extra adjustments were made with extreme difficulty and expense, as video editing was neither easy nor accurate to do.

By the late 1960s, actors in Britain started to take television more seriously. In 1966 Judi Dench appeared in John Hopkins' trilogy for the BBC, *Talking to a Stranger*, which the *Observer* called 'the first authentic masterpiece written for television'. And in the same year Ken Loach directed his gritty groundbreaking film *Cathy Come Home,* which used a new realistic documentary style and was so powerful that it affected government policy on homelessness.

Over the years there have been classic series with quality acting like the original *The Forsyte Saga* (and, lately, the remake), *The Jewel in the*

Crown, *Auf Wiedersehen, Pet*, *Tutti Frutti*, *Our Friends in the North* and *Edge of Darkness* (now released on DVD) but these have always been the exceptions and are getting scarcer.

We still see outstanding work in television dramas like *House of Cards* with Ian Richardson, *Longitude* with Michael Gambon, Judi Dench as *The Last of the Blonde Bombshells*, David Suchet in *The Way We Live Now* and Kenneth Branagh heading up the excellent cast of the discomforting *Conspiracy*. And, of course, there are excellent American series too – like *The West Wing*, *Six Feet Under* and *The Sopranos*.

But these will never, unfortunately, be the main fare on offer. In television, ratings rule. And with the multi-channelling of digital television and the needs of independent programme makers to produce commercial products, it can only get worse. It is significant that people still talk about really good television performances with a kind of surprised reverence.

Nowadays, though video cameras are much smaller and more sophisticated and there is easy digital editing, some of the earlier programming style remains. Because television is still the poor relation in terms of budget, the actors often have little rehearsal. And they have to hit those white lines in order to stay in shot during much longer takes than those usually done in film. There are some compensations for the actor in television, though, as these longer takes mean there is more continuity. Far fewer lenses are used than in film and the scene is shot from fewer angles, so the progress through the story is not broken up as much by having to stop for close-ups and reverses.

But the acting style has, for the most part, remained less naturalistic than film, especially in situation comedy. There have been some fine comedy performances done in this genre over the years and there are perennial favourites like *Dad's Army*, *Fawlty Towers* and *Rising Damp*. In the best of these, the actors have found a heightened reality that we recognise. But they're rare.

Soaps have developed a kind of shorthand telegraphed style that we accept in order to follow the plot. But, to be fair to the actors, they are usually shooting one episode while learning the lines for the next – an even shorter time scale than in old weekly repertory theatre. There isn't much time for deep characterisation, subtle choices or ambitious camera work.

Because television programmes run at a shorter length than films, scripts are about story line and situation rather than character. There is little time to uncover subtext or work in depth, so the actors tend to rely on 'playing the lines'.

In America, there has been very little cross-fertilisation between the two media until fairly recently and actors like George Clooney, who have moved between them, have been unusual. For the most part, television has always been pretty much despised by the film industry and even now I still meet technicians who won't put their television credits on their CVs.

And in spite of all the technical advances and the perfection of picture quality, video still has a different look to film. Film works like the eye – the foreground is in focus and the background blurs – whereas video has a much flatter look and, unless a very specialised lens is used, the background stays sharp. This makes film appear more lifelike to us. And film has been developing its own way of working and its own acting style.

When he was directing *The Fifth Element*, Luc Besson asked me if I knew the difference between theatre and film acting. Then he said, 'Give me your arm,' and ran his fingernail over my shirtsleeve: 'That is theatre acting.' Then he rolled up my sleeve and drew his fingernail over my bare arm: 'This is film acting.' I personally believe theatre work also has to be that immediate, that specific, albeit with a different kind of energy – but I find it a very good distinction between television and film acting.

The extreme fragmentation of short takes repeated many times out of context and the magnified exposure of large close-ups are both the strengths and the challenges of film. The actor has the satisfaction of seeing the subtlest thought show on camera but has to repeat that thought afresh again and again without being able to do the scenes that lead into it. And the final version on screen is in the hands of the director.

A film is made three times: once in the film-maker's head, once in the studio and once again in the cutting room. Cutting a film can completely change its content, mood, rhythm and pace. Not to mention all the visual effects that can be added. This gives the actor less control than on television and certainly far less than in theatre. Many an actor's 'best' scene has ended up on the cutting-room floor.

And yet film acting can be the most satisfying of all because it is the most distilled, the most exposing and the most demanding. Everything you do on film is vividly highlighted. You can't cheat the camera.

Gene Wilder once said, 'The eye of the camera and the eye of God are very similar, I think.'

THE CASTING EXPERIENCE

'Come up and see me sometime...' (Mae West)

So here you are, with a chance to be seen by that all-seeing camera eye. You may have a general meeting with the casting director alone. This will just be to get an idea of you so that she or he can put recommendations to the director. Following on from that there will be a session with the director who may be accompanied by a few other people like producers, the writer or the dialogue coach. Each interview is different but it usually includes a chat and reading a scene from the script or perhaps some improvisations. It will be videotaped so that it can be shown to the producers and other interested parties and so that the director can refer to it later.

Try to be yourself. Easy to say, but so often actors put on a mask in interviews to provide what they think is needed. I know some actors try to 'be' the character and there may be a case for adopting the accent the character will use or wearing clothes that are within the parameters of what the character might wear. Over the years, however, I've noticed a strange phenomenon. The interview that happens suddenly so you haven't time to prepare, the one you're not bothered about, the one where you fall over or your zip breaks – these are the ones you get. Also the times when a steely resolve takes away your nerves and you think, 'Right – this one is mine.' Whereas the interviews where you try really hard to please and to give them what you think they want, those are often not successful.

Incidentally, you can look up the director on the Internet Movie Database site – www.IMDb.com – and check out what else he or she has done so you get a feel of the possible style. The film itself may have an entry with a summary of the plot, the leads already cast and maybe even the budget.

When I was a young actor, I used to think that directors were perceptive super-beings who could see through my mask of mock-modesty, my fears and my reticence to know that it was my part – that I'd be wonderful. Now I know that's rubbish. They only hear what you tell them and see what you show them. They may be wonderful judges of acting talent but they're not mind readers. Unless you've got a great track record, they are not going to risk casting you if you are too frightened to show them what you can do at the audition. They are as vulnerable and as insecure as you are. More so, probably, because the responsibility is so much greater.

Many years ago, when he was directing *The Go-Between*, Joe Losey turned his blue eyes on me and asked, 'Are you a good actress?' I believe I mumbled something about hoping so, before I stumbled away (probably into the proverbial broom cupboard). Not exactly designed to impress!

Be positive about what you've done. Be proud of your work and don't apologise for its having been a small part on the fringe or in a student film. Try to eliminate those little lead-ins – 'I'm afraid it was only...', 'It was just ...' Simply tell them the work.

You may have been lucky and have been sent the script beforehand or you may be given it only ten minutes before the interview. Be a detective. Look for the clues to the given circumstances. If you take a strong line and it's wrong, then at least it will be interesting and the director will guide you into a different reading. If you try to keep your options open and stay on the fence, you will just be boring. You can ask the casting director questions before you go into the session like, 'Are they about to break up?' or 'Is she his sister?' if it isn't obvious from the script. But don't worry too much about pronunciations or facts that won't affect the reading.

Remember to breathe and stay relaxed. In the discussion, listen carefully to the director's ideas and feelings about the film. When you speak, try to be clear, honest and confident without being pushy. Ask any questions you have, either about the scene or the film. If you're asked about a previous job, don't gossip about anyone or knock your last director – they'll know you'll be doing this about them next time round! Of course, if you can tell a funny incident that makes them laugh, so much the better.

When you come to read, remember that they're not testing your reading – they want to know if you're right for the part. These days you should be able to get the script in advance, either by fax or email. Get as familiar with it as possible. Casting director Karen Lindsay-Stewart says, 'This is a huge thing. If you have an opportunity to learn it, learn it!'

Sometimes things don't work out – you're coming back from holiday, your agent's fax is broken, the script isn't ready or they decide to do an extra scene. So it's worth spending time at home practising cold readings. It is very rarely taught to actors and yet it's part of how you get a job. Nina Finburgh, with whom I was lucky enough to train many years ago, runs excellent classes at the Actors Centre in London on sight reading for auditions. When you pick up a script you need to extract all the clues to the situation, how the characters feel about each other and what they want – and then risk a decision. Learn to do that detective work and rely on the punctuation to show you where you think and therefore where you breathe.

For the videotape you may have to say your name and agent straight to the camera at the start of the reading. Don't let that throw you; just believe you're telling a friend. But speak clearly. Then give yourself a second to pick up your character's thoughts before you begin.

When you read, don't hold the script too high or it will mask your face and don't put it on the table or hold it too low or you will have to look down too far. Holding it to the front and a little to the side is the best place. Put your thumb at the edge of the script and allow it to travel down the page with you as you read the scene. That way you can look up and interact with the other person. Learn to read ahead – a line, a clause – and try to stay up for the last word of the thought. Don't look down to find your place until the thought is finished. It's much better to have slight pauses and really be able to take the words off the page. They won't mind waiting if they can see your eyes.

If your partner has a few sentences to read, look for the cue. That way you can give them your full attention until you hear the key word, then you can look down at your thumb marker. The director will see your reactions – see you really listening. And listening is what you need for film acting.

Sometimes you may read with the director, sometimes with the casting director and – if you're very lucky – with another actor. The person reading with you may not read well. Try not to pick up their style or rhythm. Just use extra imagination to fill in the gaps and respond as your character.

One reading may be enough to show the director what he or she needs. If you are asked to do it again, take it as a good sign, not as a criticism. He or she may want to perfect the performance but, equally, may be seeing how well you respond to direction. Usually you will be sitting down but if you are invited to move around, then do so, as the director may want to see you in action. Equally, if you need to stand or move for the scene, then you can.

If you are given an improvisation, don't worry about making up lines. All you have to do is to believe in the situation, follow the character's actions and any words will happen automatically. Never start an improvisation by buying time – go right to the heart of the matter. You are like an editor: your scissors can snip out the boring preamble and start with the meat of the scene. So, not 'would you like a cup of tea?'

but right into 'I've been meaning to ask you something'. Generally, any improvisations are likely to be very specific and occasionally even silent, like reading a letter, or opening a door and seeing your lover with someone else, so the director can see reaction shots. But every casting session can hold a new challenge. So feel ready for anything.

Beyond this, you may be asked to do a proper screen test with full costume and make-up and some crew. And with the script learnt. You are now being considered seriously. Think of it as a filming day and not an audition and use all the preparation work suggested for the real thing. At this point you might be given the whole script to read.

Read it the first time as if you weren't involved, to get a sense of the story and how your character fits in. On the second reading, do some work on the character. Find out who you are and what you want. Even though you are going to test with just a couple of scenes, this work on the whole script is really worthwhile to make you feel secure in your character. You also never know what else they'll throw at you – an extra scene or an improvisation.

Sometimes you might be sent to an outside acting coach for help with this preparation or for an assessment at an earlier stage of casting. This is a role I have found myself in sometimes and there is a nasty rumour going around that if you knock me over you get the job! There is a grain of truth in this.

When I was helping a director to cast a science fiction film that needed a very particular look, he asked me to have long sessions with lots of top models to see if they would cope with the acting demands of the script. I had to see them in their hotel rooms and make an assessment about their acting potential. A successful model has had to learn how to interact with a camera and already has enormous charisma but may not have ever tried characterisation work or dialogue before, so I set up improvisations which became more emotionally demanding as the session went on.

I started each session, however, with this simple test. Having established that they liked animals, I asked them to imagine that their favourite pet was in the hotel bathroom, unconscious and about to be used in a nasty experiment. To rescue it, all they had to do was push me out of the way and go and get it. I then placed myself across the doorway that led to the bathroom.

This set up all sorts of dilemmas. I was a stranger, in a position of some power (if they wanted the job), and a lot older than them. In order to carry out the designated task they would have to commit completely to the imaginary world that I had set up.

Most could not. Their shyness, politeness or sense of the absurd got in the way. They giggled, played at it or simply refused. One, however, who later starred in the movie, questioned whether I really wanted her to do this as she was stronger than I was.

'Certainly,' I said. And then picked myself up from the floor. The rest of the afternoon confirmed her as an actress of extraordinary power and emotional depth.

When I was later asked to do similar exploratory sessions into the acting potential of some heavyweight boxers, bodyguards and bouncers for another film, I decided not to use this particular exercise!

Now, with or without knocking someone over, you've got the part and the hard work begins.

QUICK TIPS FOR READING AT CASTINGS

- **Practise a lot.** Read out loud whenever you can – to any willing children, your lover, yourself.
- **Learn to be a detective.** Choose scenes from scripts or plays. Make decisions. Then refer to the whole text to see if you were right.
- **Go to sight-reading classes** – or scene classes.
- **Get familiar with the script.** Break it into units or chunks of sense.
- **Find** all the changes of thought and intention.
- **Learn** the script if you are sent it beforehand.
- **Decide what the character wants** – and play the action to get it.
- **Hold the script** in a comfortable position where you won't be dropping your head or masking your face.
- **Use your thumb** as a marker and look up as much as you comfortably can. Then you can give your fellow actor or director your full attention.
- **Use punctuation** – to think and breathe. A new breath is a new thought.
- **Keep eye contact** to the end of the thought. Don't drop your eyes on the key word.
- **Keep your voice strong** to the end of the thought.
- **See pictures** in your head of whatever or whoever you're talking about.

IN FEAR AND TREMBLING

Auditions, film tests and performances don't always work out the way we want. The old familiar wail of 'it was so much better at home/in my bath/in front of the mirror/in rehearsal...' is a very real problem for actors. We talk about the need to be 'centred' or 'rooted' in the body and about staying relaxed. But how do you do it?

Certainly an actor needs to clear away unwanted tension. But during filming you need the freedom of movement a cat has when in a state of alertness. You need to be watching, listening and ready to move emotionally and physically in any direction on the instant; a heightened awareness within a body freed of tensions; a kind of energised relaxation.

Adrenalin can be a powerful ally in this super-reality – it gives you strength, enhances your visual concentration and heightens your sense of hearing and smell. But it can also be enormously damaging to performance if it is not harnessed.

When adrenalin hits the bloodstream, the body tries to protect itself: the stomach contracts, the chest concaves, the shoulders rise, the neck tenses, the tongue goes stiff, the jaw locks, the throat closes. The body gets smaller, the voice goes weaker and higher and eye contact wavers. The actor tries desperately to hide from the film crew or the camera: a curtain of hair here, a turn of the head or the hips, the arms folded, the chair in front – anything to gain some private space. If you are playing a confident character, you have a constant battle between the character's need to take up space in the world and your desire to make yourself smaller to protect yourself.

Many actors have suffered from debilitating 'stage fright', including Derek Jacobi, Ian Holm and Laurence Olivier, who called it 'an agonising dread'. In my first television role after leaving drama school (which, as a point of history, was in the first TV drama ever broadcast in colour), I remember the director calling, 'Turn to your left.' Nothing happened. 'Turn to the left.' Again, nothing – my neck had locked tight. 'Can't you hear me? Look left!' I turned, by moving my whole body from the waist. Nerves had completely immobilised my neck.

Even without these extreme reactions to the adrenalin surge, tension is often responsible for loss of voice or overreaction in the face as the actor tries to compensate for the body's defence mechanism. This protection is a natural part of your survival kit: when a lion jumps out of the bushes at you, the body takes in a high quick breath. This releases hormones into the bloodstream including adrenal steroids that allow you to take immediate action, reduce pain and activate responses in every area of the body, especially the brain. This fight or flight mechanism allows you to hit the lion with your handbag or run away. Then the body will gradually return to its natural breathing patterns.

But an actor is fighting lions for hours on the set and if you stay in the fight, flight or fright position too long, with rapid shallow breathing, the lungs can't oxygenate the body properly. You will feel tingling or numbness in your hands and arms, your voice will feel out of control. Taken to extremes – as in a panic attack – you will eventually either faint or have hysterics. Anything to get the body working properly again. And that's not greatly to be recommended on a film set!

Try this little experiment: hold your stomach in tightly and without letting it go take a deep breath. What did you feel? Probably some tightness in the chest; some constriction in the throat. After three more breaths you are likely to feel slightly light-headed. Let your muscles relax and your breathing return to normal and this will quickly clear.

Sometimes it helps to know that these unpleasant sensations, although initiated by your psychological state, have a totally physiological foundation. The instant stimulation of the senses brought on by gasping in air is very temporary. If you stay in this breathing mode, even in a less extreme form, the body is unable to cope. Because you are breathing out too much carbon dioxide – which is acid – the blood pH balance is disturbed and becomes more alkaline and you start to suffer respiratory alkalosis. This can cause shortness of breath, sweating, trembling, palpitations, nausea, shakiness and headaches. The oxygen doesn't reach the body organs properly, including the cerebral cortex.

This lack of oxygen in the brain leads to forgetfulness, loss of words and thought structures and an overall inability to think clearly or take decisive action. Stress can upset bowel and bladder activity (we all know that problem!) and even change mucus production in the nose leading to the sensation of having a cold. Long-term stress causes muscle stiffness, heart problems and weakens the immune system.

Knowing all this at least gives you a reason for all the unpleasant side effects we associate with nerves. Relaxed abdominal-diaphragmatic breathing has an instant calming effect on the body. Regular breathing work encourages the body to breathe ergonomically under stress. But you must supplement this by making it second nature to check whether you are holding in the stomach. If you are, release it to breathe in. Are you holding your breath when you are tense? Remember to keep breathing!

With the frenetic pace of urban living, we tend not to breathe deeply enough and some medical researchers believe long-term shallow breathing is bad for our health. And when we keep muscles permanently tensed, we lock in our emotions. When deep, relaxed breathing becomes second nature, your voice will respond naturally to your thoughts and feelings, even under pressure.

Most people breathe effortfully when they do it consciously. If you asked a hundred untrained people to take a deep breath, about ninety of them would take a clavicular breath – that is a high tense breath – raising their shoulders and pulling in their stomachs. And yet when they are relaxed, they will breathe in by expanding their stomachs, thus allowing the diaphragm to work properly.

Just before you go to sleep at night, slide a hand on to your belly. You will find it rising towards the ceiling as you breathe in and going down to the mattress as you breathe out. Yet during the day, you may reverse this process and interfere with the way the body functions naturally. It is only tension that gets in the way.

There are other positive things you can do to combat nerves. Try to switch off any negative or censoring voice within you. Don't ever feel a fraud or worry about not being trained. Most successful people still have an illogical fear of 'being found out'. Intelligent people always want to be better at what they do and set high standards for themselves. It's only untalented people that feel fully satisfied with what they've achieved. If you're just starting out, learn to tell people that you're an actor or director – and believe it.

Engage fully in the moment and commit to the character's thoughts and needs. Listen to the other actors. See the pictures in your head as you talk about places, people and situations. Enjoy where you are and what you're doing. When you are not acting, try to find out everything about your environment and the technical wizardry, give support to your fellow actors and generally keep your focus away from yourself – outwards and not inwards.

The best time I ever had as an actor was when I was taking part in a writing workshop where we had to instantly prepare and act out scripts. Because I was concerned only with serving the writer, it took the heat off me as a performer. Trying to tell the story well is a good strategy for combating nerves. Remember that the director and the other actors are nervous too. Making things easier for them will give you confidence.

* * *

THE DESIRE TO PLEASE

When you approach your part, it's easy to think only about the problems you may encounter. Concentrate on finding the character – knowing which aspects of yourself that you can draw from and which things are different from you. Leave aside thoughts like 'I must lose weight', 'I can't do accents', 'I'll never learn to horse-ride' and all the other myriad fears that come rushing in once the euphoria of getting the job has faded away. If you need to do any of those things, be practical and positive – you can get professional help to achieve them.

Try not to let your insecurity lead you to ask for reassurance all the time. People want to be helpful and readily offer all kinds of notes but are they really in a position to help? All that will happen is that you will have lots of conflicting advice: from other actors, the stand-in, the dresser, the props man, your mum, and your work will become ungrounded. Take practical advice from the technicians – that is invaluable – but only take acting advice from the director, the coach, maybe one experienced actor, and smile and ignore the rest.

If the director says nothing, then rest assured you're on track – film is far too expensive a medium to let you get away with something that isn't right for the film. But directors are busy people and they haven't time to make you feel wanted if what you're doing is fine. So keep reminding yourself that on a film set, no news really is good news. And find security within yourself.

We often carry an image of ourselves, a mental picture that gets in the way. For years I saw myself as a funny little thing, too young to be taken seriously. One day that image turned into a scatty, middle-aged woman. I don't know what happened in the middle! But I do fight these judgemental shadows and these days I can usually keep them at bay. If you let them in, they make you feel inadequate or at least self-conscious.

Tom Wilkinson said during an interview about *In the Bedroom* that he felt he had become a much better actor since he discovered a kind of fearlessness. He put it down to having dropped his trousers in *The Full Monty* in front of 300 women from Sheffield. He reckoned if he could do that he could do anything! Strangely, nude scenes *can* make actors more secure afterwards. It's as if living out the bad-dream scenario of finding yourself in public with no clothes on brings liberation. If people can accept you without a cover-up, you've nothing more to lose. A long time ago, I had to take my clothes off every night in front of a thousand people at the Old Vic in *Equus*. My main memory is of learning to cope without the comfort of putting my hands in the pockets of my jeans!

We like to hide from a camera or the audience around us on set by cutting off communication – putting our hands in our pockets or behind our backs. You might protect yourself by making yourself physically smaller or putting up barriers like folded arms. Or you may try to reach out to the other characters by sticking out your chin and craning slightly forward. This reduces resonance in the voice, makes you lose power and takes you away from your emotional centre. The larynx gets trapped so the voice gets shriller, higher or breathier. The character may need to 'lean back' from the situation, take space, play cool, but our desire to please fights this so that the character becomes pushy or looks unconfident.

But there's something else even more damaging that we do in our desire to please. And women are particularly vulnerable to this physical manifestation. We smile. All the time. We have been encouraged to do so all our lives – by our mothers, by photographers, by the local builders, by our lovers – we don't even know we're doing it. Instead of finding the direct simplicity of a part, this signal of wanting to please, beguile or placate, muddies the communication.

Actors often justify this by saying, 'But it's a social situation, it's natural to smile.' Well, is it? Watch people around you. They smile in greeting and they may smile between sentences and when the other person is talking. But they don't smile all the way through their own dialogue – at least, not after the first few sentences. Or if they do, we register them as being superficial, unconfident or wanting too hard to be liked. As soon as they feel relaxed, they stop smiling. Be sure it's your character that needs to smile, otherwise it is yet another filter that comes between your words and the straight honest needs of the character. As if we are frightened by our own inner power, we weaken it to make it more palatable.

That little unconscious self-deprecating smile says, 'Please don't take me seriously.' Dare to be unlovely. Don't sugar the pill for us. If you experiment with not smiling you may find something very powerful happening and you will allow free access to your feelings. And not smiling can be very sexy! Try it and see.

THE AUDIENCE AND THE CRITIC
Any judgement about acting will be, to a large extent, subjective. We all inhabit our own reality of perception. All you can do is work with integrity and commitment, try to serve the script and be guided by the director. If a lot of people like the film then that is a bonus. However many do, there will always be some who don't. And sometimes no one will like it and yet it may be hailed a long time later as a work of genius.

Usually there is a kind of shared public consensus about what is 'good' acting and what is 'bad' acting but even within these broad definitions, tastes will differ wildly and may be governed by our culture, environment and view of the world. Fashions and preferences change as well. The Victorian actor, adhering to a set code of gestures to express emotions, might seem absurd and pantomimic to us now. In the same way, a modern performance would have been incomprehensible to a Victorian audience.

Critics attempt to be the arbiters of public taste, but they are not immune to changing fashion. Several films I've worked on originally met with a luke-warm reception from the critics, but now when they turn up on television they are called a 'classic' or a 'jewel' of a film. And different critics can offer radically different views on films.

Audiences often respond well to a 'bravura' performance where they can see the acting. You will sometimes hear the criticism of an excellent but more understated actor that 'they can only play themselves'. Which is an odd remark because surely, as an audience, we should believe the character and the actor are one and the same. And this actor is working off scripted lines and actions and is making it seem so natural that we believe that no acting is going on and that they *are* the character. Isn't that true acting? I suspect this remark is really a reference to the fact that the actor tends to play the same kind of character in different films.

Some actors immerse themselves, chameleon-like, into many different roles and some draw their roles deep into their own psyches but alter little outwardly. Of course, some actors are incapable of reaching any depths and reduce their characters time and again into the limits of their own personas. But critics and audiences are also responsible for this very typecasting of actors that they criticise – expecting similar performances from them in every film and so this is how they are cast.

All this means that you have to be wary of listening to criticism or taking too much unsolicited advice. Believe in the film while you're making it and don't listen to the prognosticators of doom. Doggedly ignore helpful advice from friends, family and lovers who are not in the business or you will just get confused. Many potentially wonderful actors have been sent down the wrong path by hurtful comments or bad teaching.

If you are a young actor, avoid acting and speech medals and diplomas. The criteria for these are not based on the needs of the profession and preparing for them can be positively harmful to your acting health. Only go to good accredited drama colleges or teachers of repute within the business. And never allow praise or blame to stop you from seriously working at your craft.

Critics can be hurtful. Some offer constructive criticism, but most don't. Only you know whether you're up to reading them. Many top actors don't. If you decide to go for it, just remember – it's only one opinion.

QUICK TIPS FOR NERVES

- **Keep breathing** – stomach relaxed, not held tight – feel the breath dropping in deeply – keep throat open. Do regular relaxation and breathing work.
- **Keep posture strong** – feet firmly on floor, shoulders free, neck lengthened, but don't lock your knees. Relax shoulders and hands.
- **Allow yourself to stop** and breathe – don't let panic overtake you.
- **Find something else** to absorb your nerves: a task, a prop, a piece of furniture.
- **Focus** on what your character wants.
- **Send energy outwards** to the other characters, not inwards to yourself. Listen and watch.
- **Don't hide** from the camera – watch body position, hair, eye level.
- **Become unafraid of your power** – try not to smile unless the character needs to.
- **Only take advice** from the director and those you trust.
- **Remember _you've been cast_** – they want _you_.
- **Conserve** your energy. Rest when you can, drink and eat regularly, go into the fresh air when possible. On location keep warm between shots.

THE CHARACTER'S WORLD

Every human being sees the world uniquely through her or his eyes. When I look at a tree, it is with all the past experiences, references, resonances, associations and memories that I have built up about trees. I may not be aware of them – I may hardly glance at the tree – but this knowledge will be there all the same. Even my perception of the frequency of light called 'green' may not be the same as yours. If it were not so then we would all have the same tastes, wear the same clothes and be in love with the same person. If someone sees the world too differently from ourselves, we brand them as misfits or outcasts. We put them in prisons or go to war with them. To operate within society we assume a shared reality of vision, and yet to some extent this is patently not so.

You are in the business, as an actor, of seeing the world through another person's eyes. Not to be limited by a subjective view of reality, but to observe different truths and to experience them as your own. You will not, though, start from a blank canvas. We all have our own experiences and observations, empathy and understanding to draw from. We are all capable of many emotions and actions. We are like prisms that contain all possible colours within us.

Lauren Bacall has said that the privilege of being an actor is being able 'to live many lifetimes in one lifetime'. We have to view the world of the script from the perspective of the character and never judge them. It would be unusual for someone to see themselves as bossy or mean, a nymphomaniac or a cheat. Instead they would argue it from their own angle – standing up for themselves, looking after their own interests, seeking love or getting what they deserve. Unless the perpetrator is deranged, even the worst crimes must be done from some kind of logic or from a situation that has led to an uncontrollable emotion. We need to understand the character's mindset – Jack the Ripper may have been trying to purge the world of wicked women. The teenager who commits mass murder at the school has some unbearable pain or outrage, even though this solution seems horribly out of proportion with the injustice from an objective viewpoint.

The film itself may seek to portray such people with condemnation or sympathy, but the actor playing the character has no such view. You will have to justify or at least accept your character's actions. While you might find their actions repulsive, you must have felt a flicker of their emotions in your life. To commit murder in a film, you need only to have felt a moment of red rage. Or have lashed out for a second. Or viciously killed a mosquito. We only need an acorn that we can imaginatively grow to the oak required.

You may want to play an unsympathetic character because the film itself is saying something important to you. Once you decide to take on the role, you have taken on a commitment to understand the drives of this character. In the moments you are playing the part, they need to become your drives. But because of the nature of acting, they will be yours only for those moments – they will not take over your private life, although they may temporarily inhabit your dreams. It is important to keep this separation. Too many marriages in Hollywood have ended because the actor and the character got confused. As Bette Davis said, 'The character I am playing stays behind in my dressing room at the end of the day, and is waiting for me there the following morning.'

Equally, a 'good' character may have underlying motives at odds with the surface that you need to uncover. The character who makes you cry when you first read the script may not feel sorry for themselves. They are struggling to survive – battling through life. Feeling sorry for the character can be as useless to the actor as hating or despising them.

Say 'I' and not 'he' or 'she' when you talk about your character. You need to be inside the character looking out, not the other way about. Depending on who you are playing, you may be called upon to adjust your gaze fractionally or enormously, but seeing the script through the eyes of the character is the first vital step for the actor.

YOU OR YOUR CHARACTER

John Gielgud said that the character is 90 per cent you, and Ingrid Bergman observed that 'what you bring to a part is what you have within you'. The actress Liv Ullmann, who had a close working relationship with the great Swedish director, Ingmar Bergman, writes that she can never completely hide who or what she is; that the audience meets a person – neither a role nor an actor.

Certainly, by the time you come to film, your role should feel part of you and you shouldn't be aware of the joins. Even if the character is not like you, temporarily they have moved in. For the moment of acting they have totally inhabited your psyche.

In the end, however many wigs you try or shoes you wear or however you walk, it is your body that you will use. You and your character share the same bloodstream, heartbeat and brain. They may have different needs or say things differently but you provide the emotional impulses.

We pursue the character's objectives and actions but we carry them out through the normal functioning of our own faculties – our body is not 'acting', it is responding. Angelina Jolie, talking about her role in *Lara Croft: Tomb Raider*, said that when she was dodging obstacles at high speed, she wasn't acting. It was her that was running, not the character.

At the moment of performance there can be no separation. It is *your* eyes that are really looking – not pretending; *your* ears really hearing – not faking; *your* skin really feeling and responding. But these reactions are propelled by your inner reality, which bears no relationship to the outer reality of the set or the one being experienced by the crew.

DEALING WITH DIALOGUE

Sometimes we feel really connected to the character. We've decided what he or she is thinking. We know what they want. Our feelings and impulses are engaged – until we have to speak. Then somehow, hearing the sound of our own voice blocks out any inner sense of reality. We feel false and disconnected from our internal vision. Sometimes the very act of speaking gets in the way.

Making a sound is a really big deal. In order to speak, the brain has to send about 140,000 signals a second to the relevant muscles so you've got to really want to do it! In life we never make a sound without a reason, even if it's an unconscious yelp of pain or whistling to keep ourselves company.

Simple emotional needs can be voiced without words, like a baby crying or a yell of outrage when someone runs off with your wallet. When we want to make a point, win an argument or get what we want, we use words. Sometimes without thinking; sometimes chosen with care; sometimes as cleverly as playing a game of chess. Sometimes we mean them; sometimes they cover up our true intentions. Words are dangerous, irrevocable. Once said, they can't be unspoken. They take enormous energy and decision to make.

Try this experiment:

- Lie down or lean back comfortably in a chair. Close your eyes and relax before each step and observe your reactions.
- Step one: Breathe out slowly.
- Step two: On the next breath breathe out slowly on a sustained 'Shh' – like telling someone to be quiet.

- Step three: On the third breath make a good strong sustained 'Aah'. Not a weak breathy one – a good full sound.
- Step four: Now say in a normal speaking voice, 'What am I doing?'

I imagine that you found step one fairly easy. We breathe automatically anyway to keep ourselves alive, so you simply put the action into your conscious control.

Step two, though needing a certain amount of willpower, was probably not too hard. Shh is an unvoiced sound, which means that, although you needed to take the decision to move your tongue into position to make the sound, your vocal folds remained open. (You can check this by gently putting your hand against your throat – you will feel no vibration.)

Step three is much harder. You can really feel the energy needed to commit to the decision to create sound. In order to make the sound Aah you had to go all the way to a fully voiced sound and bring the vocal folds together so that they could vibrate to create a sound source. (You can check this by putting your hand against your throat again. You will feel a vibration – all English vowels are voiced.)

You might have cheated a bit because you were tentative or felt silly. You might have allowed some breath to escape between a gap in the vocal folds making a breathy sound that sounded shy or unsure. You might have held the breath back so that you sounded creaky. You might have tensed the larynx so that the sound was harsh.

Step four is potentially the hardest of all. As soon as you change to words, the brain has to cope with the meaning as well and all kinds of associated tensions to do with 'performing' creep in. Actors will often get a good free sound on open vowels but when they use words, their voices change. You might have tensed your neck, stuck out your chin or raised your shoulders. Your voice might have sounded higher or harsher, thinner or quieter.

All these are natural ways of shielding ourselves from completely committing to the words. The decision to make them is not strong enough or you are feeling tense about not saying them right or you are listening to the effect of the sound.

If you did all the steps quite comfortably, well done. Even if you didn't pull back from the sound, you should have felt yourself summoning up the energy you needed to make it. To make it harder, try it again with someone else in the room or in a public place.

If you still doubt the mental energy needed to provide the impulse to speak, watch the inexperienced presenter up on a platform in front of their peers, or the schoolboy admitting guilt or the enormous effort someone who is really ill makes to talk. Words are the first thing to desert us when we are confused or weak. Especially words spoken with full voice rather than on a whisper. It is said that the energy an actor needs to do two hours of dialogue at performance level burns more calories than it takes to work all day on a building site.

Words are enormous! We choose them with great precision and mental energy. We dig into our storehouse of memory, select them carefully, reject them, find new ones and then add another. We weigh them up against a visual memory, remember how we felt and finally invest them with enough vigour for the listener to share the picture in our heads – all in a millisecond. Or we decide to keep our feelings private and set up verbal decoys instead.

Once the words are written down and repeated, you are in reverse. All this energy has gone and the words become flat, lifeless and generalised, divorced from their original impulses. For an actor, words on the page are too easy. They mean nothing till you have the need to say them. You need to re-find the original energy and make the words specific and individual – the extension of your real impulses. If there is no impulse that leads organically to the words, you will start thinking, 'How shall I say it?'

Sometimes the actor feels the impulse but then the brain steps in and censors the thought. So the breath is held or is let out on a sigh and yet the words still have to be said. When the actor finally speaks, there is no energy left to propel them into the world. They are flat and lifeless and the actor feels false. To combat this, the actor may add effort and tension. Now the words are pushed but still disconnected from the impulse. They feel 'acted'.

When what you want drives your words, they come out as easily or as forcefully or as carefully as they do in life because nothing comes between the impulse and the words. The in-breath is the thought and the out-breath carries the materialisation of that thought with nothing in between. Unless you are consciously censoring your words because they are dangerous or difficult or you are lying, you don't usually think how to say something. You just say it. So don't impose anything on the words. Don't colour them with any emotional quality – just let them arise as a necessary extension of your action.

I suggest that you always whisper the lines slowly first when you are preparing. This allows you time to connect up to the thoughts and you'll feel the words travelling over your lips, but without the distraction of hearing your own voice and speech patterns. When you finish whispering, go straight to speech, without thinking. The words will sound truthful and spontaneous.

Get used to the shorthand in scripts – POV: point of view, CU: close-up, ECU: extreme close-up, MS: mid-shot, LS: long shot, VO: voice-over, MVO: male voice-over, FVO: female voice-over, FX: sound effects, SFX: special effects.

If you have a long speech, divide it into chunks: find where your thoughts change and think of it in sections. There is a danger that you'll want to speed up in order not to bore us, but it will be much more interesting if you take the time to follow the character's thoughts. On the first reading, you can allow yourself pauses to find the impulses, but then take them out completely. (But still breathe! The breath should come in quickly, silently and effortlessly through your open mouth with each new thought or extension of the thought.) The thought needs to power the breath, which goes straight into sound. Only take a pause if the character *really* needs one.

You may find yourself adding little preamble words like, 'well...' or 'anyway...', which will weaken what you are saying. Repeating a word like, 'I'm ... I'm sorry' or 'it's ... it's difficult' may be truthful if the character is searching for a word, but it shouldn't become a stylistic habit.

Punctuation marks are your clues for thought – and breath. A comma takes you on a detour or adds something; a full stop or other major punctuation completes one thought and starts another. If your lines end in a dash or peter out in dots (ellipsis) you need to decide what is happening. Are you being cut off by the other speaker? (This is usually indicated by a dash.) If so, know exactly what you were going to say, and go on talking until you are interrupted. If you are interrupting or censoring yourself (usually the dots) then you need to ask why. Was it hard to find the right word? Was it emotionally difficult to talk about? Did something else catch your attention?

In life, we often carry out a secondary activity while we deal with life-changing conversations. Chopping an onion while we carry out a violent argument with our lover in the next room; clearing up the classroom during revelations about childhood traumas; packing clothes in a suitcase as we give last-minute reassurance to the relative going into hospital.

Give yourself a real physical task that has to be carried out and completed while you use your dialogue. Don't cheat: make sure you give it full attention as well as being alive in every moment of the text. You'll be surprised by how real you feel and your voice will carry the energy of your movements. Actors never have any problems, text-wise, in the sword-fighting scenes!

When you are rehearsing, alternate between speaking about something real – your journey this morning or what you're going to do next – with speaking your text. Make sure you are not changing your pitch or level between this real conversation and the written scene. If you are working in your second language, move between your first language and the one you are using to check that you feel as free in both. Working in another language adds an extra layer between your thought and the words. If you can, try to think in the same language as the one in which you are speaking during the scene.

Enjoy words. Babies get enormous tactile pleasure by experimenting with sounds. Often all that is left for adults is the pleasure of swearing – using fricatives and plosives against the lips. Be silly in your bath: babble – gurgle – sing. Be aware of the physical sensations of making sounds. Choose a favourite word – say it ten times, each in a different way. Use lots of different texts as well as screenplays – poetry, Shakespeare, fairy stories. Say your own name – and like it. Because we tend to hear our own names only in formal situations or when loved ones are annoyed, a lot of us don't like them. Find a new way into your name.

Experienced actors get very good at noticing changes in their sensations and sound. At first you may need a tape recorder to hear what is going on and to reassure yourself that the changes are smaller than you think or, indeed, are happening at all, or to monitor whether you're using a different energy with improvised speech than when you're working on text.

We all hear our voices differently to the way we are heard by the outside world. This is because our ears are on the sides of our heads. So it is like standing at the sides of your loudspeakers and hearing more of the bass. Plus, we get the feedback through bone and skin. Our voices tend to sound lower to our own ears, so everyone gets a fright when they hear their own voice taped for the first time.

You can check this out for yourself. Cup your hands behind your ears so that you funnel the sound forward and count to five. Your voice should now sound more like the tape. You'll hear more overtones, which will make your voice 'brighter' and appear higher.

You'll soon get used to hearing it and be able to judge when it's free and communicating what you want. Work to find your own unique sound. For film you will need to use your whole voice at a normal speech level rather than a half-voice that carries no emotional resonance. We talk about 'the ring of truth'. When your voice is naturally resonant and free, we will instinctively believe you.

DEALING WITH MOVEMENT

Just like words, movements have to come from a need to make them. As you read the script and work through what your character wants, follow any impulses to move as you feel them arise. If you want to get up because you can't look your partner in the eye and you need to buy some time, or to adjust an ornament on the mantelpiece to avoid your mother's awkward questions, or to go to the window to see the picture in your mind's eye of your dead lover more clearly, do so. Learn to trust these instincts.

I often observe young actors, working on a text, suddenly squirm or twitch a foot. 'Did you feel the need to move?' I ask. 'Yes,' they confess, 'but I didn't know if I should.' If you give in to shyness then you'll play every part glued to your seat, arms folded and eyes averted. *You* may not want to move but *your character* needs to. It is your responsibility to honour those needs.

Of course, during filming, you often end up working the other way round. The director supplies the moves and you have to find the impulse. This is no different from working from prescribed dialogue. You need only to work out why your character needs that move. And if you start by supplying instinctive movements with the first rehearsal, the director may choose to sort his or her camera work around a lot of your choices.

Observe how you use gestures when you relate a specific incident. Repeat the same story when you're on your own and find those natural gestures again – go back to the original impulse that made you use the gesture the first time. Give yourself props to use while you rehearse: really pour drinks, take out cigarettes, put on a sweater, lace up your trainers and teach your hands to stay dextrous during pressure.

Actors often ask what they should do with their hands. They feel odd with their arms by their sides. This is another effect of nerves – in life you don't worry what to do with your hands except in awkward social situations. When you are at ease, you keep your arms relaxed until you need to use them – to make a gesture, pick up a glass or write a note. You also carry things, open doors, touch your face or pat the dog without ever thinking about it. Sometimes you fold your arms or put your hands in your pockets.

Hollowing your back and lifting up out of your sacrum (like a child or a ballet dancer) when you get nervous, disconnects your thorax from your abdomen. This leaves your arms swinging out of your control and can cause little displacement wiggles around the hips which means you don't look 'centred'. If you never look still on camera, check that you haven't held in your stomach or narrowed your back. If you lock your shoulders back or forward, your arms will hang stiffly and oddly by your sides. Lift your shoulders and just let them drop to free them again.

If you still feel awkward, then hang over from your waist, letting your arms and neck hang completely free, as limply as a rag doll. Make sure your head feels really heavy and you are not holding on to any neck tension. Now build up the spine slowly, putting one vertebra on top of the other, like a child's building blocks. Let your arms stay completely relaxed and they will take care of themselves. Bring your head up last to balance on top of your spine. You should feel strong but relaxed, ready to move in any direction.

Combine movement and text. After all, when you act you won't be separating them – they must both be part of the communication process. Try running across a room, then turning quickly round to face into the room and speaking your lines before you allow yourself to add any preparation tension.

If you have a big space, or it's summer and you can use the park, try rolling gently over and over, letting the words 'fall out', then gradually come on to all fours and then up to standing without putting in any tension. Now you should feel a new freedom in speech and movement. And you are ready to work!

GETTING READY TO WORK

'Ready when you are, Mr DeMille . . .'

This is the famous – probably apocryphal – story of the making of one of this director's epic films. Because so many thousands of extras were involved, Cecil B. DeMille decided to play safe and use many cameras placed at strategic positions. Camera C was up on a hill and would see the whole action: the horses charging down the valley, the thousands fleeing, the Red Sea parting and the riders toppling into the waves. His was a key position.

Action was called and the cameras rolled. Everything went perfectly – the wagons jolted down the hillside, the soldiers died horribly, the thousands fled. At the end of the shot the director called, 'Cut!' and then checked out all the cameras through his megaphone. 'How was it for you, camera A?' 'Perfect. Couldn't have been better.' 'Camera B?' 'Got the lot, guvnor!' 'Camera C?' 'Ready when you are, Mr DeMille . . .'

You, on the other hand, will be ready when they call. You are going to prepare so well beforehand that you'll be able to absorb any new information and never be thinking, 'What do I want?' or 'What do I say?' in those precious moments of last rehearsal.

Even if you are told that you will have two weeks rehearsal with the director, you'll still need to do this preparatory work. A film rehearsal usually means a few hours a day with the director and cast, mainly rewriting the script. The rest of the time will be taken up with costume, hair and make-up. You may also be learning to ride, shoot or fight at the same time.

It is very rare to have much rehearsal in the theatre sense, even if you have extra hazards like accents or new skills to cope with. A few major stars will be booked far enough ahead to prepare over a longer period of time and some directors with theatre backgrounds do rehearse scenes in depth. But they have to fight for the time because a lot of Hollywood stars don't like this kind of rehearsal anyway. (There are exceptions – Paul Newman insists on it!) You are more likely to have a few weeks of private preparation and just a few days of rehearsal if you're lucky.

Start preparing now, long before you get your part. See as many films as you can. Not only the current ones but also foreign language films, old films and films of every style. There are lots of specialist companies that offer these on videotape or DVD. If you are in London then join the British Film Institute on the South Bank where there are regular showings. Watch as a professional. Keep seeing movies – good and bad. Bad movies and television can be very rewarding homework. Why is it bad? Try to put your finger on the problem. It may be very subtle: not enough subtext – playing just 'the line'; actors not listening to each other – no clear relationships. Or the most common problem, actors 'showing' or 'signalling' to the audience how they ought to feel and react.

Go to art galleries to get a feeling of people in different periods and places and in different emotions and moods. Read good screenplays, novels, Shakespeare, poetry. Read out loud. Write your own!

Best of all, buy a camcorder and film yourself. Play it back enough times to get over the initial shock we all feel when faced with ourselves on screen for the first time. Start to see yourself objectively and learn how what you think transmits to the screen. Most actors hear a director tell them to do something that they know they are already doing. It's no use saying, 'I'm already doing that' if the director's not seeing it. So learn what's coming through and what's not. And how little you can do if you think hard enough.

PART TWO
THE ART

INTRO

'There is really no question of my method or your method. There is only one method, which is that of organic, creative nature ...' (Constantin Stanislavski, 1936).

There is no one way for an actor to approach a role. We respond to our individual needs and the needs of the script, the style and the period.

The poetry of Shakespeare, the dark world of the Jacobean writers, the wit of Restoration, the knockabout of commedia dell'arte and the surrealism of Theatre of the Absurd all enrich us and put our period into perspective. You can only gain by reading the great writing of all periods: Stanislavski, Brecht, Artaud, Grotowski, Boal and Peter Brook and all the other great theatre practitioners. Much of the work will be equally relevant to film. Similarly I urge you to see all the plays and films, photographic and art exhibitions you can from every period and genre. The more material you store in your subconscious, the more useful that subconscious will be to you as an actor.

All these practitioners have had their bearing on the work we do today. The biggest influence on screen acting has been the Russian director Constantin Stanislavski. There is no doubt that we owe Stanislavski an enormous debt. He started working in a theatre that had lost its organic roots and was filled with formulas and rules. Actors were admired for the sonority of their voices and the magnificence of their gestures. Stanislavski was trying to bring back to theatre the epiphany – the magic time-stopping, living-in-the-moment connection between actor and audience.

Stanislavski made an attempt to forge a system to help his company. This was first made public in 1921 and has since been changed and re-invented by countless practitioners, not least Stanislavski himself. The actor who mumbles and scratches in the hope he is revealing something profound, has misunderstood Stansislavski's method. It is about matching the appropriate voice and movement to the character's world, personality and need to take action. Otherwise it becomes a 'style' and just as disconnected from the truth as the formal gestures prescribed by earlier systems. His system or method, along with its later offshoots – the work of Michael Chekhov, Lee Strasberg, Stella Adler, Uta Hagen, Sanford Meisner and all the many other methods of 'method' – has left its mark indelibly on film through most of the twentieth century.

I've always been enthralled by films and film acting. When I was a child growing up in the middle of Central Africa, I prayed it wouldn't rain – it usually didn't – as I sat in the back seat of the car on a cushion at the drive-in cinema, pretending to be sixteen, for the latest Debbie Reynolds' movie. I crossed my fingers that the projector wouldn't break down in the community hall at the third reel of the weekly movie – it usually did.

The projector held up long enough for Tom Courtenay to experience *The Loneliness of the Long Distance Runner*, which solidified my desire to be an actor and sent me off to a drama school in London. Since then I've been able to see the work of master directors from Altman to Zinnemann without having to worry about missing the end of the film. I've watched actors from Lillian Gish to Mia Farrow, from Spencer Tracy to Kevin Spacey and from James Dean to Johnny Depp. Aren't we lucky to live in an age when we can see around a hundred years' worth of great acting on screen?

I'm also lucky to be on the shop floor of this world and to watch quietly from the monitor as many directors take their own route to making a film and many actors give astounding performances. And to try to work out why some don't.

My experiences as audience, actor, teacher, director, theatre and film coach have given me a ragbag, into which I dip and steal to help actors make the work come alive. When I am involved in a class, workshop or rehearsal with a director or teacher, I try to enter it innocently and to engage in it fully. Only then do I evaluate it and often I find something that sticks fast to be owned and used later by me. And that is what I urge you to do. My work has undoubtedly been shaped by each of these encounters.

So we all pass the baton on – using what's come before us and adding something of our own. We are all after the same thing: to communicate that story or to evoke those particular thoughts and feelings to an audience and to make them believe it's happening in this very moment for the very first time – to make the work live.

And since everyone's unique, the ways of working are infinite. Different approaches work better for different actors and styles and media. So you can work from the outside, through technique, and the inside will follow. Or you can work from the inside, and if you're really centred, the technique will be right. You might start with the character's clothes or you might start with his fantasies. You might start with her way of walking or you might need to know her innermost thoughts first.

If you work from the outside first, observing other people, finding a walk, putting on a jacket, gradually you will start to feel part of you in the character. The only watch-point is that you have to feel that you fully inhabit the role that you create. You can't observe your character objectively or put morally loaded descriptions on to the character – wicked, dishonest, cheap, miserly or nymphomaniac. Very few people are that self-knowing. Or if they do give themselves labels, it may be from a sense of self-loathing that is out of kilter with the facts. You need to see how the character views and justifies his or her actions.

If you work from the inside first, you need to accept the premise that, in embryonic form, you are capable of almost anything. You don't need to have experienced what the character experiences, but you have to be capable of understanding and feeling the impulses within you that could give rise to these actions and reactions. The watch-point here is not to bring your character into your own 'habituality' – to pull the part down to where it's comfortable for you but to allow yourself to grow to where the character is. You can take extraordinarily brave choices as long as they are propelled by your own innermost feelings and visceral imagination.

Working as an acting coach, I realised that when someone wasn't 'rooted' in the breath and the voice wasn't working, they couldn't fulfil their acting visions. But if they found a free resonant sound, the acting became free too. So I trained as a voice coach because voice, acting and movement are inextricably linked in the acting process.

Through all these many paths I've taken into the work, I find my old ragbag is overflowing and I could call it a treasure chest – though a male colleague frowned when I told him this and said that he called his a toolbox!

MAKING IT COME ALIVE

Film always seems to take you by surprise – to be over before you've even warmed up.

I wonder how many directors have cast the perfect actor from the casting session: the one who looked so right, spoke so passionately and was so moving in the improvisation that the clever director set up; they even did well at the cold reading. But they never provided the performance they had promised. Their voice sounded different – higher, tighter, breathier. The confident stance had gone and they always seemed to close themselves off from the camera's prying eye. There was no magic between them and the co-star, no electrifying moments, no emotional connection.

And every time the actor hopes it will be different. You know you're good at cold readings. You know you're good at improvisation – you can catch the moment on the wing.

And then you have to do those lines again – and again. And each time it's harder. Why does it seem so flat and lifeless?

Or maybe you're a model: you have such magnetism, such rapport with the camera. But what happens when the dialogue arrives? Where is that energy? Why that tension? And why, why were you better in the bath at home?

Jean Seberg once said, 'I was a better actress the first day I auditioned for Otto Preminger than all the time we worked together.'

There is an answer – one so simple that it seems too obvious. Acting is the wrong way round. In life we never make a word or gesture without some impulse driving our need for it. We rarely prepare what we are going to say next, and even when we do, it seldom works out as we expected. We react to all the stimuli around us on the moment and our energy goes out to meet it through words and actions. Or we recoil into ourselves and remain silent, alive with thoughts.

When the words and actions aren't our own but are dictated by print on a page and someone else's vision, we are working backwards. We are committing an unnatural act.

Make-believe is natural. We all did it as children and can re-release that capacity within us. To empathise is natural – we do that whenever we feel sympathy for another human being's situation. Communication is natural. But to take someone else's words and actions, to repeat those words endlessly in front of a camera and hundreds of crew members without necessarily even seeing the person we are talking to – these are not natural acts.

Add to that the adrenalin pumping through your veins, the corset holding your ribcage, the make-up making your eyes water and the temperature of over 100 degrees, and you start to realise that this is a job that needs respect, a craft that needs a technique – maybe a vocation – that allows it to *seem* natural.

Somehow we have to learn to turn life around so that those prescribed words and actions become ours – the only ones that we can use in that situation. When we watch you on film, you and the character have to merge in our imaginations so that we believe every word is happening spontaneously, every moment is taking you by surprise.

We don't want to feel that you are working from a script. We don't want to admire your acting – not till later. We want to be involved – to believe in your screen life as firmly as we believe in our real life. For film is mainly a naturalistic medium.

In life, everything is specific. Nothing is generalised. When you talk, you are flashing up pictures of who you are talking about, where you've been, what you want. Your scripted imaginative life must be just as vivid, just as precise, just as specific. No millisecond must pass you by, without you completely being in that moment of thinking and reacting as that character.

Then we will believe you really exist. Then we will want to be involved with your screen life.

THE ACTOR'S QUESTIONS

It is really useful to have a disciplined format that you can bring to bear on the life of any role. These exercises are meant as preparation and homework for the part – to make your character-work specific and know what drives you to speak and act. They are not meant to hold you up in performance, make you careful or require you to analyse an action while acting. Matthew Broderick said in an interview, where he talked about his extensive preparation for a role, that 'in order to be instinctual, you have to do a lot of work'. Use this work systematically in your rehearsal and fly free in performance.

First read the script thoroughly. If you haven't understood it, read it again. Try to resist the impulse to skip through it, looking for your character's lines (or, if your curiosity overwhelms you, do that first, then approach it freshly for this proper reading).

Now ask yourself what the film is about: what is its purpose, its main themes and preoccupations? Which characters are the protagonists driving the action, who supports them and who opposes them? Where does your character fit into this? If it's a really complicated plot, you might want to do a simple outline so that you make sense of it. Or try telling the story out loud to your best friend or your dog. (The dog's safer – the film may be highly secret at this stage!) Director Raoul Walsh's dictum was 'if you haven't got a story, you haven't got anything'.

The script provides the given circumstances of your make-believe world. These can be any situation that the writer puts you into: moving house in *The Chain* or in a chain gang like *Cool Hand Luke*; taking part in a psychological experiment, with terrible consequences, as in *Das Experiment* or preparing for a *Monsoon Wedding*; finding the Titanic is sinking or realising that you are mutating into a monster.

When you feel that you are fairly familiar with the script, then it's time to work on your role. Here is a list of questions to ask yourself on this second reading. Some questions will be more important to some roles than others, but it is worth making the effort to go through the whole list for everything you play, however small. The questions are interrelated: *who* you are can be dependent on *where* you are and the given circumstances. But it is still a good discipline to go through each in turn. Filming requires enormous concentration and imagination. The more concrete and specific you can make that imagination, the easier your task will be.

WHO AM I?

'Who am I?' is the first question on the actor's list. There is an ancient Maori saying: 'Until you know who you are, until you have a place to stand, you have no voice, you cannot speak.'

Read the script carefully, noting every time you are mentioned:

- Start by making two columns and note (1) what others say about you and (2) what you say about yourself. Either might be true and neither might be true, but it's a place to start.
- Then write two more columns under the headings: (3) 'Things I know are true about my character' and (4) 'Things I assume about my character'. Column (3) contains facts about which there is no argument. Column (4) is where you start building your character. For example: we know Hamlet lives in Elsinore; we know his father is dead; we know his uncle married his mother. We may only guess that he loves Ophelia; that he hates his stepfather; that he despises his mother. You can change your mind, add or subtract choices at any point. Use any information gleaned from your first two columns and any other textual evidence to guide your choices.
- Now, within all these columns, cross out everything that is true about you, yourself as well as the role, and highlight all the things that are not true about you as a person but only true for your character. You only need to work on the highlighted items. I think this is really important – television sit-coms are littered with attractive twenty-somethings trying to play what they think is an attractive twenty-something, and ending up with a caricature instead of a real person. If the character is your age and lives in the time and environment that you live in, then that is 'given' – you don't need to enhance it or 'show' us that you share these traits. You need instead to work on the differences. Similarly, don't make generalisations about the character – a nun, a policeman, a drug addict – you need to find what makes them individual and different from other nuns, policemen or drug addicts.
- Next, write a short autobiography of yourself as the character. It's a really good discipline to write it rather than to think it. It's not set in stone; you can always alter it as your preparation progresses. Write in the first person. Always think and talk about the character as 'I'. Pick up all the clues from the screenplay and from any meetings with the

director and writer and add only things that are really relevant. For example, if your character is a well-balanced human being then why write in a schizophrenic mother, if it's not in the script? If, however, your character is afraid of water, then do find a specific incident in your past that set that off, even if it's not referred to.

In writing the autobiography, remember that 'Who am I?' takes account of the period you live in and how that affects who you are plus all the given circumstances. The character is you – as if . . . you lived in 1800, as if . . . you had to kill your friend to get the money, as if . . . you were an astronaut, and so on. For example, Strindberg's powerful eponymous heroine, Miss Julie, is tied completely to the strict social codes of her small town in Sweden in the year of 1888. It is because she is rebelling against those values that she sleeps with Jean, her servant, and it is because of the pressures or guilt caused by those values that she commits suicide. (Incidentally, *Miss Julie* has so interested film-makers that it has been made at least six times. The 1950 version won the Grand Prix in Cannes and Mike Figgis directed it most recently, in 1999.)

So many films, like *Pleasantville*, *The Wicker Man*, *The Fifth Element* and countless more, including time-travel films and many westerns, are about strangers entering an environment new to them. They act as a catalyst to the inhabitants who suddenly see themselves through the stranger's gaze, their petty lives and weaknesses exposed. How do you feel when you visit a foreign country for the first time? You will be having new sensations with every glance, touch, sound and smell. You have to carry that detail of observation and experience of a different culture and values into your new imaginary world – which might be as extreme as another planet. On the other hand, you may have to deal with a stranger entering your safe environment.

Apparently, for *Gosford Park* Robert Altman, much loved by actors for the freedom he gives them, asked each character to find some secret quirk or tick, either physical or mental, that only they knew about. This particularly suited his film, which was about secrets, but it can often be a useful device. This private knowledge could be a hidden pregnancy, a secret fear of spiders, a dislike of someone else, claustrophobia, etc. You might try this although, if it is anything obvious, it must be discussed with the director – and beware of overloading a simple role with unnecessary complications. But if it's something private and subtle that enriches your inner life – like always wishing you were taller, wanting to be outdoors, or trying to hear other people's conversations – then this is another way of being specific, creating a well-rounded character.

Another good device is called 'Hot Seating'. Put yourself (in the role) in the 'hot seat' and interview yourself (better still, get someone else to ask the questions). Ask yourself everything from little things like your food likes and dislikes to big things like childhood fears or your attitude to sex. Ask practical questions like where you go on holiday, how you vote and what newspaper you read. Find metaphors for your new self: if you were an animal what would you be? if you were a car? if you were a drink?

Chart the journey of the character. In all good stories, characters change. Be aware of when you change, how you change and why you change. Mark the script with these changes.

If the film is based on a book, read the book. If the hero has a favourite sport, go to a game. If they mention a song, find it and listen to it. If the film is based on a real person, read the biography. See if you can find some footage. Or find a real person or an amalgam of people to base your character on. The more you surround yourself with reality the better. You might find a character model by looking at paintings and photographs. For example, in London, the National Portrait Gallery offers pictures of real people divided into periods and is an excellent place to start. Most cities have similar galleries and photographic exhibitions.

Whether they're fictional or real, it is always beneficial to research some of the experiences and environments of your subject. For example, if the film is based on a famous novelist, like the recent *Iris*, and you are playing her, it will be important to at least read the book you are supposedly writing at the time. You are bound to find clues into the thoughts, dreams and rhythms of the character.

Some actors, like Jim Broadbent who did a marvellous portrayal of Iris Murdoch's husband in *Iris*, and Russell Crowe who played John Forbes Nash Jr in *A Beautiful Mind*, prefer not to meet the living subject that they're playing in case they get a false idea of their character's younger selves, or they might tip into doing an 'impersonation'.

On the other hand, Al Pacino chose to get to know his subject well for *Serpico* and Will Smith worked closely with the boxer for his role in *Ali*. Will Smith made the interesting distinction that impersonation is what you see and what you hear; interpretation is what you feel. His preparation was rigorous – he had to learn to box and trained like a professional athlete for months, as well as learning a dialect and watching all the original fights and newsreels. Robert De Niro not only had to learn to fight but also had to put on enormous amounts of weight for the second half of his role as the boxer Jake LaMotta in *Raging Bull*.

You may not need to go to those extremes, but do some of the physical work that your character would do.

If your first ideas stop working for you, be brave enough to throw them all away and make new ones – don't feel trapped by these early decisions. By going off in all sorts of directions you will gradually be drawn inexorably to the centre of the character.

WHERE AND WHEN AM I?

Even if the script is set in your own city but your character inhabits a different environment – the opulence of a millionaire or the deprivations of the streets – then you might as well be in another country. Or the film could be set in a foreign location, even another planet. You have to do enough research, both imaginatively and concretely, to feel at home there. Sometimes, where you are can have physical effects on your character, like being in a desert without water, in a prison cell or weightless.

'Where am I?' is inextricably linked to 'When am I?' Every period will have a resounding influence on all your other questions. Even the recent past is going to offer a different social and moral landscape. As in the famous first line of LP Hartley's novel, *The Go-Between*: 'the past is another country: they do things differently there'.

Make the imaginary world as real and specific as you can. Use picture references, literature research and documentaries to immerse yourself in that environment. Sometimes an artist can capture the mood of a particular period, like William Hogarth did of eighteenth century England or Edward Hopper of 1940s and 50s small-town America. A particular painting can crystallise a mood or a feeling of place.

Using films to research a particular period is fine up to a point, although they tend to reflect the period in which they were made as much as the time that they are portraying. So *Cleopatra*, with Elizabeth Taylor, may tell you more about 1963 than about Ancient Egypt.

Play the music of the time. Choose a few pieces that might mean something specific to your character – music is a very powerful affective tool. When rehearsing, find some authentic objects to use or substitutes that remind you of that world. For example, if you are in a film that's set in 1900, then try washing in cold water from a bowl one morning. If you have a real fireplace, then try a day without central heating.

Find out as much as you can about the geography, politics and social mores of your character's world. The British Library has a newspaper archive at its Colindale site in North London where you can browse through articles of the period. Read contemporary writers. Go to museums – not just major museums, but the little ones that offer insights into everyday life. If you can, visit the area and you might turn up a lot of information, even actual buildings your character might have been in.

In Dublin recently, working with a young actor on *The Count of Monte Cristo*, we found a square with houses from the right period. He took a walk alone late one night wearing clothes that felt right for his character. He said afterwards that hearing his footsteps on the old streets, his shadow on the Regency glass doors and touching the old stone walls was a tremendous help when he had to work with the painted equivalents in the studio.

If the location is abroad and you can't go there, then get books on the area. Or go into a travel agency and get brochures. The Internet can offer enormous amounts of background knowledge. Just use a search engine like www.yahoo.com, or www.google.com – type in a key word and be prepared to spend an hour or so sifting through all the references to find what you want.

In theatre there is time for directors to get their casts to research different aspects of the play's background: the role of women; medicine and hygiene; the art of the period; a working day at the factory and so on. You will be working alone on film, but you will still find it valuable to take a few key topics to explore.

This kind of detail will put you in touch with the world your character inhabits in such a particular way that you won't be tempted into generalisations or choices gleaned from other movies. Of course, you will be restricted by time, so if you're a late entry into the cast, don't worry. A few specific things to relate to – a song, a picture or a poem – can make all the difference.

'Where am I?' and 'When am I?' also need to be asked about each particular scene in the film. Films start a new scene every time you change location – even if you go out of the back door. Know what and how far you see; what time of day it is; where the sun is; how warm you are; what you can hear or smell; and where you've just come from. Some sets or locations will give you substance around you to believe in. Others will tax your imagination to the utmost.

This is not hypnosis. You have to fuse your inner reality with your acceptance of the outer – the set around you. You can live in your imaginary world and the sight of the crew and the smell of bacon butties at one and the same time!

WHAT ARE MY RELATIONSHIPS?

You need to think about your relationship with every character you interact with and how that relationship changes through the course of the film. You've made a list of what they say about you. Now note anything you say about them. Is it true? Why are you saying it?

What is your status in respect of each character? Does it change? Is there a scene where you are struggling for a stronger position in that relationship? If so, you need to mark the rise and fall of your status blow by blow. How has the relationship grown? How long have you been together? Are you locked into ever repeating patterns – like two people crossing a field by the same worn path every day, never noticing the wide, green spaces around them? Or are you learning about each other moment by moment?

Think about your relationship with everyone you mention, even if they don't appear. I may say lightly, 'I must pick up my son from school,' and yet, however quickly I say it, there will be a lightning flash of connection to my son – a fleeting image. And that relationship will be more important to me than the one with the person I'm talking to. If you've done your background work – know what your son looks like, what the school's like, what happened last time you were late – you won't have to dwell on the line or make it heavy. You'll say it just as lightly as you would in life and the image will flash by as fast as in life.

Think about relationships to people that you don't mention but who have shaped your life or are governing your choices of action – your parents, teachers or those who have influenced you for better or for worse. They may not appear in the film, but if their faces flash up for you at key moments, then the words will come alive. We also have relationships with our ideologies: with work itself, our beliefs, our political leaders and our heroes.

Don't forget animals and pets, birds and insects. These relationships for good or bad might be as powerful as the ones with people. A farmer will have a real relationship with animals. Witness the heartbreak of so many farmers during the 2001 foot and mouth outbreak in Britain. A blind person relies on a guide dog literally to steer a course through life. A loved cat could be more important to its owner than any person and feeding the birds can give real solace to a lonely pensioner.

Equally, you may have a phobia about snakes (like poor Sid James who had to play a snake-handler in *Trapeze*), loathe spiders, fear red ants. These relationships can affect your life in deep ways. (I once had an agent who was horribly afraid of pigeons and she worked near Soho. Every lunchtime was a real trauma to her and crossing the square was as terrifying as walking through a prehistoric jungle.) Plants, trees and gardens can be really important as well. The success of a crop of rice can mean the difference between life and death. A garden can assuage grief for someone bereaved who sees the growing plants as evidence of continuing life.

We also have relationships with inanimate objects: places and things. You will have a relationship with your house or flat, your old school, your work place, your room. With your clothes – 'my ancient jumper'; your latest CD – 'it makes me cry'; your favourite book – 'I've read it ten times'; with your chosen newspaper, radio and TV programme; with all the important objects in your life, even your old hairbrush.

If you are dying of thirst in *Ice Cold in Alex*, where the characters have arduously crossed a desert in wartime to reach the haven of the bar, you are going to have a different relationship with your glass of beer than a character who has wandered into the local pub for a drink!

Not all these categories will be relevant, but try to identify all the significant relationships in your character's life.

WHAT ARE THE CONDITIONING FACTORS?

Conditioning factors, or 'given conditions', can be anything from being blind to being blinded by love. They can be physical or emotional conditions. You can't play an emotional state – it just is. You accept it as a given. But you can know what caused it and what you do because of or in spite of it.

Conditioning factors can be unique to you as the character or come out of the environment. For example, your character might have vertigo or a limp or have to cope with the physical hardship of war, the heat and thirst of a desert or the icy cold of a polar landscape.

The tiredness of the ambulance crew in *Bringing Out the Dead*, the stench of cholera in *Death in Venice*, Alzheimer's disease in *Iris*, Spencer Tracy coping with one arm in *Bad Day at Black Rock*, or Donald Sutherland's private grief for a drowned daughter in *Don't Look Now* are all conditioning factors.

They can be temporary or permanent, like being old, beautiful or crippled. They can also be ones that are not scripted (given) but ones you decide for yourself, like being hungry, cold or having a headache. Make a note of all the conditioning factors that affect your character in each scene.

WHAT DO I WANT?

In life, we do not play the conditioning factor; we play our need. If you see me standing in the snow and flapping my arms about, jumping up and down, I have the objective, 'to keep warm'. I will not be playing the objective, 'to show how cold I am', unless I'm angling for pity from the owner of a spare fur coat. Being cold is the conditioning factor; 'I want to get warm' is the objective and my physical action is to flap my arms about. If you really play the action, physical or psychological, which stems from the objective, you will always be truthful.

When emotion overwhelms us, it comes as a by-product. If we are angry and want to prove our point and we start to cry, we brush our tears aside to carry on with our objective. The tears are annoying; they get in our way. Fighting through the tears, we try to regain our composure and deal with the task in hand. If you wanted to tell the police what your lost child was wearing and tears choked you up, you would struggle through them to get those details understood. Maybe your objective is to leave someone for their own good. The given conditioning factor is that you love them deeply. If you really play your objective until the impulse to hug them is so strong that it overwhelms you and makes you take a new objective and action, it will move us more than if you try to show us how heart-torn you are.

It is this bravery that we recognise and which moves us when we watch it. Sometimes emotion does sweep us away but it is in spite of ourselves, not because we try to find it. Let the emotion take care of itself and drive your objective.

So, human beings are driven by needs, which lead to words and actions. The stronger these needs are and the greater the obstacles that have to be overcome, the more dramatic the action. Even if the needs are in the subtext – hidden by the words – they will still be driving the characters. Different practitioners use different terminology for these needs, but I shall stick to the term 'objectives'.

Be strict about putting your objective into the form, 'I want …' and choose positive rather than negative objectives – they're easier to play. So 'I want to be alone', rather than 'I don't want to be touched' or 'I want to avoid work' instead of 'I don't want to work'. These positive objectives are active rather than passive and will lead to actions to achieve them. Alan Alda, best known for his role in M*A*S*H, has said that he would like to put a sign up above every stage (or sound stage!): 'WHAT DO YOU WANT?'

Look for the main objectives first – the ones the character is pursuing long term. You might find these needs changing through the course of the film – maybe two, three or more large shifts. Let's call these major units. (The director will also need to identify the major units of the whole action of the film.)

The actor's major units are decided by the overall objective for those sections as opposed to the immediate wants that the character pursues at any given moment. For example, in Unit 1 of *Romeo and Juliet*, Romeo wants to be in love (he talks of his idealised love for Rosaline) but later, in Unit 2, when he meets Juliet, he wants her and only her. In Unit 3 he wants to avenge Mercutio's death, then, in Unit 4, to reconcile himself with Juliet, and in Unit 5 he wants to bind himself to her in death for ever.

The Jack Lemmon character, Bud, in *The Apartment*, wants promotion at the start of the film; then he wants out of the arrangement to lend his flat; later he wants Shirley MacLaine. Lester, played by Kevin Spacey in *American Beauty*, wants to keep the status quo at the beginning of the film; in the second unit he has an epiphany when he sees his daughter's friend and his objective changes; at first it is to bed the friend, but then it changes again. I don't know what Kevin Spacey chose for the final unit, but it might have been 'to refind myself', 'to recapture my awareness of life', 'to love' or 'to see beauty in life again'. These main objectives chart your character's journey through the film.

Now try to identify the character's super-objective. This is the deepest need permanently within the character that he or she may not even be aware of. It may not become clear that this need is there until the end of the film. The super-objective may be simple for a villain in a Bond film, like dominating the world. A more complex character may never come to recognise what drives him, but his hidden super-objective may instigate the path he takes.

Romeo's super-objective may be to find someone to give himself to utterly: his soul mate; Bud wants to be valued; Lester is searching for beauty, or kindness, or himself. These decisions are not absolute; they are for each actor and director to deduce from the text. Uncovering the super-objective will unlock the heart of your character's life and govern the choices that you make.

BUT ... during the film, you can only play your objective in the scene, and at any given moment. This can change during the scene and may not agree with your super-objective or your main objective. For example, your super-objective may be to find love, and at the start of the scene you may want to marry the hero, but at this point you just want to throw him out of your room because he's treating you too casually. At this moment, *this* objective is the *only* one you can play.

Although a given situation can endow you with mixed feelings and ambivalence, *you cannot play more than one objective at the same time*. This is important. If you try, the result will be muddy and unclear. But though you can play only one need at any given moment, you can swing to another in a split second. Don't bleed one moment into another but jump thought in an instant. If I'm walking down the street thinking about what I'm going to wear at the party and someone claps me on the back in greeting, I don't continue with my thoughts and then react – I enter the new situation in a split second.

Jogging round the block, thinking about this book, I noticed a frog stranded on the pavement. I picked him up and deposited him in some cool leaves in a nearby garden. While dealing with the frog, I had no other objective but to rescue him. Returning to the run, I vacillated between wanting to get to the top of the hill without expiring, wanting to ignore the pain by thinking about something else and, taking the pain as a given condition, trying to work out the next chapter.

Similarly, don't enter a future objective before it happens. If the scene begins with you welcoming a long-lost friend and then finding out she's seriously ill, don't pre-empt that knowledge. This is particularly important in film as you'll be redoing it over and over and will have to jump from the emotional consoling back to the joyous welcoming, time and again.

Sometimes though, a character may see something or think of a new objective while still having to say the words that reply to another character's last question. We will see your look – or read your new thought as subtext – as a new objective, while the words relate to the one before. So when you are marking your objectives, they don't necessarily pertain to the lines but to the inner needs of the character.

The change from one objective (or action) to another is called a 'beat'. It stems from Stanislavski again, although it may have been his Russian accent getting in the way when he was really saying 'bits'! (And indeed, early translations of his work do call them 'bits'.) Anyway, you'll hear many directors using the term 'beats'.

The movements from beat to beat are called 'transitions'. The speed at which your character changes beats reflects the rhythm of the character. Some people dwell on one thought for a long time, needing to find out everything about it; others dart from one need to the next. It's worth marking all the changes of objective in the scene – all the beats. Start by breaking the script into the major units, then find smaller units that you can give names to: 'I want to ask for a date', 'I want to drink away my sorrows', 'I want to make him pay' and so on.

This is very useful for a director to do too – by thinking in units and having titles for them rather than just scene numbers, the cast will have a handle on the content of the scenes. The director can use titles that apply to all the characters like 'the lovers' meeting', 'going wild', 'the row to end all rows' and so on. A film is really long and tiring and everyone will forget what scene 33 means. This gives them a useful shorthand. These units will reflect the overall action of the script and not be tied to a specific character's units as one character may change units when another does not.

Now divide each unit into beats – that is, note each time you change your objective. You will no longer see a scene as a single event or a monologue as one long speech. Exits and entrances, by the way, are nearly always new beats, as anyone joining or leaving a scene will cause a reaction in the other characters. Exceptions would be if your character is so wrapped up in his or her own thoughts or actions or so engrossed in conversation with another character that the arrivals and departures go unnoticed. I would argue that, for the director, exits and entrances of major characters (rather than background action) are always new beats.

If you can play only one objective at a time, what is the use of the super-objective – or 'spine' as it's sometimes called? (Patience Collier called it 'the pith'.) I've pondered over this a lot recently and I think that it affects your choice of immediate objectives and actions. This could be by causing an opposing reaction. For example, if you have decided that your character is looking for love and someone rejects you in the course of the film, you may take the objective, 'I want to make them pay'; and the action 'to humiliate'. If the character had not been looking for love, the reaction to rejection might not be so fierce.

If Hamlet did not have problems avenging his father's death and the super-objective, say, 'to find strength to act', would he have the same relationship with Horatio or use the same actions to play the scene where he cross-questions his mother and ends up killing Polonius? Obviously the text makes many of your choices for you, but the intensity of your actions and the precise nature of your objective is under your control. If it were not so, then every actor playing Hamlet would do it the same way – and that is clearly not the case. (Incidentally *Hamlet* has been filmed more than 25 times and played by, amongst others, Sarah Bernhardt in 1900, Laurence Olivier in 1948 and Kenneth Branagh in 1996. The classical actor Robert Stephens said that the part was so complex that you couldn't play it – you could only give an opinion of it!)

So although you can only play what you want *now*, at this precise moment, this inner knowledge of your character's super-objective will govern how you choose to get it. Even if your character has not recognised her or his super-objective, you need to be able to. Only then can you find an inner drive for the character. We may not identify what drives us through life, but it drives us all the same.

But that doesn't mean that you can change the script to make it fit your view of the character. Warning lights go on if I hear an actor say, 'my character just wouldn't do that' or 'I wouldn't say that'. If the script is incoherent or really badly written that may be so. You may need a script meeting. Or a little shared improvising. But be sure you are not just making it easy for yourself. Your character may sometimes act unpredictably. Film scripts are often open to some discussion, but beware of making your character too bland. Actors used to working with fixed scripts in theatre don't ask whether a character would do something, they accept that he or she does. It becomes their job to make the emotional leaps that allow it to happen. This can be a liberating approach for the film actor.

Jack Lemmon said that you shouldn't ask what your character 'would' do but what he 'could' do. We do not act consistently in life and your immediate objective might oppose your super-objective as we've seen. Doesn't it annoy you when you take a new decision and your loved one says, 'that isn't like you', or 'but you never enjoy that'. It is the crazy thing, the unexpected shift that makes a character have depth. It is your job to take all the pieces of the jigsaw and create a living, breathing, wonderfully human character. To create a logical journey through an illogical terrain.

An excellent game, derived from a workshop many years ago with the theatre director Clare Davidson, for honing the skill of driving objectives is as follows:

- Two strangers (they might have seen each other at a distance but don't know each other) sit in a neutral space – say a train station, a bus or a dentist's waiting room. They each take a strong objective that relates to the other character but they never reveal that objective. It could be an emotional objective – 'I want you to like me', or 'I want you to know I despise you'. Or it could be a practical one – 'I want to get a date', or 'I want money'. Or it may be a really devious one – 'I want to know if you're the woman who stole my husband' or 'I want it confirmed that you're responsible for the all-night parties'. Try all the kinds at different times.

Here are the rules:

- Never state your objective.
- Drive your objective with everything you say. (You can keep changing your action depending on your partner's response.)
- Don't get swayed by the other person's objective.

So for example, if one person is playing, 'I want you to know I worship you' and the other person is playing, 'I want you to know I despise you', you might get:

'You have beautiful eyes' (*action – I compliment*).

'Well, they don't want to look at you' (*action – I insult*).

'A glance is all I need' (*action – I plead*).

'Just leave me alone'; *she turns away* (*action – I reject*).

'Your back is magnificent' (*action – I worship*).

And so on. This exercise often gets very funny and is not meant to be naturalistic, although it's often uncomfortably like life. If you do it in a group, the others can guess the objectives at the end of the exercise. If the two have chosen conflicting objectives it works very well, if the objectives coincide, then the scene will be very short!

If you look at Act 1, Scene 2 of Shakespeare's *Richard III*, you will see this game being played. Anne has great reasons to hate and despise Richard. He has killed both her husband and her father-in-law. Her father-in-law's body lies on a bier between them. Richard woos her. Every time he compliments her or tries to touch her, Anne rejects him. And that rejection gives new fire to his purpose. She responds by humiliating him further. And yet by the end of the scene, she has taken his ring. His objective has finally overridden hers. Is it just his stronger willpower? Or is there an enormous sexual attraction in spite of his deformities? When does her objective change and what does it change to? Why does it change?

So far I haven't included 'Why?' in our list of questions. Actors often do need to ask why but I've left it out so far because it can lead you astray. If you answer, 'because I'm sad' or 'because I'm aroused', then you are stating a given conditioning factor. That's fine if you just accept that condition, but you can't play it. When you ask the question, 'Why?' the answer must lead to new objectives and actions. The detached viewer might see that Anne takes Richard's ring because she loses strength or feels drawn to him despite herself. It's more useful for the actor to turn that into 'I want to get away' (objective) so 'I buy time' (action), or 'I need to touch you' (objective) so 'I accept the ring' (action).

I used to set up an improvisation based on that scene. The characters became a gangster and a young woman whose boyfriend he had just killed. The body lay between them. The place was a disused, locked garage where they were alone at night.

I gave the man the objective, 'I want to get you into my bed' and the woman, 'I want you to know I despise you'. The rules were as the game above with the extra proviso that although threats were allowed, no force must be used.

At first the actors would find it absurd. Then they made it work and it was always very powerful. It was, in the end, usually the woman who gave in first, sometimes willingly – in spite of her horror and disgust.

Then I would ask them to read the original scene in Shakespeare's *Richard III*. Most agreed that if they had not done this exercise first, they would have considered it unplayable in a naturalistic style. And yet by playing objectives, the scene had acquired an emotional integrity and enormous excitement.

If you want to see how different actors coped with the scene, watch Laurence Olivier directing and acting in the famous 1955 film, Ian McKellen playing the part in a version set in the 30s, and Al Pacino exploring the character and charting how he worked on the role in *Looking for Richard*.

If it were important only to understand the words of a film, you could read the screenplay. It is what lies beneath those words that makes you go to watch it and that brings it to life. Your objectives provide the subtext to make your version of each role unique.

WHAT GETS IN MY WAY?

What makes for drama is the character's inability to achieve her or his objective. What gets in the way is the obstacle. This can be within the character's own psyche or a situation or circumstances outside the character's control.

An example would be what the Ancient Greeks called 'hubris': when the character's arrogance challenges the gods; pride comes before a fall – like Oedipus or Macbeth. Film characters who suffered from hubris might be Bonnie and Clyde or Butch Cassidy and Sundance. Sometimes it is a lack of strength of purpose within the character that prevents them from achieving what they want – like Hamlet, who could not find the resolve to kill his stepfather. Or the weakness might manifest itself in alcoholism or drug addiction which gets in the way of the character's objective and happiness.

The obstacle is often outside the character's control. As in *Romeo and Juliet* or the musical version, *West Side Story*, the lovers are from rival families. In *Brief Encounter* she is married and the social times and her sense of loyalty make her end the love affair. There might be war, power struggles, disasters, villains or poverty to battle. Whatever the screenwriter invents to throw in the way of the heroes and heroines becomes the passage of the film.

If it were not for obstacles, no film could sustain more than a few scenes. There is no audience involvement in a play where the hero achieves his quest without hindrance: 'a holy grail, my lord? No problem – I've seen one lying around here somewhere ...'

The obstacle might be a major one that stops you achieving your super-objective or it might be one that stops your immediate objective. Not succeeding in realising your objective will make you change your actions. The other actors in the scene will constantly throw up reactions that deflect your original decisions. You need to be alive to all the changes that happen in an instant. Don't be caught as in *The Two Ronnies* version of 'Mastermind', answering the question before last!

Traditionally, heroes usually achieve what they want eventually – unless they get killed off at the end. But on the way they are stopped, just long enough for us to enjoy the struggle.

HOW DO I GET WHAT I WANT?

The Shorter Oxford English Dictionary defines an actor as someone 'who conducts an action' or 'a doer'. When you try to get what you want, you do it by actions. These might be physical or psychological. Either are the outcomes of the character's objective.

When you don't immediately get what you want, like Richard III in that wooing scene, you change your action: everything from, 'I flatter', 'I appeal', 'I seduce' to 'I blackmail', 'I humiliate' or 'I threaten' – although the objective or need stays the same.

During your preparation, it is a good idea to write down your possible actions next to the appropriate moments in the script. Use verbs. For example: 'I cajole', 'I threaten', 'I plead', 'I hope', 'I manipulate', 'I provoke', 'I defend', 'I cover up', 'I entertain' and so on.

People get very hung up on how to phrase these actions or what verbs to use. Some acting handbooks even give you lists of possible verbs, but if the words don't hold some inner connection for you, they won't be useful. I don't think it matters what words you use as long as they are driven by the character's needs. You can phrase your action as 'I try to make him see' or 'I persuade'; 'I hide my tears' or 'I show her I'm brave'; 'I face the truth' or 'I accept' – it all depends on what works for your instincts.

Just avoid words that denote feelings which can lead you to colour your work with a generalised emotional wash and are the conditioning factors: 'I am angry', 'I am in love' or 'I am brave'. Thus: 'I remember my dead mother' rather than 'I am sad', 'I confide' rather than 'I am lonely'.

If you add adverbs to your action like 'I shout loudly', 'I kiss her lovingly', or 'I strike out bravely', it means you're looking at how you do it judgementally – from the outside. Always cross out any of these words the writer might have used.

Sometimes it isn't easy to separate your objective from your action. So what! It *can* be hard to make the distinction. Generally an objective is phrased as 'I want' and the action is the verb that you play to achieve it. Objectives tend to stay in place longer than actions, which can change rapidly. But that's not always so – you might have a character who keeps changing objectives. A lot of comedies do and the 'slalom', as Maria Aitken calls it – as the actor changes abruptly from one need to the next, like a skier swerving round the posts – is half the fun. As long as you've identified the changes and you're acting, doing, thinking, who cares?

Like objectives, it is easier to play positive actions than negative ones, so try turning 'I don't want her to know I'm hurt' to 'I cover up my pain' or 'I protect her'. You can use any kind of colloquial or personal language but active verbs are more useful than passive ones.

The great Italian actor, Eleonora Duse, had to make an explosive noise of disgust in a play she was doing in 1882. In the margin of her script she wrote, 'Stand erect, summon to the spirit all the words spoken, feel again all the torments of the love that is dead, reflect, realise that *he* never loved her in return: sum up all this in a single exclamation: puah!'

Duse was pre-Stanislavski, but see how many action words there are: 'I stand', 'I summon', 'I feel', 'I reflect', 'I realise', 'I sum up'.

I'm against getting too hung up on formulas. It's interesting to try to clarify our thoughts about them but, in the end, the only purpose in marking your objectives and actions is to make sure that you are not playing the emotion or the results – that you are working off drives and impulses as we are in life. So take all these ideas and then find your own way of phrasing your actions.

In early preparation, you can say your action out loud before you say your line. This sharpens your awareness of how the actions keep shifting to achieve the objective. Sometimes actors prefer to work by speaking the subtext of the character – the hidden thoughts behind the words. That's another way of finding these drives, which we'll explore in a later section.

Actions can change very quickly. I can try many different actions to gain my objective: for example, to get my son to do his homework, I might cajole, admonish, make him feel guilty, plead and threaten, all in the space of a couple of lines: (*cajole:*) 'Go on, it's easy. (*admonish:*) You always put it off. (*make him feel guilty:*) If you knew how much we've spent on your education! (*plead:*) Please, love – for me. (*threaten:*) If you don't write this essay tonight I'm not taking you sailing on Sunday.'

You get the idea. Sometimes an action changes very fast through an outside intervention – someone arriving, a phone call or a bomb going off outside.

Whereas objectives remain pretty fixed by the needs of the script and you can make decisions throughout preparation and rehearsal, keep your choice of actions fluid so that they can shift depending on how you bounce off the other characters. While it is helpful to write down possible actions at this early stage, these can only be provisional. In life, we may know what we want but the way we get it depends on how the other person reacts and what obstacles they put in our path.

Your preparation has given you an idea of the kind of choices available to you, guided by the character's scripted reaction. But you can play a line in many ways. You shouldn't stick to your pre-decided actions. If you pursue your objective, you will respond instinctively with different actions depending on your partner. Acting is reacting and interacting with the situation and the characters. Respond on the instant to your instincts. Anthony Hopkins calls it 'a tennis match'.

In theatre you rehearse in depth with fellow actors and respond to their input but for film you will usually do your preparation in isolation. So it is important that you don't stick to a programmed response when you get on set. Acting is about being alive in the moment so be sure you keep open to your fellow actors. In performance, like life, you don't have to think what action to take – you just do it.

I've just knocked over my coffee cup and my expletives were out before I even realised it – I didn't stop to think 'I swear' or 'I release my anger' first! If you let your preparation go on happening as you act, your head will get in the way of your organic responses and put a filter between the impulse and action. Then you will be imposing the worst kind of 'method' style on your work. It will be untruthful.

Here is an exercise to free up your actions. It is like a week's rehearsal in ten minutes. It is best done with a partner but you can do it alone by pretending that your partner never speaks or responds (use an empty chair for something to focus on):

- Sticking to our updated Richard III, let's write the line, 'I'll never want to be with you' for Anne, and for Richard, 'But you know I've always loved you'. These are the only words each of you can say.
- Keep repeating your lines or part of your lines, speaking in turns or together but in response to each other. You can move anywhere or do anything, but you can't say anything else. Start by consciously trying lots of different ways of reacting to your partner. Keep changing

objectives and actions every time you speak: I want you to know I despise you, I want to make love to you, I flirt, I tease, I humiliate, I repel, I seduce. Just keep pushing yourself in lots of different directions. Take the words out of context and don't get into a pattern. You can play against the lines so that 'I'll never want to be with you' could mean, I want you really. There could be moments that this is true for Anne – after all, she does accept Richard's ring.

- Soon it will become almost impossible to speak the words. That's OK. You're allowed silences. But drive through that block and keep going until the scene draws you along. You will find a great freedom and intensity. Eventually you will be reacting spontaneously and feel you're playing the original scene and really connecting to your partner.
- Then just hold each other's gaze and whisper the lines.
- Stop and have a hug (if you've got a partner!) – it can be quite draining.

Ideally you want someone watching to push you a little and stop you letting yourself off the hook until you're connecting emotionally with your partner.

You can also do the exercise by choosing and saying fixed objectives instead of the lines, such as: 'I want you to know I abhor you' and 'I want to get you into bed' but keep how you achieve the objective – your actions – flexible. While the first exercise is great for early exploration when you are still trying to find out what the characters do want, this version will give you enormous force and intensity once you've established the objectives. And it allows you the freedom to get what you want in a million different ways before you hone your possible choices.

You can also do this exercise with the lines or objectives for all the major beats of a scene and find its backbone very clearly and how the transitions work between them. It can be an amazing exercise. When we first look at a script we think, 'Oh, I know how to play this.' This exercise puts you through the limitless possibilities in the scene.

No one has put it better than Shakespeare in Hamlet's advice to the players: 'suit the action to the word, the word to the action'.

THOUGHTS ON THINKING

A quick word on 'thinking'. It is a word that I use a lot in this book and yet it needs defining. Having written at length about the need to think at every second, I found myself writing 'don't think – it will get in the way'. Well, that's confusing, I thought. What do I mean?

We're thinking all the time we're awake (and probably when we're asleep). Sometimes these thoughts are unconscious and sometimes they're conscious. The unconscious thoughts spring from an instinctive response to the situation, the conscious thoughts engage our intellectual reasoning and logic.

The actor has to deal with her or his own thoughts – of both kinds – and the character's thoughts – of both kinds. Let's call the actor's unconscious thoughts A1; the actor's conscious thoughts A2; the actor as character's unconscious thoughts C1; and the actor as character's conscious thoughts C2.

If the actor allows his or her own unconscious thoughts (A1) that are responses to the stresses of the surroundings, insecurities or a loss of energy (and which are nothing to do with the actual performance moment) to take away from the intense focus needed to engage in the scene, the work will become muddy and confused.

If the actor lets the conscious thoughts (A2) that have been part of the preparation work impede the natural flow of the scene, then the performance will be too cerebral and will not feel organic. So you cannot think, 'what is my action?' in the middle of playing a scene. Neither can you think the 'action', 'I reject you' and then be left to say the actual line, 'Leave me alone'. The action should be so instantaneous that the line will travel on it before you even know you've thought it.

Your unconscious instinctive responses in the acting moment become the character's unconscious instinctive responses (C1) and will keep the performance alive at every second. Breath, thought and action will work organically as in life. This 'thought' is so immediate that you and the character become indivisible at some deep level.

But the character also has 'in the acting moment' conscious thoughts (C2). If you are listening to another character, working something out or wrestling with an internal debate you will be aware that you are thinking as the character. This is part of an intelligent performance. It can't get in the way as long as these thoughts are springing into your mind as part of the scene. If you are signalling these thoughts to the audience, then you are standing outside your character.

So at the moment of playing your scene, your thoughts should be only in the C1 and C2 categories.

QUICK TIPS ON SCRIPT PREPARATION
- **Prepare yourself thoroughly** – through work on voice and body.
- **Get a feel of the whole script**, not just your part.
- **Find the story** (the given circumstances) – don't add things that don't help you pursue your course through the film.

- **See the world** through the character's eyes.
- **Don't judge** your character or hate or despise or feel sorry for them.
- **Justify** or accept your character's actions.
- **Who am I?** What is said of me? What is true? What do I surmise? What is like me? What is not?
- **Write an autobiography.**
- **Research** the period and environment.
- **Explore** your relationships with the other characters, the people you mention, animals, places and objects.
- **Identify** the conditioning factors.
- **Know what you want.** Find strong objectives – identify major units (the character's journey) – the super-objective (the spine) – then subdivide into smaller units and beats.
- **Have one thought** at a time.
- **What actions** do you take? Keep actions open and spontaneous.
- **Don't anticipate** or jump beats – a beat can be mid-sentence.
- **Be innocent** – your character doesn't know what will happen next or how it will end.

FEELING OF EASE

The acting teacher and director Michael Chekhov (who was Anton Chekhov's nephew) preferred the term 'feeling of ease' to relaxation. For him, it summed up a state where you have energy but not tension. Being relaxed is of no use if you are like a rag doll: without tone, without power. But before you start any kind of vocal or physical warm-up, it's important to minimise the unnecessary tensions that have accumulated in the body during the day and allow the breath and energy to 'centre'.

Frederick Matthias Alexander (1869–1955) was an Australian actor who kept losing his voice when he performed. By observing himself carefully in a mirror, he discovered that he pulled his neck back and down when he acted. For the rest of his life he worked on the importance of neck and spine alignment, developing what is now called the 'Alexander Technique' and this work has been used widely in training actors and as a basis for voice work.

Alexander believed that mind and body are one and that tensions and trying too hard for results mean that we put unnecessary effort into carrying out physical tasks. The extra work that we do, trying to achieve the task, actually hinders the action. For example, if you get out of a chair, you might hollow your back and tilt your chin upwards as you stand. This is a waste of energy. You need only to plant your feet firmly on the floor and let your thigh muscles do the work. This is really important when you're filming, as these extra movements take you out of frame or make you look awkward.

Performance tension often leads actors, like Alexander himself, to hold their necks out of alignment with their spines. Instead of the head moving freely on top of the spinal column, it is held up at an angle or tucked in at the chin. This disconnects the voice from its breath support, making it thinner, breathier or higher. But it also disconnects you from your emotions. Your head and neck alignment is crucial to the way the rest of your body will interact – the way your arms swing, your hips move and the free movement of your ribs and diaphragm.

When you stand, it's useful to think of an invisible thread of energy going from the crown of your head up into space and from your feet down into the centre of the earth. Your shoulders should feel that they are radiating to either side of the room. Don't allow your knees to lock or your back to hollow. Really feel rooted to the floor – imagine your twin, your doppelgänger, upside down beneath you. Keep contact between the soles of your feet and your twin's. Don't let your twin fall into the centre of the earth.

Lying in an 'Alexander' position is a good way to let the tensions in your back and neck muscles ease and to prepare for work. You have to stop before you can go.

- Lie on the floor on your back on a blanket or a mat.
- Give up to the floor – it won't collapse under you. Don't hold any muscles to support your weight.
- Put a paperback book under your head. Adjust the height of the book so that your neck lengthens at the back and your chin is neither tucked in nor jutting up.
- Shut your eyes.
- Bring your knees up; feet on the floor, shoulder-width apart.
- Let your arms lie comfortably alongside your body, palms up.
- Allow the floor to take your weight. Don't hang on to any muscles.
- Go through your body, tensing and releasing the muscles. (It's really hard to relax your muscles without contracting them first.) Tense your toes ... relax; tense your legs ... relax; tense your buttocks and stomach ... relax; tense your hands (lift them a little) ... relax; lift your shoulders up ... relax; press your shoulders down into the floor and away from your ears ... relax; press your head lightly into the book ... relax; screw up your face lightly ... relax; wiggle your tongue ... relax.
- Now just listen to the sounds around you. Don't think about your breathing – just give up to the floor for a few minutes.
- Slide a hand on to your stomach – quite low with your thumb on your navel.
- Relax again and listen to the sounds around you and just observe your body.
- As you get more relaxed, so you will feel the hand on your stomach rising on the in-breath and falling on the out-breath.
- Increase this movement (but don't hollow your back) so that you really release your abdomen with the incoming breath. Feel that your breath drops in deeply.
- On the out-breath, consciously allow your stomach to pull gently inwards and upwards (as if making yourself slimmer).
- Breathe in for a count of 3 and out for a count of 6, in for 3 and out for 7, in for 3 and out for 8, in for 3 and out for 9, in for 3 and out for 10.
- Now find your own natural rhythm of breathing.

You may want to find some relaxation classes. Your local gym will probably have lots of these on offer – stretching and relaxation, Swiss-ball, yoga or t'ai chi. The traditional hatha yoga is better for relaxation than the fast astanga forms. Stanislavski incorporated yoga into his work to focus 'prana' – the energy you radiate out to reach someone else. Yoga, t'ai chi and chi gung can put you in touch with your energy – chi – in an extraordinarily vivid way. Paul J. Underwood, who is an acupuncturist and a t'ai chi and chi gung instructor, says that these exercises are particularly useful for actors, 'as they involve not only the physical body, but also the emotional, mental and spiritual aspects of the person, enhancing their self-image, memory, confidence and ability to focus'.

If you go to an Alexander teacher, expect the work and progress to be slow. Make sure you choose one who works with actors and understands that when you work you have to just 'go'. There is a danger inherent in Alexander work that it can make you too careful. The work of Moshe Feldenkrais is a later offshoot of Alexander's work. The good thing about Feldenkrais is you can do it in a group, using a wide range of movements and it can be more liberating to an actor.

Pilates is popular and good for back problems. Pilates teachers urge you to contract your stomach muscles to protect your back. This is good practice while you perform the activity but some Pilates teachers ask you to hold your stomach in permanently. This is no use to actors. So if you do Pilates, remember to release your abdominal muscles to allow full released breathing again after completing the session.

Sometimes massage, like osteopathy, acupuncture, chiropractic and even deep breathing work can temporarily make you feel a little emotional. That's because it has released tensions that we lock into our bodies to protect ourselves. It will pass and as an actor you need to release these tensions. I knew an actor who was so pleased with the benefits of massage that he wanted to share them. He started a facial massage parlour in Chelsea in the 1970s. In the end he had to pay to have a counsellor on hand to comfort his wealthy weeping clients. They felt better afterwards though!

Exercise is also relaxing. It helps to oxygenate the bloodstream and utilise lactic acid, making you more alert and focused. Swimming, jogging, walking, rowing or carefully balanced weight training can help you to relax at the end of a hard day, as well as keeping you fit. Some people swear by starting the day with a cold shower. Personally I prefer relaxing in a hot bath. At the end of a long day at the studio it can help you to unwind – and the steam is good for your voice!

THE BREATH OF LIFE

The breath is literally at the life of everything. Our breath and thoughts are inextricably linked. When we have a new thought or an extension of a thought, we draw breath. The word for having an idea is 'inspiration' and when we breathe, we 'inspire'. You as an actor will inspire others. The audience in the cinema actually starts to breathe at the same pace as the actor they identify with, to hold their breath when the heroine holds hers, to gasp when she does. If the actor's breath is flowing freely, we are relaxed; if it is not, we start to feel uncomfortable. Our speech rhythms and even our thought rhythms are thus directly connected to our breathing rhythms and you can find the unique tempo of your character through these connections.

Some characters are so full of energy that they barely manage to rush a breath in before the next thought and they drive their thoughts to the very end of their breath. Others breathe out before speaking. They are so filled with the cares of the world that they cannot commit the breath energy to the word. So they sigh out what they say.

Sometimes people need to breathe often while they speak, as they choose, discard and select each word with enormous difficulty. Sometimes the words flow along on a river of sound – a free-flowing breath stream.

The quality of voice is directly related to the breath. Too little breath and the sound will be strained and creaky with no resonance. When you are tense, the larynx gets held a little high in the pharynx and the pitch goes up. If you allow the breath to escape through a chink in the vocal folds so that they don't meet fully to vibrate, you will sound unconfident and unfocused with no resonance. When breath is harnessed effortlessly to sound, the voice will respond to every thought and feeling. It is the most subtle instrument imaginable.

While you listen to the other actors, make sure that you are breathing. It is quite common to hold your breath in this situation. In order to protect ourselves, we instinctively hold everything static and this stops us reacting freely and blocks our instant responses.

We feel emotions in our solar plexus where all the sympathetic and parasympathetic nerve endings meet. We talk of literally 'aching with sorrow' or having 'butterflies in the tummy' when we're nervous. We get a 'stab of fear' in the stomach, anger 'clenches up our insides' and 'sick with disgust'.

This is also the area where the large double-domed sheet of the diaphragm, contracts and flattens downwards to allow our breath to fill our lungs and releases effortlessly to expel each breath. If the stomach is locked and the breath is held, then this channel to the emotions isn't open. When we are connected to these feelings, the voice automatically drives from the centre – what voice teachers mean by 'rooting' the sound. Righteous anger produces an enormous voice that sometimes surprises the owner, and heartfelt emotion, freely confessed from this deep area, has an open honest sound.

Sometimes actors are unable to release their emotional energy through the words. They end up with the kind of forced overemotional work you sometimes see on the worst of television soaps. The voice goes up, the face overworks and the acting seems melodramatic. If they fully connect breath and sound, the work becomes truthful and grounded and they have immediate access to their feelings. When you breathe freely without effort, you have a direct connection between breath, thought and voice. The channel is open and you can contact your feelings and communicate them through your actions.

As soon as the body senses danger, it protects you by getting ready to close off the larynx. When the throat is constricted, the channel to the breath isn't open. Try this:

- Put your hands over your ears, breathe through the mouth and hear your own breath coming in and going out.
- Now tell yourself to make it completely silent in both directions. You should feel the throat as more 'open'. You may also feel more movement in the abdominal area as you use a deeper breath.
- Now speak. Don't use a breathy voice. Stay on a full sound but keep the sense of 'openness'.

Releasing constriction in the throat enables free access between feelings and words. You will feel more vulnerable and open to the world around you. When we speak, we often leave the throat slightly closed. This gives the voice a 'creaky sound' as there isn't enough breath fully to power the voice. You will hear this voice quality in teenagers, when it's not cool to use too much effort, or old people, who haven't the strength to open up fully. It is also a feature of some accents – in Los Angeles, for example, people often go to 'creak' at the end of a sentence.

By closing the throat, your body is protecting you from choking on your cup of tea. When you eat or drink, your body shuts off your air passage and sends the food down the oesophagus instead. When the body senses danger, the throat closes up, so you need to consciously keep the breath flowing when you are tense.

In camera close-up, any tension in the breathing mechanism will show as tension in the face. You will be slightly 'pushing' because there won't be an organic connection between thought and breath. The camera will spot these little telltale signs – a twitch of an eyebrow, a furrowed brow, a tense mouth, a slightly high voice and a lack of emotional connection. You will look as if you are acting and not 'being'.

Unfortunately, the body doesn't care about your acting – it only wants you to survive. So with adrenalin racing through the body, it tries to protect your vulnerable abdomen by tensing your stomach muscles. Then, when you take a breath, you draw the breath into the upper chest. This is called a clavicular breath and is part of the body's 'fight or flight' mechanism. Clavicular breathing makes you feel unconfident and uncentred as an actor. It also gives you less lung volume, so you work really hard for little reward.

As we saw in the section on Feeling of Ease, it is really important to be able to release the abdominal muscles to allow you to take a natural relaxed breath when you are tense. Sitting comfortably in a chair, or lying on your back:

- Put your hand on your stomach, quite low with the thumb on your navel.
- Let the breath out slowly on a sustained Shh (like telling someone to be quiet) feeling your stomach flatten towards your spine.
- Relax the stomach muscles at the end of the out-breath and feel them release back out into your hand as the breath comes in.
- Now consciously pull your stomach inwards and upwards again as you let the breath out on three short beats – Shh-Shh-Shh. (Make sure you really say 'Shh' rather than just a breath release – it gives you resistance to work against.)
- Again on the in-breath make sure the stomach completely recoils to the starting point.
- Repeat six more times.

The diaphragm is contracting downwards as you breathe in and the abdominal muscles need to be relaxed in order for it to descend unrestricted so your stomach releases outwards.

When you breathe out, the diaphragm relaxes back upwards and the abdominal muscles contract to help expel the breath so your stomach goes inwards.

This abdominal–diaphragmatic breathing exercise strengthens the muscles, helps them remember to work automatically in the right direction and encourages flexible release. If you perfect this recoil method of breathing under stress – which is, after all, your natural relaxed breathing method – you will never have a noisy intake of breath and your voice will sound resonant and be able to respond to your intentions.

You will find a full voice workout at the end of the book. By training yourself to release your stomach muscles for a new breath at tense moments, you will breathe freely in all situations. Even in close-up!

THE SCAFFOLDING

As we've said, nerves will affect your posture. Posture also affects your breathing. You know the old song, 'your hip bone's connected to your thigh bone ...' – well, the larynx is the only jointed structure in your body that isn't joined to another. Because the larynx is suspended only by ligaments and muscles, a good alignment of your neck and back is really important to keep your breath flowing freely and your vocal tone free and resonant – it provides the scaffolding that ensures everything is in place.

You can easily test this for yourself:

- Stand or sit with your shoulders relaxed and free. Imagine a string pulling upwards from the crown of your head so that your chin is neither tucked in nor lifted up, but is parallel to the floor with your neck lengthened at the back. Have your feet flat on the floor if you are sitting. If you are standing, feel your weight evenly distributed on your feet and don't lock your knees. As you breathe, feel your stomach moving outwards on the in-breath and inwards on the out-breath.
- Shut your eyes. Feel the breath coming in and out comfortably while you breathe through your nose. Now lift your shoulders. Try to breathe – and feel the difference. Drop them again. Now concave your chest. Note the constriction. Finally stick your chin out slightly. You will find a real difficulty keeping the breath flowing. (This position also affects the tone and volume of the voice, which is why you will never see an opera singer in this position.)
- Now return to your well-aligned posture and free breathing.

You can see that when you make postural character choices, you need to be sure that you are not restricting your breathing or increasing your anxiety by choosing a posture that is too closed or tense.

QUICK TIPS FOR BREATHING

- **Feeling of ease** – not de-energised. Tense muscles first – then release them.
- **Feel feet** are firmly grounded: crown of head pulled upwards by an imaginary string, shoulders wide and free (not braced), knees not locked. Try not to take character choices too far from this ideal.
- **Work for alignment** of head and neck – don't stick out your chin. Lengthen at the back of the neck.
- **Don't take a breath in on 'Action'**. If you are in 'fight or flight' mode, it will just jam everything up. Trust you'll have enough breath, go and the body will catch up naturally.
- **Release your stomach muscles** (out) when you breathe in, contract them (in) when you breathe out. Find a natural unforced recoil movement. Don't take the breath into the upper chest.
- **A new thought** is a new breath.
- **Keep breath flowing** – don't constrict your throat.
- **DON'T HOLD YOUR BREATH WHEN LISTENING OR TENSE.** THIS IS THE SINGLE MOST IMPORTANT ADVICE I CAN GIVE YOU.

MUSCLES HAVE MEMORY

Our bodies reflect the lives we lead or have led. The way we move, our physical habits and how we set our bodies are a unique testimony to our personal choices throughout our lives, coupled with our individual genetically moulded physical characteristics. You can't do much about your genetics, but you can change the other aspects of your physicality.

One way of getting physical character choices to feel organic and not to drift into stereotypical generalisations is to find a way of patterning your body by living out an accelerated version of your character's life. You need any body changes to be really specific.

Let's start with age. Usually you will be cast within your own age range, but there are parts that may require you to age from, say, thirty to seventy. Obviously the make-up department will make you look wonderfully old, but how do you feel it in the body? Here is an exercise which will increase your kinaesthetic awareness – even if you never have to age on film. Try out the movements and thoughts and feel the effects of the changes in your body. This is one particular character's path through life:

- Start at age 7. Move around the room feeling how little gravity affects you. Expend your energy with no regard to the future. Feel how little relationship with the floor you need. You can change direction and attention in an instant. You can jump and roll and yell. You like to look at the world upside down or on your back. Possibilities are endless and all is possible.
- Age 17. Gravity still doesn't really hold you down. Your energy has diminished very little but it is more channelled into what you need to achieve. Sometimes you leap into the air and yell as you remember something exciting. Then you feel a little embarrassed and try to curb your energy – to look like an adult. You may be slightly self-conscious about your body and close up to hide it if someone is watching you. You look as much at the sky as at the earth.
- You're 27. Still got loads of energy but you're a little more connected to the earth. More grounded. Silly to expend more energy than you need to – you've got a working day tomorrow. You're not self-conscious of your body but you're aware of the effect you have on the

world around you. You sit on the floor to relax. You hum a tune that reminds you of a lover from your past.

- 37 years old. No problems with your body or your energy yet. But it makes sense to conserve that energy – you've got a heavy day ahead. Mortgage worries are getting to you, so you sit down while you work them out. It's nice to feel the comfort of a chair and you lean back and shut your eyes. You sigh in spite of yourself.

- At 47. You're going to the gym now and proud of how you keep yourself in trim. Keeping fit has become a preoccupation. As you walk around the room tidying up, you are aware of a slight twinge between your shoulder blades. Your legs ache a little from the workout yesterday and your feet feel a bit heavy. You're going for promotion at work. You talk aloud as you take yourself through your meeting with your boss tomorrow. You're aware of gravity now but you consciously resist it. You sit in a chair and, without realising it, you use your hand on the arm to get in and out of it. Doors are closing and all things are no longer possible.

- 57 now. You wake stiffly in the mornings and are aware of the odd twinges in your back. You've stopped sleeping on your front since you did your neck in. Sleeping on your back is the most comfortable, although you tend to snore. You have to be a bit careful how you lift things as your lower back twinges. When you walk you shorten your steps a little so that you keep more contact with the floor. Sometimes you catch yourself making a little exertion noise as you get in and out of your chair. One arm annoys you, as you keep getting a frozen shoulder and reaching is painful. You try to remember someone's name but can't. It's exasperating. Gravity is pulling your body downwards, rounding your back, sagging your posture.

- Age 67. You're proud of how well you're ageing and you consciously stride out to go where you want. When you don't think about it, you walk in shorter steps with a wider stance to give yourself more stability and keep a connection with the earth. You look more often at the earth than at the sky. You know which movements cause a problem, so you hold your body more carefully – gradually your range of movement has lessened. You use a bag with wheels to shop or take the car which you've changed to get more room in the front seat. When you sit, you take all your weight on to the arms of the chair. You do the same to get up.

- 77 and proud of it. You're having a new lease of life. You've joined a gardening club and your son-in-law has built up the flowerbeds so you don't have to stoop so much. Gravity has become your friend and you walk slowly without lifting your feet much off the floor. You wear your slippers whenever you're home because they're more comfortable. You need a banister to get up the stairs and you've put a handle by your bath. You keep one hand touching something solid – an umbrella, a walking stick or the chair back – so that you always feel connected to the earth. Space feels dangerous. You've lost your sense of balance. You get vertigo.

- 87. You are soon to return completely to the earth. When you walk, you make your feet wide and make sure one foot is always connected to the floor. You may need physical support. Your eyes look mostly at the floor when you walk. You rarely see the sky. The possibility of seeing tomorrow is now your great adventure.

Your character may not age like this. I know 87 year olds who are still pretty spry and look ten years younger, and 97 year olds who are still active in mind and body. You can adjust it to your character. But do you know that, medically speaking, your sense of balance declines from about forty? Someone who does yoga or t'ai chi or a sport that requires balance can keep vertigo at bay, though, for decades longer. Different characters' lifestyles and personalities will make your ageing choices different.

Pregnancy brings obvious changes in balance and body distribution. Strap a cushion in front of you and see how you'd cope with it there all evening and what changes in balance and energy you'd make. You will tend to lean back and keep your feet further apart to give you a wider base. Crossing your legs is effortful and difficult in late pregnancy. Your breasts are heavier too. The baby needs protecting and your hand on your belly will instinctively guard it right from the early stages of pregnancy. You'll feel hot and glowing, which can be comfortable in winter and hell in summer. Your feet will ache and your ankles will swell.

Every illness has specific aches, pains and discomforts and sometimes emotional changes too. Never be generalised. Research the illness if you haven't experienced it, and feel it in just one or two particular places. (After rehearsing or shooting do a relaxation session for yourself and visualise yourself as healthy again. The mind–body connection can sometimes be too powerful!)

What work does your character do? If you are bent over a computer all day, there will be changes in your spine and vision. If you sew all day, it will change your hands, your sense of touch and your eyesight. If your character works the land, you need to do something physical in preparation to let your muscles feel that work. You can then distil this into some small movements that you can use as a preparation in your trailer or dressing room. (By the way, only really top stars have trailers on film sets – mere mortals have dressing rooms situated in the same block as the make-up and hair departments. But on location you will have your very own trailer!)

The clothes that your character wears change your body. If you need to wear high heels, then start wearing them now. If you are in a period film, then wear long skirts as you go about your daily life. Buy a light corset. Men can ditch the trainers for proper shoes and wear a jacket. All these things will have an effect on your posture and movement. Many great actors like Alec Guinness, Anthony Hopkins and Laurence Olivier started by finding the shoes of the character first. Johnny Depp says he is fascinated by feet – 'they tell you so much about people'.

Clothes and hairstyles are not unimportant for the actor. They are part of how we interact with the world. You feel really different when you wear different clothes. Try going out in your oldest scruffiest clothes one day and really dressed up the next. You'll see altered reactions from people around you. Is this because we feel different or because we look different? Probably a combination of the two.

There have been many studies carried out into people's preconceptions about appearances. In a recent one, a smartly dressed man, apparently ill, was found doubled up in pain outside a major London railway station. Hidden cameras recorded passers-by offering help within minutes. The same man was given old jeans and a scruffy T-shirt and placed in the situation again. He lay there for over an hour, moaning for help. No one stopped. Frightening, isn't it? But fascinating for the actor.

Go around the park or out to the shops in your new body. Carry out different tasks as your character – do you do them differently? I worked with an actor who was a model from New York. His body held memories of nothing more strenuous than photo-shoots and window-shopping. He looked urban, modern and cool. But he had to play a medieval peasant who lived off the land and went to war. On our first meeting, I had the poor man running barefoot through French fields trying to catch rabbits and wading in icy water looking for fish.

He did lots of physical improvisations over the coming weeks as well as walking, swimming, archery and horse-riding. Emotional physical improvisations followed: he dug graves and buried comrades, lit fires to ward off wild animals, fought battles and ran for his life. He was excited by how differently his body could move. When he came to filming, he distilled these experiences into something small that would keep alive these new muscle memories, spending the first few weeks whittling a stick in his trailer and between shots. He was great in the role. And he looked really different.

PULLING STATUS

We all carry a private space around with us. This space is forbidden territory and can only be invaded by close friends and relatives. Different cultures have different perceptions of private space. The British and the North Americans like a wider space around them than some Asian cultures, for example. If two people from different cultures have a conversation, the one with the smaller personal space will try to get closer and the other will keep backing away. You can watch them gradually progress across the room at a party until one is pinned against the table of drinks.

An invasion of personal space can cause stress. Crowded places like tube trains and lifts in rush hours can cause increased heart rates and raised tempers. People cope by cutting off from each other as much as they can by reading a paper or the adverts, thereby avoiding eye contact. If someone invades your space by touch, in this closed environment it can be very disturbing. Perhaps because city life forces people to override their natural instincts in order to cope with close body contact with strangers, they are less likely to respond with compassion to the stranger on the street. In more relaxed surroundings they revert to their innate humane responses.

Performing conditions often require us to override our perceptions of body space. Theatre – because the actors have to be seen across a distance – requires the actors to stand further apart than seems natural to them. At first it is difficult for actors not to move instinctively closer in an intimate scene. Conversely – in order to fit into the frame of the camera – actors on film are often asked to stand much closer together than their instincts dictate. So you will have to overcome the sense of having your private space invaded and your status lowered.

Our status, as perceived by us, affects the way we stand, our gaze, our gestures and the way we talk. The higher status we feel, the more space we take up in the world, the longer we hold eye contact and the bigger we make our movements. The thug who feels in charge of the street, walks with a swagger swinging his shoulders; the business man in a hurry wields his briefcase and lengthens his stride to signal his importance; the call girl who's won a trick wiggles her hips, thrusts out her breasts and tosses her hair. We increase our feeling of status with our clothes and accessories – padded shoulders, flowing scarves and cloaks, higher heels, hairstyles, hats and large cars.

In order to confer status, we award badges of authority – we give policemen uniforms, judges wigs and market researchers clipboards. We increase private space upwards or outwards: managers have large chairs and desks to protect them, teachers sit behind, or even on, tables, politicians use platforms, bankers work from large high-rise offices, royalty sits on thrones. Theatre actors have stages and movie stars look down from high billboards and enormous screens!

Actors can pull status by 'upstaging' – forcing the other actor to turn away from the camera, to respond. More often they upstage themselves – putting a barrier between the all-prying camera eye by turning away or averting their gaze. Or they make the space they take up in the world smaller, by pulling in their shoulders and tucking in chins and elbows.

We also take up the amount of space vocally that we feel reflects our position in the world. Those who feel less in control, allow their voices to become quiet and breathy. They use short sentences and fear interruption or speak for too long because they lack the courage to stop. If we feel confident, we 'support' the sound so that it carries well. We tend to use more volume and expect people to listen for longer. If we use short sentences, then it is with authority. If we whisper, it is because we choose to. We send out verbal signals with the volume, stresses and tones of voice that we use.

Professional people evolve complicated language and members of groups develop a private mode of speech or coin jargon, often inaccessible to people outside their world. Lawyers, financial experts and politicians use circumlocution and technical language. They expect you to give them the time to listen and try to understand – or they hope you won't. High status characters, like those of Oscar Wilde and Noel Coward, use language like weapons to cut and kill. It is a constant challenge to find the physical and vocal qualities of characters that may have different social and status perceptions to your own. And to 'wear' the language your character uses in the film.

In *The Silence of the Lambs*, Anthony Hopkins chose to be discovered standing in the middle of his cell waiting for Jodie Foster. The director had planned for him to be sitting at the back, but Hopkins wanted to unnerve her as she turned the corner by being ready for her – sensing her, smelling her. Immediately his status seems more elevated than hers. In *Glengarry Glen Ross*, Jack Lemmon's status in relation to Kevin Spacey and Al Pacino becomes much higher when he thinks he's made a big sale.

You will be in a different status relationship with every character in the film. One might be your boss, another your employee. Or you might be the employee blackmailing the boss so your internal status will be higher. Your status might be equal but there will still be moments in a scene, when you score a point or feel humiliated, that this status will change. This shifting status moves the scene along.

Look around a café or train station and you will see different status relationships: the mother and child, the eager husband, the bullied wife, the cocky adolescent. You will also see status changes reflected in their body language. This will sometimes be overt – like standing up in order to yell; and sometimes subtle – a slight shift of a chair or legs crossed from one side to another.

An exercise in status that will increase your awareness of how it affects our dealings with others and for which you need nerves of steel, is to cross a bridge at rush hour and hold high status. Waterloo Bridge, for example, is perfect. Pedestrians coming from the station crowd the pavement to cross into the city. If you walk against the flow determined not to give ground, you will see that people have a clearly perceived status and a view of their priority to pass across the bridge without hindrance. Most of them will be completely unconscious of this hierarchy but will be assessing status priorities from many yards away. Those who deem themselves more important will literally barge into you with their briefcases, others will stop at the last minute and give you an amazed look or a curse as they step out of the way. Others have started moving out into the road – assessing your higher status – long before you reach them. Occasionally you will find yourself doing a little dance of apologies with someone who expected *you* to move but found, as they came, embarrassed, out of their reverie, that you had thought *they* would.

Of course there are exceptions, but stereotypically, male businessmen are more likely to assume higher status and middle-aged women tend to take the widest detours. Anyone can come out of automatic pilot at any time and make a conscious decision to move, so a high-status person will move out of the way of anyone who seems a threat, like a drunk or someone behaving unpredictably, or for a disabled person or for a pretty girl.

Old people get barged a lot. This is because they haven't noticed that they've got old so they still see their right of way as stronger than other faster travellers who perceive them as lower status. This is even more extreme if they come from cultures where they are normally given due authority.

Different cultures may have different status perceptions and react differently to the local London population. Tourists have all the time in the world and don't react to the same pressures that drive people to pull status. So you may find them either avoiding you completely as you steer your course, or getting in your way because they aren't switched on to the need to assess your passage.

This exercise can be a frightening and illuminating experience!

Go through your script looking for status changes. See where you feel silly or proud or ill at ease. In preparation, mark these status changes physically by actually raising or lowering your body. If you are working with a partner, put out a couple of strong, stable chairs. If your character scores an emotional point or feels they're winning the argument, jump on a chair (the other person has to jump off to be lower than you), if you feel defeated, lie on the floor. This simple exercise really pinpoints where you change status and how this affects the relationship. Your character's perceived status will affect your whole physicality – posture, gaze, movements and gestures.

HIDDEN MESSAGES

In the old Eastern European bloc, the teaching of Stanislavski was banned in many drama colleges because the authorities were afraid people would become too sophisticated at understanding what lay behind their words. As people did, indeed, become more mistrustful of language, a new kind of physical theatre evolved. Gesture and movements seemed to expose feelings with less guile. Early silent cinema relied on our ability to understand the emotional nuances of people's physical behaviour. And that remains true, albeit in a subtler way, of all cinema. In our daily lives, we also rely on an instinctive reaction to body language in order to read people's intentions.

Become a people watcher. Watch people at work, at play and at moments of emotion. Observe them carefully: all the little body clues, all the ways they interact. When do they laugh? How do they cope with social pressure? In what ways do they show love or fear or disgust?

How do we make assumptions about personalities? We watch the complicated signals that people send out – the hidden messages. Their smiles and frowns, whether they bare their teeth or raise an eyebrow. All animals read body signals to check their safety and to see if their overtures are welcome. Humans are no different and in spite of our sophisticated use of language, we are still subconsciously reading these tiny signals. Without being aware of it, we make decisions about someone within a few seconds – whether they are friend or foe, false or sincere, understanding or judgemental, vulnerable or secure – decisions that are sometimes hard to reverse on better acquaintance. When we accept coffee late at night at a stranger's flat this is all we have to guide us. We call it a sixth sense.

Eye contact is of primary importance. We hold a gaze or break it. If we are shy, it is hard to hold a steady gaze. We want to hide by looking away or down in spite of ourselves. If we are playing very high status we might make a choice to look away to make the person feel humiliated by denying them our attention, or we will stare at them without breaking eye contact. Like the schoolteacher, who either will not acknowledge the pupil's late entrance or who glares him into contrition.

Eyes are instantly recognisable: at the beginning of *The Hunt for Red October*, we can identify Sean Connery by a narrow strip that shows only his eyes. We communicate warmth and friendship by crinkling the corners of our eyes. If someone smiles without it reaching their eyes, you will read it as insincere. Our pupils dilate when we are excited. (Chinese opium dealers know whether to put the price up by watching the buyer's eyes.) A study was done showing people identical photos of a woman, except that in one her pupils were dilated. They overwhelmingly voted for that photograph – which is not surprising, since it mimicked what happens to the eyes during sexual arousal.

So you need to be sure that your nerves don't get in the way of how you use eye contact for the role, that you don't keep blinking or buy yourself space. We have a kind of code about how much we look at someone in conversation. Unless we are showing deep concern, love or anger, we look away often as we speak. We look away to focus our thoughts or to see the inner pictures in our head before looking back at our partner to see if they're still interested or to show we're listening to them. If what we're saying is painful or difficult, we may not look at them at all. As long as you are following the character's actions, you will automatically be using the right eye contact. You might even find your pupils dilating – Eleonora Duse was said to blush at will!

In *Rear Window* James Stewart is confined to his room with a broken leg. He is a photographer (a professional people-watcher) and bored. He gets more and more involved in the lives of his neighbours and eventually, by watching their body language through the lit windows of their apartments, uncovers a murder. We constantly reveal ourselves through our gestures and movements. Some gestures are conscious and social – like handshakes, or sticking up one finger when someone cuts you up in your car. As these social gestures vary from culture to culture, period to period and from one social group to another, it can be important to know the local code. The Masonic handshake, giving it 'the high five', theatrical kisses or the brisk business grip all act as signals to the other person that you belong to their gang.

Other gestures are quite unconscious and reflect some inner drive.

These are called 'displacement activities'. You want to walk away from the boring meeting but you can't, so you flap your feet. You'd love to hit the annoying chat show host but you scratch your head instead. You're pleased with your remark so you lean back and cross your hands behind your head. You want to show the stuffy boardroom you're a modern woman so you cross your legs, putting your ankle across your knee. (This last is a male gesture of sexual pursuit which women began assuming in the 1970s.) You fancy the boss so you play with your hair and tilt your head.

Emotions are reflected by body actions – we tap tables in frustration, bite our nails as we worry, rub our foreheads to erase a painful memory or suck our thumbs when we have long outgrown our childhood. You see people in great emotional pain holding themselves tightly or rocking themselves for comfort. Allow your character's emotions to infuse your whole body.

If you turn the sound off on a video of a movie you can still tell how the characters feel about each other by the way they interact physically. We reflect the body gestures of those with whom we feel in tune. If you watch people talking, you'll see that those in sympathy with each other allow their bodies to flow in the same direction: they cross their legs towards each other and gesture with the arm closest to their companion. They lean in to each other and look at each other a lot. When people dislike each other they'll put up an arm to create a barrier, cross their legs in the opposite direction or choose completely different postures. They lean away from each other (schoolboys lean their chairs so far back from the teacher, they often tip over) and use little eye contact. We use folded arms, hands in pockets, closed eyes, sunglasses (especially the kind that reflect back the other person), desks, lecterns or even doors as barriers to ward off other people. Children, animals and audiences come more readily to people with an open body posture and no barriers.

We also take strength from furniture, handbags, briefcases, notebooks, folders, jewellery and our scripts. Actors like to move from one piece of furniture to another and are very reluctant to put their scripts down. Props can be useful if they add something to our knowledge of the character and are distracting if they don't. If it's you, the actor, fiddling with your ring, chewing your pen or folding your arms then you will be blocking us from seeing your performance. If it is the character needing this protection, then choose it with care. It is like salt on your food – it can add to the flavour or ruin the dish.

We also apologise with body language for our own social gaffes. If you trip going down the street you might stop, examine your shoe or the pavement, shake your head and mutter before you move on. If you are greeting a friend and they don't recognise you, you might change your gesture to smoothing your hair. These little pantomimes are a way of saying to the world (which probably isn't watching), 'it wasn't my fault' or 'I wasn't really doing that'. We show we don't really mean what we're saying with little gestures of apology, we open our palms in supplication when we say sorry or rub them together as we make a request that embarrasses. The French shrug their shoulders and open their hands to indicate, 'what can I do?' If they are not careful, actors show their insecurity on their faces by apologising for a bad take or a 'fluff' with a little grimace or a shake of the head.

THE PSYCHOLOGICAL GESTURE

When people recall a particular incident, they often 'echo' a gesture of what they did at the time or they make a movement which is a metaphor for their state of mind, like grabbing an imaginary post to steady themselves or stabbing an inner enemy, or, if you are Hannibal Lecter, smacking your lips at the thought of human liver, fava beans and a little Chianti!

Find a non-naturalistic gesture or movement that is a metaphor for your character's deepest needs – that gives a physical manifestation to the inner life and drives of the character. Start by finding a small movement and gradually let it enter your whole body. Now distil it into one big gesture. You are looking for an all-encompassing movement that embodies the core of the character. For example, Hamlet may be pushing away demons or curling into a protective ball; Juliet may be reaching for the sun; Caliban, from Shakespeare's *Tempest*, is spread-eagled, joined to the earth and hugging his island to him. Kurtz from *Apocalypse Now* might be warding off 'the horror, the horror'; Ivan the Terrible might be literally bowed over by his cares and fears; Norma Desmond from *Sunset Boulevard* is continually preparing for her close-up; Norman Bates in *Psycho* sits hunched and lonely as an old woman.

The movement is somehow bigger than the character. It is archetypal. Now add a key phrase from the script with your movement and repeat both together over and over again until you feel a clear sense of inhabiting the character.

You can use the work in preparation in its strongest, purest form or you can keep a shadow of it – an echo gesture – in your performance. Michael Chekhov called it 'the psychological gesture'. Anthony Hopkins uses this and you can see his character's inner pain reflected by these little unconscious movements in *The Remains of the Day*. They reveal the interior self, which is at odds with the exterior presented to the world.

You can find smaller psychological gestures for each scene or even each new objective and use them when you first start to rehearse. Now go back to your script keeping the essence of the experience in your work. The gesture will either vanish completely or leave the merest shadow behind. You can also use the psychological gesture like a 'trigger' to refind the heart of your character during filming, either by using it before the camera turns or even just by thinking of it.

Now close your eyes and visualise your character in front of you. Physically step forward and into your character. Make your gesture. Now open your eyes and see the world from inside your character. Now move, talk and carry out tasks keeping your new vision of the world.

You can go even further and find physical metaphors to rehearse the whole scene. Walk an imaginary tightrope as you choose the lies to get you out of your situation, actually push your partner out of your life or pull them towards you or turn in ever-decreasing circles as your character spirals out of control. If your character is wavering between doing and not doing something, then physically move towards what you want and away from it when you reject it.

The possibilities of this kind of physical work are endless. The beauty of it is that it stops you from getting blocked by 'doing the script' over and over in your hotel room!

BEING REAL

Many characters have a speech about a past incident in their lives. So often the actor performs it by showing the effect the story has on them – 'feeling it'. This turns the energy inwards and cuts off the listener. This is quite different from what happens when you recount something that has already occurred. Get someone to tell you a specific event from their past and watch them. You'll notice that, as they get more involved in the story, they use more and more gestures. We remember in pictures, relive the incident – and share it through these gestures. The energy goes outwards.

We also think geographically. People use gesture to locate what they are talking about in a very precise, spatial way or to clarify the internal logic of what they're saying. They also choose their words carefully, censoring them if they're not right and selecting those that will best convey their story. You will see their eye contact moving between you and their private world. They are constantly shifting between seeing and experiencing again what happened and the need to make you see it too. Strangely, they often smile or laugh as they remember the worst moments in a cathartic release or a protection from the painful memory.

Documentaries on television are a good way to watch real people telling real stories. I remember one about the liberation of Holland after the Second World War. Elderly people recounted the day that the first badly needed food parcels were dropped by Allied planes. The programme was subtitled and so my attention was held by their body language. Each of them, in separate interviews, re-enacted the falling of the parcels, getting down on their knees and miming opening them, with tears streaming down their faces. It was vivid and extreme – completely different from the internalised way that people so often remember on film. Truth has nothing to do with size of performance and everything to do with being specific.

Compare real disasters from newsreels with bad disaster movies. There is much less panic in the immediate aftermath. People have adrenalin flowing and they take action – to get out – to get help – to grab the children. They save the hysterics for later. If your child runs out in the street you either freeze in shock or run to save them. When you find they are safe, then you hug them or hit them, cry or shout at them – it is the relief that causes the reaction. When someone steps in front of your car, you step on the brake in an instant without thinking. Then you start to shake.

There was some terrible news footage of a floor collapsing during a wedding in Jerusalem in May 2001. In the middle of the celebrations and the dancing, a gaping hole appeared and dozens of people fell through to the floor below. There was an eerie silence as everyone followed an individual action. One man grabbed two children and ran to safety. Another went to the edge of the hole and knelt down to peer over. One woman stood transfixed by shock, hand over mouth, unable to move. Only then did the screams and sobs begin.

There is a danger that we pick up certain kinds of acting styles not from life or real people but from watching other actors. By deciding how we want to play the scene before we really know what it's about, by being generalised. Test your decisions against life. Observe people constantly. Don't take anything for granted. You'll find yourself continually surprised. Real people don't always behave as we've been led to believe from the movies.

SEEING IS BELIEVING

People think in pictures. We carry aural and kinaesthetic memories too but, for most people, pictures predominate. We dream in pictures. In movies we act in pictures. By finding a way to flash up subliminal pictures that are as strong for your imagined memories as for your actual memories, you will find a spontaneity and verisimilitude that the camera will recognise.

If your character is recalling a memory, is using rich descriptive language or has a complicated thought structure, then in early rehearsal use 'physicalising'. Do a movement either with just your hands or with your whole body as you say each word. By making a movement on the word, you personalise it.

Words are just black hieroglyphics on a page. They have a lexical meaning but they won't mean anything to you until you make them specific. The author visualised what she or he wrote – there were pictures behind those words. When a screenwriter puts the word 'fountain' into the script, it is a particular fountain. If you had never seen a fountain or had one described to you, the word would mean nothing. When you do a movement as you say the word, a picture of *your* specific fountain will spring into your mind. Then you leave the gestures out. But the pictures remain behind your eyes and flash up instantaneously as you speak. It is the quickest way I know of making the language your own – of not being generalised.

Try it where your character is relating a memory or describing a scene. Take your time and don't think of the words in context of the scene or even the sentence. Take each word separately as if you're building a personal dictionary – even the little words. 'Will' is not the same as 'shall', 'I' carries a lot of significance for you, even 'a' is different from the more precise 'the'. Now as you say the words – you can whisper or use full voice, but don't just think them – do a movement that somehow connects you to that word. It can be representational, pantomimic or non-naturalistic. Take the word 'sun': you might do a wide circular movement to show the sun's shape, you might point at the actual sun or you might lean back with your arms above your head feeling the warmth of the sun. The possibilities are endless. The only criterion is that the movement means something to you. Make sure you release the sound at the same time as you do the movement.

When you have finished the sentence (and you are allowed to repeat a word if it hasn't felt 'connected' the first time), say it normally with no movements other than the ones you want to make naturally, just keeping connected to the pictures you created in your head. Now trust the work is done – a faint echo of the pictures will stay with you – and don't let it slow you down. You've made the words your own and they can come out as quickly as they need to – our brains are as fast as lightning. You will find the words have more energy: the physicality of your body in rehearsal has given the language muscularity in performance. This work is also excellent for lists, always a problem. Each word has to mean something different to you. After you've 'physicalised', you can go through the list as fast as you like and each word will retain its individuality.

If you have dialogue about people or places that don't mean anything to you, you need to invest them with some reality. If you are working in depth, you will do research or create them out of your imagination. But if there isn't time for that, try this tip. Go through the lines choosing people or places that roughly correspond to those mentioned. They could be acquaintances or people you know from the media who fit the bill, and places you've been to. Having found your subjects, do the script substituting the real names you've just chosen for the fictional ones. Now return to the original scripted names and you will find they mean something to you, you have the pictures flashing up in your head and they have come alive.

FILLING IN THE IMAGINATIVE GAPS

Use improvisations to fill in the gaps of the story. If you have a scene that shows the end of a relationship, then do an improvisation about the first time you met your lover; the first night out in the restaurant; the proposal; the first quarrel. Then when you come to breaking up it will mean something – you'll have a relationship to break. Even if you can't work with your partner, you can find ways to do this alone. Try seeing them for the first time across a crowded room, making the phone call that gets you the date, reading the menu on the first visit to what will become your favourite restaurant. Write a love letter then find it much later, when things have gone sour, and tear it up. The possibilities are endless.

If your character has a memory to tell, act it out. Then when you tell it you will have already experienced it. Use improvisation to explain your character's quirks. What was it your mother told you about always wearing woollen vests in winter? Why are you afraid of dogs? Act out the night you saw the ghost.

Use improvisations with other cast members to find relationships. This is your mother: be ten again and let her bathe your knee. This is your older sister: be thirteen and try out her make-up or get tipsy on a shared glass of wine the grown-ups have left. You're a group of friends: go out after work and drink together. You're father and son: go to a football match on a Saturday or for a walk together in the lunch break. Take the other women out to a meal and discuss your men or share a sauna.

The possibilities of improvisation are endless. One actor says she will never suffer nerves again after our torturous shopping trips, where she tried on hats in Harvey Nichols as an alien who had never been near a department store. The staff had never tried selling a hat to an alien before – but they did their best!

QUICK TIPS FOR A PHYSICAL LIFE

- **Experience** the work and lifestyle of your character.
- **Use improvisations** in rehearsal to fill in the gaps in the story.
- **Be physical** – use real gestures. Observe others.
- **Be specific** in your body choices. Know exactly *where* you ache: how you adjust for pregnancy, your age or your illness.
- **Rehearse** in an approximation of the clothes, make-up or hairstyles you will wear.
- **Be aware** of the status of your character: how you relate to other characters, how much space you take up in the world, how your status changes.
- **Watch body language** – think about how people use eye contact, gestures, body positions and put up barriers.

- **Use improvisations** – to fill in the gaps.
- 'Physicalise' in rehearsal to own the words and to be specific. Find a movement for each word as you say it.
- **Find the 'psychological gesture'** for your character. Use physical metaphors to rehearse.
- **When you come to shooting** only use the merest shadow of this work. It has to feel completely real and organic.

YOUR VOICE

Although you will not need to project, as in theatre, you will need your whole natural voice that responds to all your thoughts. Regular voice practice is as important for film as for stage to ensure that your voice doesn't become strangled by nerves. The resonances of the voice not only enhance the tone but also carry an emotional honesty to the words you say. Your voice conveys your feelings as well as the linguistic meaning of the script.

When your friend rings, as soon as they speak you know if they are in trouble – our voices are highly sensitive transmitters of emotion. We talk of 'being choked up', of the words 'sticking in our throats' or having 'a lump in the throat'. A recent experiment showed that, of all the media, it is hardest to lie on radio.

If you watch foreign films with subtitles, you will find that you take in as much about the emotional content of the scene from the words spoken, although you don't understand them, as you do from the ones you read. If you doubt this, watch one on TV and turn off the sound. You'll find the film loses much of its impact. I have worked with actors from Croatia and Japan through interpreters and found I could tell very quickly when they were 'connecting' to what they were saying, even though I couldn't speak the language.

You can think of the voice in five parts: the thought, the scaffolding, the pump, the source and the filter.

1. **The Thought** or impulse which sets everything in motion and which is the most vital component for the actor. If this is strong and clear then your voice will be. You need to know what you want to say and why.
2. **The Scaffolding** – the body needs good alignment to allow the breathing mechanism to work freely and to encourage secondary resonances from the sounding board of the body.
3. **The Pump** is the breath that provides the support and energy to drive the sound. Do the breathing exercises regularly and when you speak, use recoil: simply allow your stomach to release back out when you need a breath and, if you keep your throat open, you will automatically refill. Then you won't increase tension or gasp in breath.

Having an image of your voice coming from this abdominal area (or your lower back) will take tensions away from your throat.

4. **The Source** or larynx is where the air is changed to sound by the vibration of the vocal folds. These vibrations become your unique sound when they are directed through the resonators of your body. Your natural voice quality should be neither 'breathy' nor constricted. People seem to like slightly husky voices (probably because it mimics the effect of sexual arousal) but huskiness isn't a voice quality to be recommended, as it's often a sign of vocal damage. If it persists, get it checked.

Because it's suspended by muscles and ligaments, the larynx can move up and down within your throat. If tension keeps it up too high, your voice will rise above its natural pitch; if you force it down and keep it there for a lower tone, you will get a sore throat. Your larynx needs to be able to move freely. (Incidentally, there are more nerves in the muscles of the larynx – passing through the whole system from brain to stomach and back again – than in any other muscle in the body, not to mention all the hormones that affect it. No wonder it is such a barometer of emotion!)

5. **The Filter** is everything above the larynx that affects the sound: pharynx, oral and nasal resonators, mouth shape, tongue position, etc. When you use different accents, you change various components of the filter.

You are looking for a flexible, supported voice that you can use at any volume. By a 'supported' voice, I mean that you are utilising the whole breathing mechanism to have good airflow and pressure, and that your vocal folds are meeting fully for a voiced sound. Here are a few exercises, which you can use at home or off-set to find your natural resonant sound. At the end of the chapter are a few quick tips to help with last-minute problems:

- If you swallow and then speak, you should find you have released any tensions and your pitch will drop to its natural level.
- Put your hands over your ears and hum up and down your range – find the point where your voice feels the most resonant. Your comfortable pitch level should be around that note in your voice.
- To find a good resonant sound, hang over from your waist letting your knees bend slightly and allowing your head and arms to hang heavily. Now 'shimmy' your shoulders (not your head) and shake out a loud free 'Maah' as you build up your spine gradually, vertebra by vertebra,

bringing your head up last and letting your arms fall freely into position. Keep the sound going until you are standing. Your voice should sound supported and resonant.

- Now clasp your hands in front of you and literally shake out 'Maah' by vigorously shaking your hands up and down in front of you. You can also give your hips a good shake as you make the sound or even jog up and down on the spot. The movements will stop you hanging on to tensions and release your free, resonant voice.

- Hang over again and fully release knees, neck and arms. Now count loudly or say your text. Let your head hang heavily and don't tense your neck at all as you speak. Now gradually build up your spine again, coming slowly to standing, arms free and head still heavy, speaking all the time (breathing where you like). Finally bring your head up to balance on top of your spine and carry on speaking. Your voice will sound richer and warmer and more supported. The tendency with this exercise is to change the voice on the way up. Keep it feeling the same as when you were hanging over. If you feel it is too loud or rich, remember we don't hear ourselves as others do. Cup your hands behind your ears to check the sound.

- Speak as you gently roll your head forwards from one shoulder to the other in a half circle, keeping your neck relaxed.

- Put your hand on top of your head and hum, feeling vibrations both on your lips and your hand. Put your hands either side of your nose, keep humming, and feel the vibrations there. Now touch your lips, feeling them buzzing. Next, the little hollow at the base of your throat. Thump your chest gently on 'Maah' like Tarzan and finally wobble your belly with your hand, letting the movement affect the sound. Now speak aloud, feeling all these different vibrations in the sound.

- If you wonder whether your sound has a predominantly nasal or oral resonance, try this test. Say the word 'ease' and stop on the 'e' vowel before you get on to the consonant. Keep the 'ee' sound going and repeatedly pinch your nose. If you get a sound that's a cross between a foghorn and a fire engine, then the sound is nasal – that is, the breath is coming through the nose. If pinching your nose doesn't affect the sound then you are using oral resonance: your breath is coming out through your mouth only. The soft palate, which works like a trap door, is the mechanism that decides whether your sound is oral or nasal. When it is lifted (like the very beginning of a yawn), it goes up and back and shuts off the passage to the nose. When the soft palate is dropped, the trap door is open, and the breath goes through the nose as well. An oral resonance will have a 'warmer' sound than nasal resonance. Making the sounds 'g' (as in got) and 'ng' (as in ring) rhythmically will exercise the soft palate and practising the 'nose test' will enable you to make choices in resonance.

- Only three sounds in English are made by expelling breath only through the nose: 'm', 'n' and 'ng'. In 'm', the lips stop the breath going out of the mouth, in 'n', the tongue against the hard palate seals off the opening, and in 'ng', the soft palate blocks it off. If you hold your nose, you'll find you can't make these sounds. That's why, with a cold, you'll say 'bubby' rather than 'mummy'. If your nose is blocked, try clearing it with really 'buzzy' humming. Finding lots of resonance in this area counteracts the muffled quality. Press your knuckle into the ridge of gum behind your top teeth. Take it out and think of sending the sound 'forwards' to where you feel your gum tingling. Make sure there is no tension around the back of the tongue and the soft palate.

- Put your hands either side of your face and draw them downwards, releasing your jaw as you do so. Chew with an open mouth for ten seconds, then with your mouth closed. Chew while you speak, then gradually drop the chewing but keep the freedom. This will give you more oral resonance and reduce tension around lips and jaw.

Here are some more thoughts about voice.

When you speak, find the important key words and let them carry the weight of the thought. Let the little words glide effortlessly away through the sentence. If you give everything the same emphasis, nothing will carry any weight.

When we speak publicly, we use a wide pitch range. When we are secret, the pitch range is narrower and we use a different intensity. To find a small secret sound that isn't a whisper (which won't carry any vocal 'message' to the microphone), turn your back to someone. Now really try to tell them something intimate as if you are sending the thought through your back. You should find a small secret voice that isn't just breath. We use this same tiny, whole voice when we say something private into a mobile phone in a crowded place: we know we can't use a whisper or we won't be heard. If you are angry, you will also find yourself using strong 'biting' consonants to get the message across!

Vowels carry the emotional content of what you say. In order to sing, you have to elongate the vowels to carry the tune and so song carries heightened emotion. If you have emotional dialogue, try just saying the vowels or singing the words when you rehearse, then go straight back to speaking the script. (Saying only the vowels is easier if you don't look at the words. Just think them, keep your mouth open without your tongue and teeth coming together, and send the sound forward.)

If you go to clear your throat and then release it, you will hear a little popping sound as the vocal folds close tightly and then open again. For a smooth delivery, your vocal folds need to come together gently on words beginning with vowels and the consonants need to link to the vowels whenever possible for sense. Saying just the vowels of a sentence, joining them in a continuous stream and then saying them again, touching in the consonants, will help get a natural flowing sound and smooth out any little glottal pops.

Consonants are like the willpower imposed on the vowels to drive what we say. If your character is powerful, precise or angry, try saying a line just on consonants. (This is hard, but just sound them out one after another.) Then go back to the whole words and you'll find a new power and energy. This is also good if you have any words that are tripping you up. When you go back to the script, the consonants will feel like stepping-stones and won't get in your way.

Be simple and direct: don't 'colour' the voice with external emotionality. By that I mean, don't go 'poetic' or sentimental in a way that signals to us what you think the scene is about. When people express deep emotion they just say it – straight from the heart. The more simplicity there is, the more we will believe the truth of what you say. I don't mean you have to say it lightly – on the contrary, the words might have to be dragged out of you – but you should never think of how to say them or 'comment' on them by the tone of your voice.

If you feel the character needs a different voice quality, changing the dynamics of your speech – the rhythms, inflections and personal tone patterns – can bring about the most exciting and worthwhile changes. Any changes have to be led by the script – the clues within the words and actions of your character as well as the larger picture set by the director and the film itself.

THE CHARACTER'S VOICE

Your character will have a particular relationship with language. They may be witty and articulate or taciturn; words may come easily or not at all. They may not say what they mean or they may say more than they mean to.

There may be joy in a well-turned phrase as in a Tom Stoppard script – *Shakespeare in Love*, *Enigma* – or the dialogue could be full of unspoken thoughts and subtext like a Pinter screenplay – *The Servant*, *Accident*, *The Go-Between*, *Betrayal*. Gangsters may be lyrical as in

Tarantino's *Pulp Fiction* or be unexpectedly funny like the ones in Guy Ritchie's *Snatch*.

Words may be as hard to spit out as stones. In Sam Shepard's *Paris, Texas*, the characters' inability to communicate is given a physical metaphor as they literally talk through a glass wall. Vivien Leigh as Blanche in Tennessee Williams' *A Streetcar Named Desire*, directed so brilliantly by Elia Kazan, uses words as lightly as a butterfly to conceal the pain beneath.

You can't take words back. Once out in the world they remain with the hearer for ever, whatever you do to make up afterwards. Even if you speak aloud when alone, you are making a decision to expel the energy of your thoughts into the world.

You can tell if someone doesn't want to say something, or doesn't understand what they say. You can actually hear the energy drop. You have to need to say the written words in the same way that the character needs to say them. They have to be as hard to choke up or to choose as they would be in life, or to sound as smooth and as glib as a rehearsed lie, while the truth bubbles unseen beneath the surface.

A well-written script (and there aren't enough around) will differentiate each character by the rhythms of speech. Writers like David Mamet – *Glengarry Glen Ross*, *Wag the Dog* – or Anthony Minghella – *The English Patient*, *The Talented Mr Ripley* – find a use of language that is unique to the user. The character may speak in short phrases, or have monologues, use hard consonants like bullets or talk in a stream of consciousness. They may never be able to finish a sentence, cut off other people's sentences or speak in iambic pentameters.

A comma or full stop is just another way of showing an extension or change of thought. In life, we breathe for new thoughts. If you obey these punctuation marks to find the new energy of each new idea, your speech will sound spontaneous. With good screenwriters like Pinter or Mamet, sensitise yourself to their speech rhythms. Learn to trust them and to obey their instructions for pauses and silences. Find why you need the pauses, what you are thinking and why the character can't speak. But don't add extra ones.

If your character has a long speech or a list, there is a danger that you will run all the thoughts together. You know what you are going to say next but your character doesn't. Rehearse by walking around the room changing direction on every punctuation mark or thought. Or pick up a different object each time you have a new thought. If your character is following some kind of internal dialogue, then put out two chairs to sit on and change chairs at every full stop or major punctuation mark. Then the argument will become very clear.

This puts you in touch with the internal rhythms of the character – the rhythm of their thoughts as well as their speech. The above exercises are based on the work of the voice director of the Royal Shakespeare Company, Cicely Berry. Her book, *The Actor and the Text*, will offer you lots of thoughts for further work on text.

Although a character will occasionally have a monologue, or you may be working on an adaptation of a classic text, most film scripts have little dialogue of any length. Because a film is working primarily on our visual senses, you may be trying to find a voice for a character with no more than a few words to go on. One way to do this is to combine some physical work your character might do – at work or play – together with improvised dialogue until a voice emerges. Keep combining words and movements they might use until you feel that there is an organic fusion between the two.

For example, I recently worked with a softly spoken Welsh actor who was playing a sixteenth-century blacksmith. He had never ridden before but had to do a lot of scenes with horses and, in preparation for the film, was having horse-riding and grooming lessons. I suggested that he did his lines on horseback and while mucking out the horses. Out of that came a particular rhythm and an earthier sound that was subtly different from his own and which fitted the character.

With emotional dialogue, you can do an exercise to 'drop the words in'. Suppose you are marrying against your will and your line is, 'I will be lost':

- Sit on the floor and shut your eyes. Now say each word very, very slowly and separately, simply and truthfully, feeling it dropping into your solar plexus.
- 'I': what does being 'you' mean? – your sense of self – uniqueness.
- 'Will': it's active – not 'should' but 'will' – your will.
- 'Be': to be – the sense of being.
- 'Lost': what does that mean to you? What feelings does the word stir up?
  (You can repeat a word once or twice till you feel it connect – you'll recognise when it does.)
- Now open your eyes and just say the sentence as lightly as you like. The words are now your own. Instead of passing from the script *into* you, they are flowing outwards *from* you – you are finding the words to express your thought.

There are many ways to get the words to flow freely. You can sing the lines. This will release you from your spoken patterns and you will find new rhythms and the words will open out to you in a new way. If your character is in emotional distress, you can chant like a child with your eyes shut to ward off terror. You can find a dance for your character and do your words with the dance. You can close your eyes and whisper them very slowly. These games will stop you seeing the lines in one fixed way and will release your imagination. They will also ensure that any changes in your voice grow organically out of the text and are never forced.

I know of actors who, either at their own or their directors' instigation, have screamed for hours over cliffs or down in quarries to give their voices a particular harshness. All this will achieve is the likelihood of losing your voice halfway through the film and the possibility of vocal nodules! In the search for the character's voice, any changes should be healthy and never hurt. Pitch changes particularly need to be very subtle. Too high and you will alienate us, too low and you may damage your voice. And you have to feel it is *your* voice.

In the end, your task is to communicate the story through the specifics of your character's needs and words. You have to reach the point where you can use only those specific words spoken in that particular way at that given moment.

UNCOVERING THE SUBTEXT

When what you say is what you mean, you reveal the meaning with the words. There's no subtext – nothing 'under the text'. When what you say is not what you mean, you conceal the meaning with the words. That's subtext.

Subtext is another way of looking at how underlying objectives affect how you play your lines. For example, I'm giving a party and the doorbell rings. My best friend is there and I say, 'How lovely to see you!' and mean it. Next time the doorbell rings, it is my mother's friend who I've felt obliged to invite and I say, 'How lovely to see you.' This time I mean, 'Oh, she came. What a drag. I'd better be polite.' Finally the doorbell rings and it is my ex-husband who has come to make trouble. There are other guests watching and I don't want a scene. I say pointedly, 'How lovely to see you', meaning, 'You bastard, how dare you arrive. How hateful to see you.' The words have now taken on the completely opposite meaning. I could also have an unconscious subtext in all these greetings – to show how charming I am!

Thus, there are at least three different kinds of subtext. There's the subtext that you know you're thinking, but you don't want to be understood, like the second example above or:

'Where have you been?'

'I've been seeing my mother' (*I've been out with my lover*)

'Do you like this dress?'

'It looks lovely on you' (*the white lie – you care about the other person*)

Then there's the subtext that you know you're playing and you want the other person to know you're using it, like my remark to my ex-husband at the party or:

'Do you like babies?'

'Adore them, especially when they're wet and soggy!' (*irony*)

'Does this look good on me?'

'Wonderful, darling. It takes years off you' (*cattiness – you're using a put-down*)

Then there's the kind of subtext that you don't even realise you're using, like me being the charming hostess. Or as in these two people in the bar:

'I've got a brand new Mercedes' (*clever me*)

'I can't even afford a car' (*poor me*)

They're probably not aware that they're playing 'I want to impress you' and 'I want you to feel sorry for me'. People can go on talking all evening without relating to each other at all, just driving their own needs through the subtext. The character may not know they're doing it, but the actor needs to.

If things go wrong, it's often because the actor has chosen the wrong kind of subtext – which is another way of looking at the problem of 'signalling' – showing us what you are thinking. And it will make your work untruthful to the situation. You need to identify what you want: your objective.

If you have the line, 'Would you like a cup of tea?' it might be a genuine offer of a warming beverage, a gesture of friendship. But it might equally mean 'let's change the subject', 'I need you to stay because I'm lonely' or 'I am trying to be polite but I want you to go'. You need to decide what kind of subtext this is. Do you want them to read it or not? In the examples – changing the subject and asking for company – you may not want them to know what you are thinking, but in the last one, you may. If the other person reads your subtext then they will take the hint and go without you having actually been rude. We do it all the time.

If you are in an Agatha Christie film, however, and you have the line, 'would you like a cup of tea?' and the tea has arsenic in it, then you want it to sound like an offer of friendship. If you let the other person read the subtext, 'I'm offering you poison', then that's signalling – and they'd be rather foolish to accept your offer!

In *The Band Wagon*, Jack Buchanan, who plays a madly over-intense director, has just written the terrible line, 'Did you ever try spreading ideals on a cracker?' which Fred Astaire does his best to deliver ironically. Buchanan gives him this direction: 'You know about icebergs, don't you? One-eighth above the surface and seven-eighths beneath? Give me eight-eighths – the whole eight-eighths.' The result is ludicrously funny as Astaire gives enormous weight to each inconsequential word, trying to play it at face value. You have to know when the character has subtext.

When rehearsing your script, say the character's thoughts out loud. Say them before you speak your lines and while the other character is speaking and you are reacting, and especially in the silences. (If these thoughts are the same as the line, it means there's no subtext.) Pinter, Shepard and Mamet texts are excellent for this work. With these authors, adhere strictly to the notated pauses and silences, but don't add any long pauses of your own. Speak your thoughts aloud in all the gaps.

These writers use a lot of subtext, as do most modern movies. Sexual games are full of subtext – look at Humphrey Bogart and Ingrid Bergman in *Casablanca*, Hugh Grant and Andie MacDowell in *Four Weddings and a Funeral* or the subtle dances of *Betrayal*. The Mafiosa films of Scorsese and Coppola are pervaded by subtext – Al Pacino and Robert De Niro are masters of this art.

When you've identified your subtext, you can find clues to your character – and also the style of the movie – by how much you use. A character in an action movie may not use much, but the protagonist in a psychological drama certainly will. William Goldman, the screenwriter, wrote that 'movie heroes need mystery'. The tip of the iceberg hides the depth beneath the surface.

As Algernon remarks in *The Importance of Being Earnest*, 'The truth is rarely pure and never simple.' Except when they're taking action, dealing with facts or expressing emotion honestly, human beings do speak with subtext. They have some 'agenda' behind their words – a hidden goal.

A character who never says what they are really thinking will have flashes, though, when the veil drops and the camera can capture a private moment when their vulnerability or inner desires are revealed through their eyes. Seek these moments out and allow us to see what you feel by connecting truthfully to the real thoughts of the character.

Martin Scorsese, in his excellent *A Personal Journey with Martin Scorsese through American Movies*, dates the start of the heavy use of subtext in films to the 1950s. This coincides with the rise of 'method acting' when Lee Strasberg brought Stanislavski's work to America, and directors like Elia Kazan made films with complex characterisations like *East of Eden* and *On the Waterfront* (Elia Kazan said of the young Marlon

Brando that he had 'an ambivalence essential to depicting humanity'). But it could also be part of the post-war loss of innocence, which meant words could never be taken at their face value again.

QUICK TIPS – VOICE AND TEXT
Here are some quick thoughts and exercises you can use on or off set:

- **Make sure** you are in your own natural pitch and that you haven't gone breathy or constricted. It should feel like *you* speaking.
- **Use a whole, resonant, 'connected' voice** but at a natural level.
- **Emergency tip** for a voice going higher with tension: open your mouth as you gently tip your head backwards. Close your mouth and swallow on the way back down. Now speak. Your voice should revert to its natural lower pitch.
- **If your voice sounds 'breathy'**, waggle your finger as if you're telling someone off and go 'Uh Uh', 'Uh Uh'. Now take that firm sound into speech.
- **For a clear sound** put your hands over your ears and hear the breath coming in and going out through an open mouth. Now make that breath completely silent. You should now feel more 'open'.
- **Take this further** into tiny silent panting for a few seconds. Again keep the 'open' feeling when you speak.
- **If you feel nasal**, shut your eyes and relax. You will probably feel part of your tongue cleaving to the roof of the mouth. Just release the back of the tongue very slightly – a millimetre (don't press it down at all) – and you should feel a tiny burst of cool air in the mouth. When you speak your voice should sound 'warmer'.
- **To re-energise the voice** or soothe it: make a tiny 'ng' or 'n' sound from your highest note to your lowest, like a little siren. This literally stretches out your vocal folds after hard work and they will work better afterwards.
- **For resonance:** shake out on 'Maah' by clasping your hands in front of you and wiggling your hips as you 'shake' out the sound. (This cheers everyone up on the set!)
- **Imagine** sending your voice to the sounding board of your back. This will keep away extraneous tension in scenes that need more volume.
- **Energy of words**. We choose our words (whether we are in subtext or not) and that takes energy. If the words aren't your own, you need to find this energy to keep them spontaneous and immediate and connected to the action you are driving.
- **Keep the energy to the end** of the thought.

- **Find the words that are important** to the thought. Although there may be other stressed words in a sentence, there's usually only one major inflection where we change the pitch. If I say, 'Where are *you* going?' I want to know about your proposed movements, not anyone else's. If I ask, '*Where* are you going?' then I haven't heard the location the first time or I'm amazed by it. Each new piece of information will change the inflection: 'I have a *dog*', 'I have a *brown* dog', 'I have a *large* brown dog', 'I have an extremely *ferocious* large brown dog'. Let the unimportant words go lightly – don't stress everything.
- **Use variety.** Keep your pitch free, find the rhythms of your character. Find the new impulses and thoughts. Let them enter your voice. Just for fun, start each new thought on a new note to explore what possibilities are open to you.
- **Be specific**. Know *exactly* what you mean. Have a picture in your head. Make the words and thoughts your own.
- **Know the subtext** – what you're thinking as you say the line and whether you want the other person to know it.
- **Think *on* the line**. Sometimes we censor ourselves or think first and then still have the line to say. Plunge in on the thought – let line and thought be one.
- **Dare to take breath.** Don't rush through thoughts.

DEALING WITH EMOTION

Frank Capra once said, 'I thought drama was when actors cried. But drama is when the audience cries.'

When I suggest that you play the action and not the emotional state, I don't mean that you won't feel emotion, that you mustn't explore fully what emotions the character is experiencing. What I mean is that you mustn't indulge that emotion or allow it to overwhelm you and deter you from the action, unless that is truly what happens to the character in the scene. If you have strong objectives that you commit to, then feelings will arise naturally.

In life, energy goes outwards and not inwards as soon as an impulse gives rise to any physical movement or vocalisation. Even if you are hunched up, eyes shut, on a bench in a railway station – unless you are asleep, drugged, drunk or meditating – you are thinking. If you open your eyes, then you make the decision to do so and if you look at a passer-by you will have an objective: 'I want you to go away', 'I want you to give me money', 'I want to know if you are real'. That will lead to an action: 'I reject you', 'I beg you', 'I recognise you' and so on.

If your impulse leads you to speak, it needs enormous energy. As we've seen, to change breath into voice takes a really strong impulse. Try it yourself: wherever you are, make a sound. Any sound. Could you feel the commitment that needed? If alone, you may have made a loud sound. If in a crowded space, it may have been very small. You may have made it willingly, unwillingly, out of duty, amusement, impatience or interest or for any other reason but you would have felt yourself having to make that commitment. The decision to speak may come instantaneously like a cry of surprise or slowly and with enormous difficulty like telling someone something you've bottled up for years.

These objectives, thoughts and desires bubble away the whole time. Feeling can lead to an action or an action can create a feeling. We don't usually *try* to feel, the feelings just happen and we decide how to deal with them – what to show and what not to show. Emotion is like a pot of water boiling away underneath. It goes on furiously bubbling. But most of the time you choose to put the lid on – the feelings are the subtext and are concealed by what you say. We don't often want the world to know about these feelings. Your job as an actor is to be very sure when you need to take the lid off or when it gets blown off by the force of the steam.

And even then, unless the feelings completely overwhelm you, you will go on trying to achieve your objective. We don't decide to have an emotion, it just happens out of the circumstances. Remember, it is bravery in dealing with emotion that moves us – not the tears themselves. And yet most actors, when they begin, seem to worry more about crying than anything else. They get frightened that they won't produce real tears when it comes to the big scene, and they won't produce them time and again. Well, it doesn't matter. The important thing is that, because of your bravery, you move us.

Katharine Hepburn took some acting advice from John Huston on *The African Queen*. He told her that she was playing the beginning of the film, after the death of her brother, too solemnly and that she should handle strangers like a hostess – chin up with a society smile – like Eleanor Roosevelt visiting soldiers in hospital. Katherine Hepburn says in her book on the making of the film, 'that is the goddamnest best piece of direction I have ever heard.'

I set you a task: next time you are watching a video or DVD of a film and you come to a scene where you cry as you watch it – stop. Rewind and see if the actors are crying. I bet that, in more than half the cases, the main character is not. (In a western, if the focus is on the dying man, he will be being brave while the one cradling him will be crying buckets. If the focus is on the friend, he will fight through the tears while the dying man moans in agony.) And how many times have you watched an actor and thought, 'Great crying' but been unmoved? The point is that if the tears come, fine, but if you try to make yourself cry, your energy will go in the wrong direction and we won't care about you. No one cares about someone who feels sorry for themselves. The tears should come in spite of yourself.

Having said that, the next two sections and the later one on crying will help you to feel emotionally connected – which is important. And you may end up with real tears too in case you still want them!

WAKING UP THE SENSES

One of the main tools in your store is your memory. The memory of pain and happiness enables you to empathise with another person's suffering. It is also your memory of the feeling, sight, sound and smell of all you've experienced in your life that allows you to fill your imaginary world so intensely that you can feel, see, hear and smell those things again as clearly as if they were present. This is sometimes called 'affective memory' because memories truly affect us.

Some actors get worried that sense memory doesn't work for them because they expect to go into some kind of hypnotic trance and conjure the imaginative world into a concrete reality. 'I'm not really seeing it,' they confess, 'it's not working.'

Remember *le jeu* – the games you played as a child? You know you are in that cardboard box or playing with those plastic cars on the back step, but you see the imaginary world as well in your mind's eye. This is not hypnosis; it is the same thing that happens to you when you smell a particular mixture of sweat and cleaning fluids and feel the misery of the school changing rooms again.

Smell is particularly evocative: aromatherapists use scented oils to stimulate or ease our aching bodies. But is part of the benefit the associations the smell brings with it? Scents carry a past history: the odour of disinfectant that takes you back to hospital, a scent of lavender that reminds you of your French holiday, the perfume of an ex-lover, or the smell of coffee or new-baked bread that gets your taste buds going and saliva forming in your mouth. They say you can sell a house by putting a loaf in the oven (or a drop of vanilla on a baking tray) and letting sense memory do the rest.

Music also takes us back instantly to the time we first heard it. The songs that were connected to our most powerful adolescent emotions stay with us for the rest of our lives (that's why compilations of past hit records sell so well thirty years on!). By remembering the feel of cold snow under your fingers, you can start to feel cold. By imagining floating in water, your muscles will start to relax.

Colour can be a powerful emotional tool. Colour affects our whole sensory system. Restaurants have discovered that using red in the colour scheme affects the appetite and makes us hungry, white is used to make us think of hygiene – think of the so-called 'white goods' we use in our kitchens – and green or blue is supposed to calm us down. We use colour in our emotional language: 'seeing red', 'black temper', 'the blues', 'browned off', turning 'green' with envy or 'yellow' with jealousy. We talk of people being 'as green as grass', 'as good as gold', 'silver-tongued', 'as black as sin', 'pure white', or 'grey and boring'. We 'paint the town red', 'feel in the pink' or write in 'purple prose'. Mediums claim to see auras around us that, depending on their colour, show the spiritual point we've reached. Purple, being the colour of gods and kings, showing a particularly advanced inner life.

Some people actually hear in colour (synesthesia) and Scriabin, the composer, who probably did, invented and scored for a colour organ to play with his music – a sophisticated precursor of disco lights. Try making sounds and associating them with colours. Find words that link to colours. Imagine your scene in different colours – does it affect your perception of it and arouse different feelings in you? Film designers and cinematographers use this link between colour and emotion to affect the mood of a film.

Taste is another memory trigger and you can feel yourself salivate at the thought of a mouth-watering meal. Try this test: shut your eyes and see your kitchen. Now see a bowl full of yellow, waxy lemons. Reach out in your mind's eye and pick one up. Put it on the cutting board and cut it in two. Smell the citrus. See the juice. Now pick it up to suck it. You can probably feel your lips beginning to pucker and your mouth starting to water as you remember the sour taste of the lemon.

You can exercise your 'memory muscles' to use this mind and body connection:

- Sit on the floor and close your eyes. (I know this is a problem, doing the exercise from a book, but after reading each instruction shut your eyes again.)
- Imagine that in front of you on the floor is the cup or mug from which you last drank – preferably your favourite or usual one. See it first: its colour – its shape – its shadow.
- Don't pick up your imaginary cup yet, just run your fingers around it. Is it rough or smooth? Embossed or indented? Run your finger around the rim. Does it glide round or are there chips? Is the china thin or thick? Or is it made of something else like plastic, glass or metal? If it has a saucer, how does that feel?
- Run your finger round the inside of the handle – if it has one. Is it square or curved? Sharp or smooth?
- Cup your hands around it. Is it warm or cold? Full or half empty?
- Now put one hand underneath it to take the weight.
- Lift it a little and feel the weight.
- Lift it up towards your face until, if it is hot, you feel the steam. Smell it. Is it comforting? Sweet-smelling? Does the smell wake you up? Does it smell of nothing?
- Lift it higher and take a sip. Taste it. Feel the texture, the temperature. Feel the warmth or cold sliding down your throat.
- Put it back on the floor. Keep your eyes closed. Keep your hands on the cup.
- Where were you when you last drank from this cup or mug? Were you sitting or standing? What could you see? What could you smell? What could you hear? Were you alone or not? What were you wearing?

What were you about to do? Where had you come from? Were you in a rush or relaxed? How did you feel? Were you looking forward to the day? Were you worried about anything, nervous, happy, tired? What were you thinking? Can you feel those feelings again?

- Gently come back to the present. Make the cup disappear and open your eyes.
- When you drink from that cup again – check it out, feel it – how accurate were you?

I once worked for weeks on undoing the power of sense memory with that actor who had to play an alien experiencing a human environment for the first time. We would push the table back in a boardroom at Pinewood Studios and she would touch everything as if for the first time, exploring innocently how things felt, trying to take away her memory of them. Obviously this is not really possible as we can never fully block out our stored knowledge, but it was an interesting exercise to attempt. She would try dressing for the first time: using a comb or trying to put on make-up. Then, to store new sensations, she would take her shoes off and walk on dozens of different imaginary surfaces in a hundred different atmospheres, gravitational pulls and strange lights and colours. All her senses became hypersensitised and awake.

Here is an exercise that will show you how strong your memories are and lead you gently towards the next section where you will explore the power of emotional memory:

- Remember a room that you haven't been into for at least five years and that has some strong emotional associations for you – your bedroom, your school dormitory, your grandmother's kitchen. (Choose a room that you are happy to share, not one that is so horrific that you don't want to think about it yourself. This is not therapy; it is only a memory exercise.)
- 'Show' a friend or imaginary visitor around it. Actually walk around the imaginary room, coming in through the door and showing them everything you remember. If you are doing it with a friend, they can help you by asking questions: 'What's on the floor?' 'Do you have shoes on?' 'How is it lit?' 'What's under the bed?' Be very specific.
- Look out of the window, if your room has one. What do you see at this particular moment in time you have chosen? Describe it. You will be amazed by what you remember.
- Then shut your eyes and feel the temperature of the room. What do you hear? What do you smell? What do you feel?

- Find the 'trigger', the one tiny peripheral thing that brings that room back to you. Something that sums the place up that may not have been important to you at the time but now you see vividly – the way the curtain falls, the vase, the wallpaper.
- Then come slowly back to the present and to where you are actually standing.

Don't be dismayed if you feel sad now even if it was a happy room. It is just that you have temporarily been back to a lost moment of your life. The feeling will pass very quickly. Now you need never visit this room again – just see the 'trigger' and all the feelings that this room aroused in you will come flooding back. You could do this exercise with a range of different rooms that make you feel warm and secure, lonely, ill at ease and so on.

This exercise hones up your memory and observation skills. It helps you to create an imaginary reality and, almost by the by it can find you some emotional triggers for your emergency kit.

EMERGENCY TRIGGERS

When you remember an event in your life that affected you emotionally, scientists tell us that your body reacts as it did when you experienced it for the first time. Bio-feedback can show you these real measurable changes to your heart rate, blood sugars and hormones. Studies have proved that the mind–body connection is so strong that even thinking through your weight-training exercises can make you stronger and concentrating on your big toe can make it grow longer!

So recapturing an emotional state you experienced in your past will mean that your body will reproduce all the inward and outward signs of that emotion: a quicker pulse, tears, blushing – real symptoms of pain and anger. You won't be 'acting'; you'll be experiencing. It is linked to your sense memory work because we remember through our senses.

What brings these emotions back to us is a single emotional trigger that we associate with the event. In the same way that the smells and songs of your youth jump you back into the past, so each traumatic event in your life has its trigger.

Although scents and sounds are strong triggers, they are usually less easy to conjure up at will than the pictures that flash into our minds when we think of something in our past. Most people find it easiest to remember what they saw. But we are all different and you may respond more to touch or sound than visual images. By trying out these exercises, you will find your best triggers – the peripheral sense stimulus that you barely noticed at the time, which you can use to propel you into the right emotional direction for your scene.

Where did you go to school? Something flashed into your mind's eye – a desk, a building, a friend. Who was your best friend? Some picture formed – a smile, a hat, the back of a head – or perhaps a place that you went to – the door of their house or their bicycle.

When you are in the middle of an awful row or pleading with your lover not to go, you are seeing something else at the edge of the main scene. The dishes you are washing, the curtain blowing, the pattern on the tablecloth. You didn't even know you were seeing it then but you will refind it when you do your emotional memory work on that event.

I found an emotional trigger many years ago during an acting workshop. I had been working for some time but had never actually cried on stage. Now I know that doesn't matter, but it bugged me at the time. I relived the car journey when I broke up with a boyfriend and he was driving me back to my own flat through Hyde Park on a rainy night. It was a good one to choose because by the time I did the workshop I was happily in a new relationship and wouldn't have wanted to go back. I found my trigger – the drops of rain on the car window – and I have used it ever since. I just see the raindrops and I feel the prick of tears. I don't have to make myself cry – it just happens in spite of myself.

And that's how it works. You choose a precise situation that made you cry at the time. It must be a particular few minutes of the event – the actual time you cried. You sit quietly and comfortably with no pressure until, by going back there, you find what the peripheral thing was you were looking at (or hearing) while you felt the pain. Not the main action or the other person but something else – the little thing. That is your trigger.

It's a kind of emergency first-aid. You may never need it, but it gives you a ground base for you to prime and paint with your given circumstances, objectives and actions. It works like the song or the scent of your lost lover. It just sets up the emotional place to start the scene from. You *never* relive the whole memory again. And you don't use it to 'substitute' for the scene you are doing. You just use the trigger to bounce you emotionally into the particulars of the scene you are going to play – into the specific 'magic if' of the moment. You just flash it up in your mind's eye and you're away. And triggers seem to get stronger and more potent the longer you use them.

In an ideal world, you would find everything you need from the given circumstances of the scene. But filming is not an ideal world. It is 7.30 in the morning, you haven't had your second cup of tea and now you're into a scene about your dead mother. Or you've got twenty minutes before the crew go into overtime, the director's left the difficult scene till last, it's take thirteen and the camera needs reloading. You may have to be grieving two minutes after celebrating the gaffer's birthday or make love in front of a film crew at eight o'clock in the morning after an indigestible bacon buttie, or have an enormous row with the big star you've never met before. And do it again and again and again. This is when triggers will work like the onion that brings tears to your eyes so that you feel sad in spite of yourself.

So I suggest that you set up a store of triggers long before you get to filming: a sad one that makes you cry, a happy safe one, one that starts you bubbling with excitement, one that fills you with shame and one for searing anger.

It is really, really important that you choose only memories of things that affected you deeply at the time but that you have dealt with and don't mind about any more. I stress that this is not therapy and acting is our job. We want to do it with integrity but, in order to do so, it is not necessary to rack ourselves with grief that won't go away or open up old emotional wounds. I would never agree with a director prying into an actor's hidden pain. So don't choose the death of a loved one; find something like a broken romance that doesn't hurt any more. The tears were just as real at the time. Your memory doesn't need to be recent and is often better if it's not. Choose what you would be happy to share.

In fact, if you have a trusted acting partner to do these with, so much the better. That way they can talk you through it. Actors are always frightened that it won't work, so don't worry about that, just go through it stage by stage. I've never worked yet with an actor who hasn't found an emotional trigger. This is how I would talk you through it if we did it together:

- Relax comfortably and take yourself back into the situation. You don't want a long time scale, just the few moments surrounding the event.
- Relive it mentally, being really specific about where you are and what you see, say and think, until you feel an echo of the same emotion that you felt then. You may even feel real tears start to well up. If you do, you'll be so pleased you may snap out of the situation, so keep going back to the surroundings in your memory.
- What can you see, feel, hear or smell? Are you alone there or with someone else? Is it quiet or are you in a crowd? What are you wearing? What is the other person wearing? What are your fingers touching? What objects are around you?

When you really felt you were back there, I would tell you to take as long as you needed but that if you felt emotion well up in you or the prick of tears, you should tell me. In a little while you'd say, 'Yes, I feel something.' (If you didn't, no matter. We'd choose another memory or try another day. I would check you've chosen a really specific memory and gone to the nub of it. It will work in the end.)

- Now look around in your mind's eye until you find this other thing you were noticing at the time: the way the light falls on the glass, the lipstick smear on your hand, the torn curtains. What were you looking at while you were dealing with the emotion?
- Now say aloud what you really wanted to say that day but couldn't say then. Verbalise your grief or outrage or love. Sometimes this is very hard to do. If you can't, then let out what you feel on a sound. This can be quite overwhelming in its release, if you had been damming up your real feelings at the time.
- Now open your eyes. Hold on to your trigger in your mind's eye. Say some of your script or a poem out loud. Or just look at your friend and say something. Remember the energy has to go outwards – your feelings just *are* so let them take care of themselves and concentrate on explaining or asking for something. Don't worry if the trigger fades quickly.
- Now come back to the present place and time. Brush away the tears – the past is the past and the present is fine.

Leave the exercise but in about five minutes' time, flash up the trigger. Can you instantly feel the emotion again? It doesn't matter if it's weaker this time. If not at all, you may not have found the right trigger and it will not be difficult at this stage to go back to your memory again and find another. But if it works – and it usually does – that's it. You've got an instant trigger for life. It's better not to relive the scene ever again; simply trust the work is done and the trigger is found.

If you want a gentle way in, rather than just jumping into sorrow or anger, stay with revisiting different places, like the exercise in the last section. You can end up with some really useful, subtle triggers.

EMOTIONAL OBJECTS

Objects are important to us in life. When you rehearse, find some objects that are part of your character's emotional life. You can discard all or most of them when you come to perform.

Sometimes we reveal our subtext in the way we use objects or touch our loved ones. The girl who has not told her parents that she is pregnant cannot refrain from touching her belly; the secret thief holds the handbag with the stolen money close to her side; the man embarking on an affair is unconsciously turning his wedding ring.

The flowers tied to a lamp post, the discarded doll in the ransacked village, the mobile phones ringing unanswered in the ruins of the World Trade Center – these objects can speak more poignantly of the lives lost than any words.

By using and creating a relationship to the objects that surround your character, both in rehearsal and – sparingly – in filming, you can increase the emotional power of your scene. Try simply holding an object your character might possess. Give it a history: where did you get it? Who gave it to you? Where did you find it? Construct some emotional attachment to the object. Now find a moment to touch or hold this object while you pursue the action of the script.

This work might give you an idea for a real prop for the film. Directors are often open to this kind of suggestion. But you may not need it – just having used it to rehearse may be enough.

QUICK TIPS FOR SENSE AWARENESS

- **Play the action** – not the emotion.
- **Send energy outwards not inwards** – you are driving an action.
- **Wake up your sense memory** – touch and feel a dozen different surfaces from your imagination, explore places you've been, tastes, smells and sounds.
- **Find emotional 'triggers'** for major feelings of sadness, happiness, etc. Not the whole memory – just a flash of peripheral vision. But use them only as an emergency measure to find the starting place of a scene, then play the actualities of the scene itself – like cutting an onion to 'trigger' tears.
- **Emotion** should be like a boiling pot of water – it's up to you how tightly you put on the lid but the pot always boils!

LISTENING

Nerves can do strange things – the eyes stop looking and the ears stop listening. I can clearly remember taking my driving test and 'pretending' to look in the rear-view mirror, to please the instructor, without really seeing anything. Later, when eventually I passed, I found looking properly was rather a useful thing!

Similarly actors can 'act' listening. The character may not share your persona but does share your physicality. There is no difference between you listening and the character listening, between you watching and the character watching.

When you see young actors at work, you are often aware that they are so tied up with their own feelings and lines that they are not really interacting. They have no real need to communicate and they are not listening. Even more experienced actors sometimes seem to be working in a vacuum. There is no generosity in their playing.

We listen in different ways, depending on the situation and why we are listening. You will listen differently if you are consoling someone than if you are waiting for a gap in the conversation to jump in with your own idea. But you are still listening. If you don't, then it's very unsatisfactory for other people. In life, we tire very quickly of someone who never listens. It is the same in film.

So really listen – don't pretend. Listen without knowing what you'll hear or when the impulse will leap up in you to respond. And breathe while you listen. We often shut off at the throat and stop breathing when we concentrate. This means you've put up a barrier between you and the other person. And you can't listen properly when you're not breathing. So keep the breath flowing.

That doesn't mean you need to pause before you speak to prove you were listening. On the contrary, if you are really listening, you will be preparing thoughts, arguments and responses. Your reactions will be so natural and unprepared that they will take you by surprise. We don't often need to think before we speak unless what we are about to say has to be chosen carefully. We respond without any conscious preparation. Brian Cox says, 'Human beings are a series of reactions.'

Sometimes the line you respond with will not have a direct link to what the other person has said – a non sequitur. This doesn't mean you weren't listening: there must have been a key word or phrase that you heard that set up an internal debate or sparked a memory that led to your response. If your partner has a long speech, shut your eyes in rehearsal and repeat every word that jumps out at you. These are your key words that plot the journey of your thoughts. (Incidentally, this exercise will also help your partner by highlighting her or his key words.)

The non sequitur might be because the character is listening with certain expectations. Choose a theme you might be pursuing: guilt, money, love, forgiveness and so on. Now repeat *every* word that your partner says that relates to this idea; this will lead to your response. Often in life we hear only the parts we want to hear and that relate to our preoccupations. If someone pays us a long compliment on our performance but ends with, 'The only thing I didn't like was . . .' you can be sure that bit is all we'll remember!

The character who doesn't speak hears everything and may have the most to say, but has a reason for not saying it.

Discipline yourself in daily life, especially in high-nerve situations like interviews, to really listen – and to keep breathing.

TALKING TO EACH OTHER

Acting is about communication. Have you ever watched a play and had the curious feeling that the actors were talking *at* each other rather than *to* each other. Somehow they were locked into their lines and not reacting spontaneously. They knew what they would say next.

The great English actress, Edith Evans, used to say that you had to know your lines so well that you could forget them so that the next line took you by surprise. This is tied to the previous section: if you're listening you will respond by really talking to your fellow actor. Great actors are generous; they reward you with every ounce of their attention. They don't know how they will respond or what they will say until the moment that they need to.

Both for listening and talking *to* someone, make sure your objective relates to the other person. If, for example, someone is explaining why they let you down and you take the objective, 'I want to work this out' or 'I want to explore my feelings about this', it will cut you off from the other speaker. That's fine if the point of the scene is that you break away from your friend and won't interact. But if you are engaging with them, then the objectives, 'I want to find out if you are telling the truth', 'I want to understand your motives' or 'I want you to know I forgive you', would be more useful. Then you will look into the other person's eyes trying to see what they are thinking or showing them you understand. You will really be talking to them. And your action will also be to listen!

QUICK TIPS FOR LISTENING

- **Don't think about your following line** or cue – listen completely in the moment.
- **Find the links** – if your answer doesn't seem to follow, try finding which word or impulse in the scene keyed your response.
- **Stay** in the environment of the scene – don't drift into unrelated thoughts.
- **What do you want** as you listen. Think as your character. Relate your objective to the other person.
- **Keep breathing** while you listen.
- **If you are really listening** you won't jump your cue but you will respond instantly on your impulse.

TAKING BRAVE CHOICES

Being real doesn't mean you think small thoughts. Or that there is never a place for extraordinary physicality. Sometimes the only difference between a good actor and a great actor are the choices they take. Anthony Quinn said that great actors have 'a latent power to disturb'.

Take brave choices – take everything to the limit. Make things really important to you. Don't love someone a little, make them your whole world; don't be somewhat hurt, be devastated; don't want a small promotion, be willing to kill to achieve; don't just be interested in your hobby or work or family, be obsessive in your passion. Take things as far as they can go – to extremes. BUT ... then decide how much the character will show. Remember these are your hidden drives: you may never choose to reveal them. They are your subtext. Or they may explode out in white-hot moments of screen time.

So, in a scene with a new date, taking the objective 'I want to get you into bed' will give you a much stronger drive than 'I want to get to know you'. When you quit your job, deciding the boss was 'a monster' will give you more to draw on than thinking of him as 'difficult'. If you've been poor, then you've had to gather fuel from builders' skips, darn your clothes, work as a cleaner all night, live on a loaf of bread, not just been unable to go on holiday.

It sounds obvious. But when I ask actors to tell me their objectives, they've often chosen really weak or general ones or they qualify them with words like 'quite' or 'somewhat'. Make the stakes higher. Don't be afraid of your dark demons and desires.

In films – on the surface at least – we are usually dealing in understatement. Modern man is afraid to show too much passion. We live in a time when being cool is sophisticated, when language has been reinvented so as not to show feelings – 'bad' is good and 'wicked' is wonderful. To be mean and moody is magnificent, but to be emotional is to be naive. Modern films are about the way we are now so they will be mainly about subtext. But don't be fooled into thinking we don't care. We just bury it. Make sure your drives underneath are enormous. Be brave, trust your strong thoughts – they are what your character really wants.

Films do have moments when what's underneath *does* show and it's even more powerful when up till then the character's been hiding behind a cool mask. Movies are often about people coping with high drama, dangerous situations and risk-taking. Audiences need the catharsis of living out their fears and fantasies through horror, action and disaster films. So if you are in this kind of movie, you will be dealing with a character stretched to the edge of their resources. Let your imagination be equally enormous. By that I don't mean the 'telegraphese' that characterises much of the histrionics that are the hallmark of soaps (rightly called soap operas!). There is an enormous difference between faking or 'acting' emotion and coping honestly with extreme situations. You can't play the horror but you can experience it. And it will drive your actions.

Sometimes there is no subtext. Actors can find playing full-on emotion revealed through words quite challenging. This is hardly surprising. We live in a post-modernist age of pastiche and parody. Irony abounds and actors can get frightened that real responses will leave them open to mockery. Most of what you say throughout the day is information-based – we seldom speak our feelings. You need to feel comfortable about speaking your real thoughts, without subtext, when you need to. This is especially true if you are dealing with Shakespeare's rich language.

But you may decide that playing against the line, using subtext, is a more interesting choice. Take this dialogue:

He: 'I feel great.'

She: 'I feel awful.'

Taken at face value, he wants to share joy on his line and she wants sympathy on hers. But 'I feel great' could mean 'I feel awful' as the actor holds his head in pain, warding off a hangover. He could want that understood (irony) or want to keep the drinking binge a secret. 'I feel awful' could be said to cheer the other person up – the actor smiling with sympathy.

Don't get stuck with instant decisions or generalisations. There are countless ways to approach your part. The actor Brian Cox, who has played many interesting villains including the first Hannibal Lecter in *Manhunter* and William Stryker in *X-Men 2*, says, 'Look for the paradox' – the difference between the inner and the outer personas of the character. For instance, if you have a selfish character, play the outward generosity; look for the charm of the villain. He cites the example of Harold Shipman, the general practitioner who, at an inquiry in 2002, was deemed to have killed at least 115 people. Shipman was perceived by his patients as warm, kindly and caring – the perfect family doctor.

People can cry with happiness or laugh at disaster. Try lots of choices.

In *Mulholland Drive*, we see 'Betty' trying out a script for an audition. First, she rehearses it in her apartment with a friend, playing the overt sense of the lines. The script is about rejection and threats. Later, in her screen test, she plays the same script as a sexual come-on, whispering it against her partner's cheek. It works so much better.

Audiences like bravura performances – look at Robert Duvall in *Apocalypse Now*, Peter Finch in *Network*, Bette Davis in *All about Eve*, Alan Rickman in *Robin Hood: Prince of Thieves*, Marlon Brando in *The Godfather*, Maggie Smith in *Gosford Park*, Elizabeth Taylor and Richard Burton in *Who's Afraid of Virginia Woolf?*, Alec Guinness in *Tunes of Glory*, Jack Nicholson in *The Shining* or Jim Broadbent in *Moulin Rouge*. These performances are all exciting in different ways. They are big, brave and they worked. Film acting does not have to be mini to be real.

But not all brave choices are bravura. Some are infinitely subtle. Jim Broadbent takes different, delicate choices for *Iris*. Robert De Niro, Al Pacino, Tom Wilkinson, Adrian Lester, James Dean, Michael Caine, Liv Ullmann, Judi Dench, Tilda Swinton, Charlotte Rampling, Frances McDormand and Sissy Spacek all take brave decisions that make their performances individual, specific and powerful.

Don't minimalise the characters by bringing them down into your habitual realities to make them easier to play; instead go out to meet them at the edge of their own extraordinary lives. After all, we are dealing with drama which is, by its very nature, about extraordinary people; or ordinary people in extraordinary circumstances. It is a heightened reality or the distilled essence of reality. Look around you. Life is enormous and extraordinary. Films should be too!

Anthony Hopkins has this advice for actors: 'Be bold and mighty forces will come to your aid. Don't think about it – leap!'

CHANGING RHYTHMS

Throughout our lives, we develop inbuilt patterns of vocal and physical rhythms. Any changes to these can be perceived by us as 'unnatural', 'wrong' or 'untruthful'. If we are used to a particular way of standing or walking, of vocal strength, accent or delivery, any adjustment will feel enormous and peculiar.

It's important to experience as many changes to your 'patterns' as possible so that you are open to a freer range of expression and can feel truthful in a variety of styles and characters. In moments of high emotion, human beings break free of their conditioned reflexes. If you can allow yourself to respond freely to your instinctive reactions, your work will be continually fresh and surprising – even to yourself.

The rhythm of the characters' thoughts will, as we've seen, often be determined by the script itself, the length of the sentences and their pauses. Also, by how frequently there are new beats. Sometimes a character will firmly finish a sentence before moving on to the next thought. Another may be struck by a completely fresh impulse while still completing the sentence. Another may never finish the words at all.

Try looking round your room:

- You might see a table – describe it.
- Then your eye alights on your favourite vase – describe it.
- Now you notice a picture of your daughter – talk about her.

Now this variant:

- See the table and, while you talk about it, see the vase and think about that while you finish your sentence about the table.
- While talking about the vase, notice the picture – be obliged to finish the sentence about the vase but be burning with news about the picture.

Next:

- See the table but halfway through talking about it, see the vase – check yourself.
- Without finishing the previous sentence, go straight on to talk about the vase.
- Notice the picture and start talking about it before you finish your sentence about the vase.

Finally, this is your grandmother's room. She is dead and you haven't been back since childhood because you went abroad. It is hard for you to talk:

- You finger the table, full of memories, then choose one to share: seeing yourself as five years old, helping grandmother make macaroni pudding.
- You see the vase. You pick it up, look at it and hold it to you. You decide to take it home as a memento.
- Your eye alights on the picture of your daughter. You didn't know your grandmother had it – or that she cared. It moves you and you fight back the tears to examine it more closely.

These are certainly transitions – the movement from beat to beat – but they are also your rhythms of thought. The only proviso in this exercise is that you cannot move from one object to another until you see it either in your mind's eye or in actuality. However slowly or instantaneously you do it, the rule is look – see – think. (And all three steps can happen in a millisecond – like a camera flash.)

Children change objectives or impulses very quickly, moving from one need to the next. As we get older, our attention span lengthens and we tend to stay with one objective longer. In old age, we may get fixed on one objective and find it hard to move on to the next.

Try looking round your room again without any dialogue:

- First be five years old. Pick up something to examine it, only to leave it seconds later as something else catches your eye. Hold that for a moment, see something more interesting and move on. That doesn't do anything exciting so you look for something better.
- Now you are your own age at an auction. Lift up and examine each item you are interested in – carefully, methodically, looking for flaws. Evaluate the worth and decide what to bid.
- Finally, you are old and going to a care home. Say goodbye to your treasured possessions one at a time. One thing stops you from moving on as you go back in time to the moment you first bought it.

In each case you will have found a different rhythm of thought and movement.

In a scene, be sure that you stay true to your character's internal tempo and that you don't pick up your partner's rhythm. For example, you could enter a room knowing you have just won a great role in a film and find your partner has received a rejection slip for his novel. Even though you don't mention your news and you commiserate over the novel, your heart will be pounding with excitement through the scene. Your tempo will be completely different from the person coping with disappointment.

If you are visiting a sick relative in hospital, you may find yourself consciously fighting the sombre mood around you and becoming more aware of your own vitality and energy. You will change your tempo as a reaction to the situation. Or if you have to cope with a party when you are feeling heartbroken and only want to crawl into the safety of your bed, you will be conscious of the frenetic pace around you and how out of kilter it is with your own slower internal rhythms.

Exploring different energy, pace and rhythm through movement and voice, discovering your own patterns and opening yourself up to other possibilities will increase your character choices. You need to be alive both to the rhythms of the scene and your own internal rhythms.

Paul Newman said, 'Pace must never control the actor – the actor must control the pace.'

NOT MISSING THE MOMENT

There is a moment in life when thought, impulse and action come together on the instant. Mind and body react in the same millisecond of time. You are poised over a cold swimming pool waiting for the gun to fire at the beginning of a race. One second you are in limbo, the next you are halfway across the pool with the sound of the gun ringing in your ears. If the mind intervenes between the sound of the shot and your reaction to dive, you've lost the race.

So often you see actors waiting to take an action – the impulse rises but nothing happens. Then they move. Or you see the thought form, the reaction happen, but the line is still left to say. The words weren't caught on the wing. This is 'missing the moment'.

In its extreme form, you will hear the breath being let out before the words as the body instinctively breathes with the impulse, but the actor doesn't power the words with the breath. Usually, it is just the faintest sense that some slight veil has come between thought and action – an adjustment, a censoring. And it is enough to have robbed the scene of energy and life.

Pausing before we speak does happen, but there has to be a strong reason or the energy drops. Generally, we respond immediately and often can't wait for the other person to stop speaking. Some directors, like Robert Altman, encourage actors to interrupt each other for a naturalistic feel. Sensitise yourself to the need to speak and act on it.

There is a real difference between thinking the character's thought and thinking *about* the character's thought. One leads to an impulse – the other blocks it. The theatre director, John Dexter, used to say constantly, 'Don't think about it – just do it!' I can't put it better than that.

COMEDY

Edmund Kean, the great nineteenth-century actor, was asked on his deathbed whether dying was difficult. 'Dying is easy – it's comedy that's difficult,' he replied. He would have found film comedy even harder. There's no applause and no laughter. In fact, if the crew are falling about laughing, it often doesn't transfer to the screen. It's hard to get a sense of timing because the takes are so short and you don't feel the whole rhythm of the piece. In the end, much of the comedy will lie in the editor's hands.

Humour is particularly subjective but some films have become comedy classics. Think of *Some Like it Hot*, *The Producers* or *Kind Hearts and Coronets*. These films use heightened naturalism – they take the truth and stretch it. They are grounded in reality but take it to the utmost possibilities.

A comedy can be physical as in the art of Charles Chaplin, Buster Keaton and Jacques Tati or 'gross-out' films like *American Pie*, or rely on keen observation and wit like *Annie Hall*, or it can be based on situation as in *The Full Monty*, which celebrates the incongruities of life: working men with less than perfect physiques rehearsing a male stripper show. The best comedies have depth. There's some pain that's buried behind the absurd circumstances. *The Full Monty* is also a sensitive portrayal of families on the dole and the breakdown of relationships. So, when it exploits the full absurdity of the situation like the scene at the dole office where, to the piped muzak, the men start a subliminal rehearsal, we laugh louder because we care.

*M*A*S*H* juxtaposes the bloody horrors of a war hospital with surreal sexual exploits and the sharp wit of the characters. In *The Dish* the gentle humour comes from the difference between the enormity of the task – to keep the first moon landing's televisual connection to earth – and the inadequate infrastructure to do so, amid the social conventions and aspirations of a small Australian town in 1969.

This opposition of realities is often the basis of comedy – and tragedy too. Sometimes it's a tragedy for the character and a comedy for us. I call it 'Kafka Land'. The man who turns into a giant insect or a bridge has a very real dilemma, but his ensuing struggle to correlate his inner reality with the view of the outside world can make us laugh or cry. Normality can turn into a new horrific environment in a minute as in a disaster movie. This clash of realities can be absurd in the extreme like the world of Monty Python where the Spanish Inquisition descend on a suburban couple's teatime.

The actor has to deal with the situation with the utmost belief and we, the audience, will supply the comedy. We laugh at things that are not at all funny to the person involved: missing the chair when they sit, splitting their trousers on the crowded train or walking into the lamppost. We can be cruel in our laughter.

The writer, director and actor take choices that lead us into laughter or tears. Sometimes our assumptions as an audience are confounded. Shakespeare's *Much Ado About Nothing* starts as a comedy then, halfway, it dips abruptly into tragedy. *The War of the Roses* seems to be a comedy until the last few moments of the film, and then both characters plunge from the chandelier to their deaths. *Crimes of the Heart* deals with racism, hatred, shootings and attempted suicide and yet remains a comedy, albeit a bittersweet one.

In comedy, your reactions may change really quickly. Look at Gene Wilder in *The Producers*: 'I'm hysterical – and I'm wet – I'm in pain – and I'm wet – and I'm still hysterical!' or Zero Mostel: 'Smile and the world smiles with you – this man should be in a straitjacket.' You need to be able to leap from one thought to another really fast.

You may make different choices of objectives in comedy. For example, a character hanging herself in a drama may 'want to get away from the pain' and take the action 'I prepare for death'. The character in a comedy may 'want to be found looking beautiful' and take the action, 'I protect my new hair-do'.

The obstacles that stand in your way will be different: a shoelace that comes undone, a Martian that appears, a striptease to do when you happen to be wearing your great-aunt's bloomers, a sure-thing flop called 'Springtime for Hitler' that turns out to be a hit. The effort of dealing with them may mean that your body gets more involved: your physical choices are more extreme. Again, this is going to depend on the kind of film you are in. Is the humour something that comes from a situation within a naturalist setting, a heightened reality or a totally surreal world? Or is the wit in the language – a verbal game of tennis or a deadly war with words as weapons?

Good comedy actors have an inbuilt timing and sense of rhythm when dealing with language. Watch this art in *The Odd Couple* with Walter Matthau and Jack Lemmon, Elliott Gould and Donald Sutherland in *M*A*S*H* – or Maggie Smith in anything.

Sometimes it is about pointing up the joke – maybe with a little piece of business to accompany it – but it's usually knowing how to take the tiniest beat pause and then to throw the joke away. It's about using subtext. You can't signal to us that it's funny – you just have to think hard and let the words slide out. Comedy takes enormous focus and energy. You can't copy anyone else's style.

So apply all your usual preparation work to comedy, understanding that you'll be dealing with different kinds of obstacles, objectives and actions but with just as much conviction.

MASKS

Oscar Wilde wrote, 'Man is least himself when he talks in his true person. Give him a mask and he will tell the truth.'

Masks may seem an odd tool to use when approaching a film role but they can be enormously liberating. They can encourage stillness, focus of energy and economy of movement.

You can use any mask, from a home-made one cut from a magazine to a leather commedia dell'arte mask. You can use this work to explore different characters and it will uncover new choices of tempo. You can also use it to find a way into a specific character and the most useful mask for this is the neutral mask. A traditional leather neutral mask may be hard to find, but you can get a suitable equivalent from a party shop. Buy a plain white mask made out of plastic or paper that is cut just below the nose to allow you to speak.

Commedia dell'arte masks embody full, rich characters that you need to discover. If you are using a character mask, traditionally you should look at it for a time to let it work on you before putting it on. Then you can use a mirror to give you feedback – mirrors have long been held to reveal the hidden nature of the reflected image. Don't talk as the mask until you feel really centred in the character (and never talk as yourself). At first, carefully put on the mask, pulling your hair over the string to hide the joins. Now just stand still for a while, looking at yourself in the mirror.

Gradually, a character will start to emerge. You will find you need to make only tiny movements to have an effect. A shoulder lifted, a head tilted and the mask will spring into life. You generally need to do very little but you can go further if you wish and add a few items of clothes – a scarf or a shawl. Every mask is unique. Even two neutral masks will be subtly different.

Move away from the mirror and see if you can sustain the life of the mask. If you lose it, then return to the mirror. When you feel ready, give your character voice – at first, just a sound, then a few words. Then you can improvise some dialogue. You may be alarmed to find that you cannot always control the mask. It is as if there's already a character, hidden inside it, that will only behave as it wants to.

But that character is a part of you – possibly an anarchic or childlike part – and working with a mask can remove some of the layers you have put up to protect you in your adult life. And it can be exhilarating. Masks are liberating and you will enjoy working with them. Peter Brook calls the traditional mask 'a soul portrait'. The other name for the neutral mask is 'the universal mask'. It has the power to release what Jung called 'the collective unconscious'.

If you are searching for a specific character through a neutral mask, then follow the steps above but, as you look at yourself in the mask, let your mind focus on the character you are playing. Try to find the psychological gesture. But don't make decisions. Let the mask lead you gradually into a posture, a gesture, a word. Jacques Lecoq taught that when you put on the mask you lose yourself in that moment and 'you are what happens'.

Don't use your text until you feel you are fully inhabiting the mask. Go really slowly. Use the absolute minimum of movement and gesture and wait for each impulse to move. As in a close-up, everything will be brought into high focus. Everything will read – the smallest movement will become all-important.

Masks seem to encourage strong clear objectives. All tiny habitual mannerisms fall away and you are left with the strong, bold essence of the character. They will increase your bravery and strength. Although you cannot control the choices a mask makes, you may be surprised to find that when you remove the mask and return to the script, you are now aware of some previously hidden truth about the character.

Watch a simple game like grandmother's footsteps or musical chairs played by masks. The power of the masks lends menace, pathos and absurd humour to the game so that it becomes an extraordinary game of life played at a deeper level.

We all wear some masks in our daily life: the social mask, the smiling affable mask, the capable mask, the industrious mask, the penitent mask. Without sometimes hiding our true feelings, we would be unable to operate within society. By putting on the protection of a physical mask, you lose your invisible mask. If you can keep this transparency when you take off the external mask then you are free to deal with the truth.

STYLE

The style of the film will influence your character and action choices. It isn't a question of themes but of directorial vision. For example, one space fantasy may need big, bold choices, another may use a low-key naturalistic approach. Films based on cartoons or games like *Barbarella*, *Batman* and *Lara Croft: Tomb Raider* keep elements of the original genre. A musical generally wears its heart on its sleeve: *West Side Story* and *Moulin Rouge* are larger than life and deal with archetypal themes – life and death, love and loss.

You need to understand the context of your performance or it may be unbalanced by what is around you. You sometimes see a performance that has the curious quality of being in a different film to everyone else. You can be 'real' in any style; you simply need to change your choice of objective or action. Reality doesn't have to be naturalism.

You can use objectives and actions in any context. A clown, crossing a street, falls into a manhole because he wants to avoid the banana skin. He must play the action, 'to cross the road'. If he wants to fall into the hole to be funny, he won't be. He might also want to 'show off his shoes' or 'keep on his wig' or 'cross backwards for fun'. In a musical, you are simply allowed, by the style, to sing your inner thoughts to your partner. A journey through space can be as real as any other journey. It's just the monsters you encounter that are different – and, as they probably won't even be there when you're filming, you'll have to use more imagination.

I used to do an experiment with drama students. I'd set up an improvisation with strong objectives. Then I'd change the situation to a spaceship. For some strange reason, they found it really hard to hang on to any kind of reality – in a few moments they'd be imitating *Star Trek* acting, which I found very mysterious. I suppose, because they had no direct experiences from which to draw, they resorted to copying from the only source they knew. By working through the actor's questions and choosing suitable objectives and actions, you should be able to hang on to your belief within any genre. Never slip into parodying a style. A film may be ironic but the actor has to play it for real – within the context.

Tastes alter and styles change. We can be alienated by earlier styles: the pantomime of the silent era, the accents in *Brief Encounter* or the laughable Hays code that meant married couples were always seen in separate beds or had to keep one foot on the floor. Each generation sets out its own parameters of what it deems truthful. Nevertheless, great acting transcends fashion. And at its best, it defies time to remain perennially alive. Katharine Hepburn, James Dean, Spencer Tracy and, indeed, Celia Johnson and Trevor Howard have as much power to move us now as they ever did. And their performances will endure far into the future.

William Weaver, in his biography of Duse, recalls seeing some old silent movies at the Museum of Modern Art in New York. The audience roared with laughter at the antiquated styles of acting, including that of Sarah Bernhardt, but, when Duse came on screen, they fell into a rapt silence. Sadly, we are left with only a brief glimpse of her work in *Cenere 16*. The shift to the screen came too late for her but she could feel how film would herald a new kind of acting. She wrote, 'Something quite different is needed. I'm too old for it. Isn't it a pity.'

Different cultures prefer different stylistic approaches. Indian films, like the classic 'Bollywood' movies, employ a more melodramatic style than films made in Europe or America. European films, like those of Truffaut and Ingmar Bergman or the more recent *No Man's Land*, *La Ville est Tranquille* and *The Son's Room* often have a more documentary feel than Hollywood films and tackle subject matter that doesn't normally appeal to the pockets of Hollywood executives – films about ordinary middle-aged women, domestic homosexuality, abuse and the problems of facing old age – and European acting is of a very high quality indeed.

Los Angeles is still the world's highest profile movie centre, but India now has a vast film industry, Australia has already become a major film-producing player and gradually film work is appearing from many different countries. If funding and distribution were made more available then it could foster a welcome diversity of style and subject matter. Witness the recent fusion of East and West in the beautiful films *Crouching Tiger, Hidden Dragon* and *Monsoon Wedding*.

Technology is also changing styles. With the advent of new digital cameras of high quality and the smaller costs involved, directors can afford to experiment. *The Blair Witch Project*, done on a shoestring, set out to look like a mixture of home movie and budget documentary. The actors were directed by remote control and left more or less alone to survive and improvise their way through a witch-infested wood. It was one of the most profitable films ever made.

BRINGING IT ALL TOGETHER

As you gain experience you will gradually find your own best way of preparing and working on and off set. One actor will need peace and quiet to create the right environment for work and another will want noise and company to crank up performance energy.

Judi Dench is an actor of enormous depth and technical mastery of every style from theatre and television sit-com to truly great screen performances like the ones she gave in *The Shipping News* and *Iris*. (Billy Connolly said he had a problem on *Mrs Brown* because she was so real, he could never tell when the scene had started!) Yet she can be cracking a joke one minute and giving a totally committed performance the next. Anyone who has enjoyed her many out-takes on television 'bloopers' programmes where she burps and giggles uncontrollably will see that she likes to work seriously in a non-serious environment.

Other actors, such as Dustin Hoffman, have the reputation of needing to re-create the physical environment of the character and to stay embedded in that character between takes.

In the same way, some actors can talk at length about their preparation while others steadfastly refuse to discuss the acting process. The character builds secretly, by what Judi Dench calls 'osmosis', and they somehow fear that, by talking about it, the magic will go and their muse will elude them afterwards.

However you do it, you need to prepare. Cary Grant once said, 'It takes five hundred small details to add up to one favourable impression.' You need attention to all these details and then the courage to leave them behind. It's like driving a car – you slowly learn to adjust all the controls, to check your mirror, to watch for hazards, and then you forget about it all and let it take care of itself while you pursue your course, listening to the radio or arguing with your passenger.

In an ideal world, you will have time to do whatever preparation you need but sometimes you will be cast at very short notice. If you've been keeping yourself physically and mentally supple, you'll have no problem. Do some fast detective work on the script to find your character clues. Go quickly through all the 'actor's questions' and use the 'physical metaphor' work as a short cut to character decisions. Know clearly what your objective is for each beat of the scene and drive your actions. Then just commit and go.

The purpose of all this work is not to make you heavy or drag you down. Once it's done, you move on and you continually adjust as you need to. You may find you never need to refer to it again. Your preparation is simply so that in performance you are as free to respond as immediately as you would in life.

If you are still following an inner script of 'actions' and 'beats' when performing, you will never be free to fly and this phoney 'method' approach becomes a style in itself, as dead as any other head-bound acting technique. Your early rehearsal work was a way to understand the impulses of the character and to make the words and drives your own. Now you must leave it in the trailer, trust it to take care of itself and work off the impulses themselves in an organic rather than cerebral way. You must be able to respond instinctively to the moment – in fluid motion. (Good method actors like Marlon Brando, Julie Harris, Robert De Niro or Al Pacino do just that.) It should feel like life.

You have just been preparing for that natural and so unnatural game you are playing: finding a way to live with conviction in an imaginary world that has to become a reality for the duration of filming, both for yourself and the audience.

Tim Robbins reminds himself of his responsibility to the audience when he's exhausted on the set at 2.30 a.m. He imagines that each of them will use their last ten dollars to see the movie, having walked ten miles to get there because they couldn't afford the fare. No matter how tired you are, no matter how bored you are twelve weeks into shooting, never let a scene go. Always care. If it doesn't end up on the cutting-room floor, it will be in the film to forever haunt you.

'The actor cannot be merely someone, somewhere, at some time or other. He must be I, here, today' (Constantin Stanislavski, 1936).

SCENE PREPARATION ON *VICTORY*

EXT. SAMBURAN VERANDA. NIGHT
Lanterns. Heyst reading. Lena cutting pages of a book with a kitchen knife.
In background in the room the cylinder gramophone playing.
Rosalia Chalier singing.
She looks up at him.

LENA

I've done it. The book is ready to be read.

HEYST

Ah Good.
He continues to read.

LENA

What are you reading?

HEYST

Poems.

LENA

Read one to me.

(Pause.)

Will you?

HEYST

They're French.

LENA

You mean in the French language?

HEYST

Yes.

LENA

Oh. I wouldn't understand, would I?

HEYST

No.
Pause.

LENA

Unless you told me what it meant?
He slowly looks up.

HEYST

Why not read something yourself, in English?
Pause.

LENA

I'm sleepy.
She stands, goes to him, kisses him lightly on the cheek, goes into the house.
He remains reading for a moment, then closes the book, turns out the lantern.

This is a short scene from *Victory* written in 1982 by Harold Pinter and never filmed as funding couldn't be raised. I have chosen it as its taut spare style exemplifies film writing at its best. Pinter's elliptical writing defies any attempt at a definitive analysis and, because of this, you can try this piece using different characters and objectives for practice. Give yourself different given circumstances and see how many ways you can play it.

Note the pauses. If you obey them and don't add others, you will find the rhythm of the language. It is your job to find out why you need them.

Victory is taken from the novel of the same name by Joseph Conrad (1915), so you can read the original source material. It has been filmed four times – in 1919, 1928, 1940 and in 1995.

Here are a few character notes:

Lena:
- *Known facts*: English; working with Zangiacomo's ladies orchestra on its Eastern tour.
- *Assumed facts*: father was a drunk; now in a home for incurables after a stroke; mother ran away; now alone in the world.

Heyst:
- *Known facts*: Swedish; lives on Sambura island in the Malay archipelago surrounded by the remains of a coal mine started with a partner who is now dead; lives alone with dead father's belongings and a servant. He is known as a recluse.
- *Assumed facts*: father was a philosopher; left school in England early; father was an embittered and powerful figure to him; possibly a baron. He is reluctant to leave his island.

Here are the given circumstances:
- Heyst had been visiting a hotel on nearby Surabaya and met Lena, who was working in the orchestra. They talked and he found out she had no money or family. He saw her being badly treated and took her away with him to his island. Today, on arrival, he gives her his own bedroom and, later on a walk, tells her about the death of his partner. She confesses that she heard the hotel owner on Surabaya say that

Heyst had murdered him which Heyst denies. He makes love to her fiercely against her will – then apologises. It is late evening the same day.

Conditioning factors:
- It is hot. There is a gramophone cylinder playing.

Here are two versions (A & B) of possible objectives and actions and subtext. Remember these are two of endless possibilities and you would try many options during your rehearsal period.
    Main scene objectives:
- (A) Lena: I want you to comfort me.
- (A) Heyst: I want to shut you out.
- (B) Lena: I want to make love to you.
- (B) Heyst: I want to be sure you want me.

	LENA
I've done it. The book is ready to be read.	(A) *I want to please you/I offer* (objective/action)
	(A) (*'Sorry I pushed you away'*) (subtext)
	(B) *I want to start again/I approach*
	(B) (*'I'm not angry'*)
	HEYST
Ah Good.	(A) *I want to avoid/I stall*
	(A) (*'I don't want to get involved'*)
	(B) *I want to know what she wants/I wait*
	(B) (*'Are you still angry?'*)
He continues to read.	
	LENA
What are you reading?	(A) *I want to make up/I pursue*
	(A) (*'Please talk to me'*)
	(B) *I want you to talk to me/I approach*
	(B) (*'Look at me'*)
	HEYST
Poems.	(A) *I want to avoid/I stall*
	(A) (*'Give me time to think'*)
	(B) *I want to know what she wants/ I buy time*
	(B) (*'Is she still angry?'*)

Read one to me.

LENA
(A) *I want to reach you/I ask*
(A) *('Please look at me')*
(B) *I want you to make love to me/I flirt*
(B) *('I want to make love again')*
(Pause.)
  (A) *('I'm so lonely')*
  (B) *('Have you understood?')*

Will you?

(A) *I want reassurance/I plead*
(A) *('Please')*
(B) *I want you to understand/I offer sex*
(B) *('Will you make love to me?')*

HEYST

They're French.

(A) *I want to block/ I humiliate*
(A) *('End of conversation')*
(B) *I want to know if she means it/
    I explore*
(B) *('Are you seducing me?')*

LENA

You mean in the French
language?

(A) *I want to understand/ I pursue*

(A) *('Please don't shut me out')*
(B) *I want to make you laugh/I tease*
(B) *('French is sexy')*

HEYST

Yes.

(A) *I want you to go/I finish*
(A) *('Leave me alone')*
(B) *I want to check she's flirting/I hope*
(B) *('You're turning me on')*

LENA

Oh. I wouldn't understand,
would I?

(A) *I want to know if you love me/I
    give up*
(A) *('Don't you love me?')*
(B) *I want to play innocent/I check you
    understand*
(B) *('Do you understand I'm seducing
    you?')*

HEYST

No.

(A) *I want to reject you/I reject*
(A) *('No')*
(B) *I want to play innocent/I tease*
(B) *('I'll force her to ask me clearly')*

Pause.
(A) they try to find a way to continue
(B) they want each other

LENA

Unless you told me what it meant?

    (A) I want to make one last try/
      I plead
    (A) ('Please don't reject me')
    (B) I want to make love/I titillate
    (B) ('Don't play games')

He slowly looks up.
(A) he makes contact with her
(B) he accepts her offer of lovemaking

HEYST

Why not read something yourself, in English?

    (A) I want to soften the blow/I pity

    (A) ('Maybe you can't read')
    (B) I want you to take the initiative/
      I encourage
    (B) ('Are you asking me to bed?')

Pause.
(A) he wants her to go
(B) he waits for her to invite him

LENA

I'm sleepy.

    (A) I want to retreat/I give up
    (A) ('You don't love me')
    (B) I want you to come to bed/I seduce
    (B) ('Come to me in bed')

You will see that sometimes a new line is a new beat, but that sometimes the character stays on the same beat for several lines. You will also have noticed that the different versions affected the status of the characters. In (A) Heyst is clearly playing higher status. In (B) the situation is reversed and Lena holds the upper cards.

PART THREE
THE CRAFT

INTRO

Dividing the practical part of this book into 'the Art' and 'the Craft' was my way of separating the acting process from the technical demands of filming. Having said that, the two sections inevitably overlap. The acting work demands an attention to craft, and the practical business of filming involves creative input and preparation.

Understanding the techniques needed and doing thorough preparation releases you from some of the burdens of film-making. For the first-time film actor, the energy that you need to keep focus in the busy atmosphere of a film set and to repeat a small section time after time and take after take cannot be overstated.

In filming, you never have the cathartic release of a whole performance. But you are able to keep striving for perfection. Laurence Olivier once said that in films, there is no performance, that you just shoot a lot of rehearsals and pick the best.

But each rehearsal has to have full commitment and energy because you never know which one they'll pick!

OUT OF SEQUENCE

A film is rarely shot in order. Exceptionally, *Nikita* and *A Beautiful Mind* were shot chronologically, but I have only ever been involved with one film, *The Hole*, that shot a substantial section of the film in sequence. This was set in a Second World War bunker that became more and more filthy as the characters were trapped in it over a long period of time. This was great for the props department who could leave the food to rot by itself and just add extra garbage and insects each day. It was great for the make-up and hair people who could add a little more dirt and blood as they went along. But most of all it was great for the actors who could build on their performances and relationships as the plot thickened. It is not always so!

Usually the love scene takes place in the first week, your wife leaves you before you've even met and the armies are counting their dead before the battle's begun. The reason, of course, is economics. It makes much more sense to shoot all the scenes that take place in the same location at the same time; to put all the scenes involving the expensive actor together; to do all the ballroom scenes with the vast amounts of extras so you don't have continuity problems. And so on.

Because of this, it becomes really important to do some work beforehand to protect yourself both from losing track of the character's journey and the plot; also, for that other nasty trick that film has of changing the order of the scenes at seven o'clock in the morning.

Since you don't often have the luxury of carrying out the events of the film in real time, you have to know where you are in terms of the story, relationships and emotions. And how you fit into the film as a whole. There are a few directors who don't let the actors see the whole script, but they are the exceptions. And even if there isn't a script, the director will tell you the plot and how he sees the character you are playing. If you don't do your homework, then you will be truly in his hands – no better than a marionette. And not many actors will find this the best way of working.

David Mamet has argued in his book *True and False* that actors do not need to know the arc of the characters. That the writer takes care of these. And to some extent, the long-term objectives *are* in the hands of the writer and director. But not all film scripts are as well written as David

Mamet's or have the same coherence and not every director can guide you through your journey. And, unlike theatre, it is not a linear journey – it is a haphazard assortment of moments. In film you get so little creative input that you need to capitalise on what you have. If your integrity of character shines through, you may actually alter the way it is edited in the end.

I think there is a confusion between the actor and the character. *The actor has to know the shape of the play; the character must not.* Thus you, as the character, must play the objective and actions of the scene without jumping beats or knowing what lies ahead. But when you, the actor, choose those objectives you are to play, it is with a sense of the script as a whole that you plot your course. And as, in film, you are likely to be jumping around this course out of sequence, it is even more important that you have set your signposts.

A character will develop and change through the course of the drama. A really clever writer will do this journey for you. In *Romeo and Juliet*, Romeo talks of his love for Rosaline, his first love, in a different kind of language to the way he talks about Juliet. But if you're in a film where the language doesn't contain the same subtleties, you are going to carry more of the responsibilities for the journey of the character.

Imagine a modern film about a similar situation, written, as so many films are, by committee. As Romeo, without textual clues to guide you, are you going to play a scene with Rosaline in the same way as one with Juliet? Don't you, as an actor, have to choose different objectives in relation to these two women through your knowledge of the whole play and the route the character travels? And if you decide that it *is* the same kind of love and, therefore, the same needs you have for both, then shouldn't that be a conscious decision that has consequences for the whole endeavour, rather than something that just happens because you don't see the shape of the piece as a whole?

Take another example. If you were playing a character like Jack Nicholson's in *One Flew Over the Cuckoo's Nest* who either gets – or pretends to get – progressively mad during the course of the film, how would you know how far down that line you were, on any given scene, if you hadn't plotted your course? How would your performance have any credibility seen as a whole if you hadn't been aware of the arc of the character?

Let's assume that your super-objective is to obtain freedom. Now you have a choice: are you going to take the action 'to feign madness' in order to achieve that objective or do you actually go mad (the 'given condition') through the actions of trying to get out of the mental institution? In either case, it will be really important to chart a course for this 'madness' so that, shooting out of order, you will be on the right part of your journey. It may not be a straight line, but its course, whatever shape, has to be coherent for the whole film.

A scene cannot be seen in isolation. Once you, the actor, know the whole course – you, the character, will cope with the given circumstances innocently and drive each objective as it occurs. But your choice of objective will have been influenced by the shape of the whole.

Some actors leave all the decisions to the director, but I think you need to take responsibility as well. Work together with the director but don't rely on that support. Be prepared to discuss and justify your choices and to compromise or change them. But be prepared.

Robert Donat, the fine actor who starred in Hitchcock's *The 39 Steps*, used to make a graph charting the emotional journey of the character, and for *Goodbye, Mr Chips* (for which he won an Oscar for Best Actor) he did one for his age and appearance too. His son told me this story: Robert appeared on set as the old Mr Chips for the first time and was practising his shuffling walk. The producer, Alexander Korda, came on set and asked the director of photography Freddie Young, 'Who's that old fart?' Robert regarded that as the finest assessment of his acting career!

You journey through life sequentially and anything that happens to you will inevitably alter your actions as it occurs. You won't need to plan ahead to decide how you will react. At each moment you'll be in the 'now' without any knowledge of the next moment.

The same must be true for the character. But his calendar will not be sequential and it will only happen to him 'in the moment' if you've done your preparatory homework and know what moment he's in!

BEING READY
Go through your script as suggested before, asking your list of questions about who you are, what you want, your relationships and actions. Note all your beat changes.

Then take some ordinary record cards or postcards and prepare a card for each scene (scenes in screenplays are usually fairly short):

- Put the scene number and page number (either might change) at the top.
- Note the day and time the scene occurs and whether there's been a time gap between scenes.
- Mark where it is – inside or outside, which house, which room, whose territory, etc.

- Write down any conditioning factors like the weather, terrain or if you're hungry, cold or ill, etc. Also any plot factors that are important.
- At the top of the card, put where you've just come from and why or what you've just been doing (check whether this scene runs sequentially from another).
- At the bottom of the card, put where you're going to or what you're doing at the end of the scene.
- Put your objective at the start of the scene and any changes that occur within the scene.
- Put who's in the scene with you and how you feel about each of them at this moment (also the relationship with anyone you mention).
- Put any other information that's important to this scene. (This might be something carried over from a previous scene.)
- Then join all the cards for the different scenes together using a treasury tag or string.
- Always look at the scene card together with the relevant pages from your script before going to the set so you know where you are on the journey.
- Add cards for new scenes as they get written.

The beauty of the cards is that they're so much easier to handle than the script. The script will keep changing and it's laborious to keep writing in all the information every time you get new pages. You can look at your cards during make-up or flick through them to check the context of the scene for the following day. The script supervisor will always help, but with this aide-memoire you'll hardly ever need to ask. With some films it's essential just to keep up with the plot! (In *The Big Sleep*, though, neither the director nor the writer knew who committed one of the murders – but I bet the actors did!)

Once, on the set, we were all very tired and many weeks had elapsed between filming two scenes which, although separated within the script, followed sequentially. None of us – the script supervisor, the actor, the director or myself – remembered that the heroine had just run miles to the house that she was entering for the current scene. All we knew was that it felt wrong somehow – flat. After the second take we all remembered at the same time. Ever since then, I've done my own set of cards too!

Some actors prefer to do a collage across the wall of the trailer – tricky if you go on location. You may prefer to do it electronically on your laptop or handheld computer. Whichever way you choose, it will provide a record of your journey as a character.

QUICK TIPS FOR FILMING PREPARATION
(See 'Art' section for full preparation.)

- **Plot the character's journey through the script.** Find out what he or she wants, as a whole, in each scene.
- **Make cards** marking them with where you've come from and where you're going, time of day, conditioning factors, key plot notes, who's in the scene and relationships, beat changes.
- **Make brave choices,** bearing in mind the journey your character will take.
- **Identify your objectives.** Play your actions. Be in the moment.
- **Find a thought** to start the scene. Observe new surroundings – watch your fellow actor for reactions – listen.
- **Trust your preparation.** Don't decide how it will be – be in the moment. Don't let anything come between the impulse and the action.
- **Don't try to reproduce** the last take – go back to the original impulses.
- **'Flying'** is being able to be both actor (craft) and character (art) at the same time.
- **Filming is very tiring.** Use time off to relax. Lie on the floor and do your relaxation exercise. Once you know you are thoroughly prepared, you need to rest physically and mentally.

THE EVER-CHANGING SCRIPT

The script will keep changing. New scenes may arrive in your dressing room every day. Sometimes they even arrive on the set. Don't let that throw you. The writer can change it, the producers can demand more scenes or the director can cut some. Depending on your status in the film, you may be able to make changes to the script. Directors are usually open to small alterations from any actor but beware – you may not be as good at dialogue as the writer and you may, as we've said, be changing it because it is more comfortable for you to say. That is not a good enough reason on its own – you may not want to say it like that but the character does.

Most film writers are not on Shakespeare's level but you'd probably be tempted to change some words in *Hamlet* to make it easier to say, so be sure what you're offering is better. And when the screenplay is written by a world-class writer like Mamet, Pinter, Stoppard, Shepard or Minghella – you change lines at your peril.

When the script changes, new pages will come in different colours – to show which is the most recent – and you'll need to feed them in. Be careful not to throw pages away that haven't been replaced, particularly if the new ones come as A, B or C additions to the old number. One actor found his role had shrunk in an alarming way because he didn't realise the new sheets were only part replacing his old script!

By the way, although the finished product is a screenplay, for an actor it is always a 'script'. There is also an up-to-date pocket version of the day's scenes, called 'sides', produced each morning, which is handy to take on set.

LEARNING LINES

It is important to learn the script thoroughly enough to forget it. If you only half know it, you'll be reaching for the words. Some actors try to keep it fresh by not learning properly *but this doesn't work*. I've watched too many actors waste the first five takes fishing for the lines. You also never know when a scene might appear. The call sheet says Scene 136 but, hey, it's raining. Back to studio cover with Scene 21.

Get familiar with any technical words or unusual dialogue (even the technobabble of *Star Trek*). You have to sound as if you use these terms all the time – they mustn't trip you up. Remember to delete all adjectives (like sad, horrified, bemused) and adverbs (joyfully, wryly, loudly) that you find in the stage directions of your script, so they don't lead you into one way of playing. These instructions are for the reader, not the actor.

Being asked to improvise extra dialogue on the spur of the moment is fine. Because you are finding the words as you go, you will sound spontaneous. The difficulty here is if you have to repeat it. Don't try to remember what you said before. Go back to the objectives of the character in the scene and start freshly, as if for the first time.

Sometimes you will be given last-minute alterations or even whole new scenes. That's OK, too. You can store lines in your short-term memory for a while and keep them fresh or even improvise around them a little. It's not ideal, but it's part of the movie-making business that rewrites keep happening and happening.

There is a truthful old adage: don't learn the lines, learn the thoughts. When you learn, find all the beat changes and see how each thought links to the next. Learn the thought changes, then the words you need for those changes.

You can use a similar device to that outlined in the 'Listening' section. Find the key words, both in your lines and those of your partner. Highlight them or act them out and they will become the 'ladder' of your thoughts – what you hear and what you say. They will lead you from one step to the next through the scene. Then instead of having to remember the lines, the words will arise unbidden as the action unfolds.

When you've found the thoughts, *then* you can put a ruler over your lines, check the cue and drum them in. When you are practising the lines, don't get patterned or say them by rote or keep practising them the way you want to play them. Do them a million different ways. Say them while you engage in lots of different activities – ironing, running for the bus, digging the garden.

As you get closer to filming, do some actual rehearsals and you will find that combining the real actions with the words will help you remember the lines. (Michael Caine lays everything out for the scene ahead when in his hotel room the night before filming.) The mind works in odd ways. Do you ever go to do some ordinary action – reaching for your toothbrush, or preparing for bed – and find yourself remembering what you were thinking when you last carried out that action? You can use this same system to learn your lines, almost by osmosis.

It seems that the two hemispheres of the brain operate in different ways: the right side responds to images, colours and sounds; the left is more adept at language, analysis and sequencing. As formal education offers more opportunities to the left hemisphere of the brain, the actor may need to wake up the right side. Try this exercise which is supposed to harmonise both hemispheres of the brain:

- Simply draw a large imaginary figure of eight in the air with your right hand following the movement of your finger with your eyes. Do six more. Now repeat the exercise with your left hand. (It doesn't matter which hand you use first or which direction you go in.)

I had an odd experience once. I have always had a terrible memory for names. One day I was attending a talk by the director, Peter Brook, in a rather cramped theatre auditorium, and I decided to take some notes. As I was in an aisle seat, I did it by writing with my left hand. I haven't tried writing with my left hand for years and it was pretty illegible. But later in the bar, talking about past productions, I could remember every actor's name. I was so impressed by this that every time I have difficulty remembering something, I scribble some invisible words with my left hand. It looks pretty odd but it seems to help. Recently, I heard a neurologist advise people to do tasks involving intricate movements with the hand they don't normally use. Apparently it keeps all the synapses connecting. Perhaps writing your lines with your non-writing hand would help you to learn them!

Mark breathing places in your script for new thoughts when learning complex text. Use the 'psychological gesture' and the 'physicalising' work to keep the words energised and specific. When you 'own' the words, they're easier to learn. Sing, chant and whisper the text to uncover new shades of meaning and to keep it from getting fixed.

In the end, if you're not improvising, you need to have learnt the lines so well that you sound as if you are – with each thought newly minted.

IMPROVISATION IN FILMING

To improvise, you simply ask yourself the same actor's questions: Who am I? Where and when am I? What are my relationships? What are the conditioning factors? What do I want? What gets in my way? How do I get what I want? If you truly drive your objective and play your actions then you will never feel the need 'to make up lines'.

A lot of directors use improvisation while shooting. Some use it just for odd scenes that haven't been fully scripted, during action sequences, crowd work, scenes involving children or animals or situations that are likely to be unpredictable. Others use it if emotional scenes feel stiff or if the dialogue doesn't seem to be working well. Sometimes whole films are improvised.

Mike Leigh uses improvisation throughout the rehearsal period to carve out a final script, which is then more or less fixed; Bryan Singer used a lot of improvised dialogue in *The Usual Suspects*. Robert Altman sometimes improvises whole sections and always likes the actors to improvise at the top of a scene so that it starts fluidly. Mike Figgis used four digital cameras to shoot *Timecode* in continuous improvisation. The finished film shows each camera's unbroken take at the same time on a screen split four ways. The actors improvised the whole film fifteen times without stopping before the director was satisfied.

The important thing is not to feel obliged to be clever or witty or to keep the scene moving. Resist playing to an audience or making up lines when you don't need them. If you know exactly what the scene is about and what you want, then all you need to do is pursue your objective. That might take very few words to achieve. If you're trying to 'make up dialogue', you've lost your way.

Don't be afraid of silence. We sometimes cover up our feelings by deadening them with noise and words. Silence can expose them. There is a Zen saying that the whole truth exists only in silence. As long as you are alive and thinking, your character may not need to speak.

Learn to recognise the natural impulse that moves the thought into breath, voice or movement on the instant. Don't manufacture it and don't suppress it.

If you are a director using improvisation work, it can also be useful to film the actors between takes – plotting the scene, making coffee or telling stories. Play this back and if it is more immediate, more specific or sounds more alive than the scene, then there is work to be done.

The director can help the actors by setting the scene very clearly, making sure that the cast know their relationships and status positions. He or she can find the major units in the scene and give each actor a really strong objective to pursue for every unit. Situations can be set up to expose the needs and conflicts of the characters. The actors can be given secondary activities to pursue that will only be stopped or changed by the power of the primary objectives. If they are still worrying about 'making up lines', they can do it once without any words.

If there is plenty of time, an improvisation can be allowed to go its own way and edited later, but for continuous improvisation or more structure, the process can be tightened. The director can note each landmark moment in the scene. This could include a piece of essential plotting, a prop that has to be handled or even a line to be included. These moments can be numbered and learnt as thoroughly as any other script. In this way, an improvisation can be plotted as tightly as a written scene – by marking each change of beat within it and each change of objective for each actor. Then the actor can use these markers as stepping stones through the improvised scene.

QUICK TIPS FOR LEARNING
- **Divide** the script into units, marking beat changes – put in breathing places for new thoughts.
- **Learn the script** from impulse to impulse.
- **Find the key words** – these make your 'thought ladder'.
- **Don't get patterned.** Try it lots of different ways. It may change!
- **Use 'psychological gesture'** and 'physicalising' to own the words.
- **Lines may be improvised** or done from instant line changes, otherwise they must be learnt *thoroughly* so that you can forget them. A halfway position is very dangerous – you'll just be fishing for lines.
- **Improvisations** are like the first stage of any script. Know who you are and what you want. Identify all the beats and make these your stepping stones. Only speak when you need to.

THE EYE OF THE CAMERA

Nobody said life was fair – and it isn't. The old adage that the camera either loves you or it doesn't has some truth in it. Some people seem to light up when you put a camera on them. All their thoughts shine through without them even trying. Maybe it's a combination of cheekbones and heavy-lidded eyes. The actual topography of the face is interesting – the contours become dramatic.

Greta Garbo is an obvious example. In the final shot of *Queen Christina*, her director is supposed to have told her to think of nothing and yet we fill in an enormity of emotion behind those liquid eyes. Other actors in this category might be Humphrey Bogart, Marlene Dietrich, Marlon Brando, Elizabeth Taylor, Marilyn Monroe, Steve McQueen, Audrey Hepburn or James Dean. Then there are the ones with what you might describe as charm: an inner humour, a sardonic smile – actors like Cary Grant, Dirk Bogarde and Sean Connery. We want to watch them whatever the merits of the movie.

You won't know how your face 'reads' until you can see yourself dispassionately on screen. But whatever category you first fall into, it doesn't mean that a camera can't learn to love you. If your inner life is strong enough and your energy focused, we will be drawn to watch you and your character will become unforgettable even if you aren't a classic 'face'. Spencer Tracy didn't have perfect bone structure and yet he is commonly regarded as one of the best screen actors we have ever had. Judi Dench also ranks amongst the best ever, even though, at her first screen test, the producer was reported to have said she had everything possible wrong with her face! Her thoughts and emotions shine out of her eyes. Kevin Spacey is not an obvious 'leading man' and yet his face subtly shifts into each new character he plays.

Some faces seem so full of hidden depth that we, as viewers, supply the interpretation; other actors have to supply it for us. Bette Davis, Anthony Hopkins, Jeanne Moreau, Peter Finch, Jack Lemmon, Dustin Hoffman, Al Pacino, Robert De Niro and Gérard Depardieu work on screen because of their acting abilities regardless of facial contours. So if you haven't got a classic 'camera face' you may just have to think harder and take braver choices.

Conversely, if you're someone the camera does love, then you may have to be extra careful that you're not doing too much. If the camera catches every flicker of thought, then you have to trust that the thought is enough. You don't need to flag it up. You will need enormous inner energy and complete outward relaxation. You will have to trust in that love affair with the camera and that it sees through you to your inner life. Never play to the camera but never hide from the camera.

This is not about a dead stillness but about having extraordinary focus of thought with nothing extraneous getting in the way. James Dean is never 'still' – he is alive in every second and sometimes his responses are enormous, but they are always real. And his performances never date. Dirk Bogarde said, 'The amount of concentration you have to use to feed that camera is so enormous that you're absolutely ragged at the end of the day after doing something simple – like a look.'

Jean-Luc Godard wrote in *Le Petit Soldat* that 'cinema is truth 24 times a second'. It is this ability to make the image transparent and to show us the inner workings of the mind that is the camera's magic. Many people find film 'more real' than theatre, which is patently absurd. In theatre we are watching real human beings living at the same moment as us and reacting to our presence. On film we're watching images on celluloid – illusions fixed for ever in a frozen moment.

And yet if that moment was alive for the camera when it was shot, it will stay alive for us for ever. We will have the sensation of looking beneath the surface into the character's inmost world. The actor's art is no longer ephemeral but accessible to future generations of filmgoers, which is quite a responsibility for you, and why you have to make sure *you* are alive in the moment – every moment.

A film is structured reality and, as viewers, we have become very adept at understanding how film grammar operates. We know what signals a sudden time change, whether we're in flashback, or if it's happening in a dream. In spite of all the stylised effects used, we register it as a kind of reality.

For example, film, which is normally shot at 24 frames a second (hence the Godard quote), can be speeded up or slowed down by running the camera slower or faster. If it is run fast, we get a slow-motion effect when it is projected at normal speed. We understand what this means. If the lovers are running into each other's arms or the hero's dying – time has frozen. If it's slowed down in an action sequence, that's code for everything happening extra fast (when adrenalin makes the brain processes faster, we do actually get a slow-motion time distortion). If the shooting speed is slowed down subtly (22 instead of 24 frames a second) the resultant speeding-up effect when viewed makes the car chase really fast or the actor look like a super-athlete. If it's slowed down a lot, we're into Keystone Cops!

We will happily move our perceptions between colour and black and white. After a few minutes we will have adjusted our perceptions to allow for a black and white world and, when the film is remembered later, it will often be hard to be sure whether it was in colour or not. Like our dreams.

Incidentally, black and white can actually enhance an actor, as it seems to help us to focus on the actor's face with less distraction. Eyes and thoughts become even more powerful. Like Greta Garbo in *Queen Christina*, Marlene Dietrich in *The Blue Angel*, Ingrid Bergman in *Casablanca* or Marlon Brando in *On the Waterfront*. Recently the Coen brothers *film noir* movie, *The Man Who Wasn't There*, used black and white photography to throw the fine performances of Billy Bob Thornton and Frances McDormand into sharp relief.

By watching films all our lives, we have also learnt that anything we're shown must be important. If we see a cigarette packet lying on the floor or an address on a notepad, it's going to figure in the story. Everything adds up to the whole. The director directs our gaze and, unlike theatre, the camera only has a single point of focus.

Similarly, everything *you* do needs to add up to the whole. Any extraneous movement or unnecessary gesture will stand out as untruthful. You can be very physical on film, but everything has to serve the character in the given situation because every movement 'reads'. Whatever you do must be essential and organic to the scene. There are rules within the structure of film that give an impression of reality. Your quality of acting is one of them.

Any unnecessary facial movement will show immediately. Even a hint of signalling to us what you're thinking will strike us as false. Earlier in the book I suggested that we can tell the difference on screen between a 'real' person in a documentary and an actor (although good actors can fool you – I just caught Joanna Lumley in *Up in Town* on BBC2 and thought she was telling a real story). Some of this is to do with picture quality and production standards and some of it is to do with the material – fiction is distilled reality and doesn't leave in all the meanderings of life. But there's something else.

We learn to read very subtle clues of body language and we are finely tuned to recognise anything 'false'. It's part of our survival mechanism. For example: research has shown that people tend to look up to the left when they remember a picture, up to the right when they construct one, to the left to remember a sound, to the right to compose one, down to the left if they are thinking something through and down to the right to contact their feelings.

You don't have to remember all this or ape it, all you have to do think the character's thoughts. Real thoughts really do read. If you 'see' what you are talking about, then your eyes will flicker upwards. Subconsciously, we'll recognise that movement and believe it. If the actor isn't really thinking or turns the energy inwards to 'feel' instead of pursuing the task in hand, we won't believe them.

The camera is very perceptive. It can see beneath the skin with what Martin Scorsese calls 'the psychic strength of the lens'. So, you have to *really* listen in reaction shots. When you take action you have *really* to drive your objectives. In a close-up you need the lid on your emotional pot of water, but it really has to be boiling. You need to think hard. And that's *all* you need to do. Then you can 'own the screen'.

IN THE FRAME

A scene is covered from many different angles. Generally, it will be done in long or wide shot first where you see all the action. This is called the master shot. Then you will cover it in mid-shot or two-shot (i.e. two people in shot) and, finally, in close-up. All the major characters in the scene will be shot in close-up to cover their reactions as well as their dialogue and actions. Whatever major moves you do in the master shot will need to be repeated exactly in all other shots. Each shot will be repeated again and again until all the elements of it are perfect.

Sometimes you may have to take up a position that doesn't seem natural or to 'cheat' a scene without being able to look at the other actor. By all means, offer your own suggestions to the director during blocking, but there are times when compromises have to be made to get it all in frame. Or the director needs a particularly precise angle for the shot. The arrangement of the shot – or mise en scène – will help the atmosphere and tell us about the relationships of the characters.

Robert Donat described the actor's trials in *Footnotes to the Film* (1938). Things haven't changed:

> *The young man's behind is probably propped up on a couple of cushions or books, and the desk is raised up on wood to improve matters for the camera, so that his leg dangles at a very unnatural height from the ground, and he must gauge his movements so that at the moment of the close-up his head will be momentarily still and his eyes – almost imperceptibly – will flash their story; not into the lens itself (for the lens, though our most inquisitive neighbour, must be ignored completely if we would win it over completely), not precisely into the lens, then, but at a spot dangerously close.*

You can never tell from the camera position how close you'll be in shot, so check with the camera operator.

Long shot

Medium two-shot

Medium shot

Close-up

Learn to trust the DOP (director of photography), the focus puller, the camera operator and the director in terms of their own specialities. If they say a shot that feels awkward looks fine – it does. If they say your position is wrong, then no matter how good the performance – we won't see it.

But only ask the director about your acting. DOP David Connell, with whom I shared many dusty weeks filming a TV version of *Cleopatra* in Morocco, tells this story: he was working with the actor/director Charles Martin Smith who asked him to keep an eye on his performance during a card game shot under one main source of light: 'Once the shot was completed, Charlie asked me to comment on his performance, and all I could say was, "It was good, you only drifted out of your light twice"' – the point being that a DOP will be watching the light, not the performance!

Make friends with the focus puller and he or she will tell you the size of the shot; you can even develop a sign language to communicate with each other (useful if the camera is a long way off). Just because the camera is in the distance doesn't necessarily mean that you are in long shot. You need to know what the framing is, so that you can adjust the size of your performance and know how much of you is in shot. There are two ways to put you into close up: the camera can come closer or a lens with a longer focal length can be used. The smaller the focal length (the lens size in millimetres), the wider the field-of-view; the bigger the focal length, the narrower the field-of-view. For example, somebody filmed across a room on a 100mm lens would be in close-up; on a 20mm lens, we would see the whole room. The only way to know whether you are in close-up is to ask the camera operator.

There was something in the days of Euston Films known as the 'Euston Salute' – one hand above the head and the other waving back and forth across the chest to signify a medium close-up. There was also a useful, if uncouth, shorthand: from temple to... 1T – teeth (ECU), 2Ts – teeth & tits (CU), 3Ts – teeth, tits & tummy (or ruder variants) (MS), 4Ts – teeth, tits, tummy and toes (LS)! All very non-p.c. these days!

When deciding how much energy you need for a particular size shot, i.e. close-up, mid-shot or long shot, think of the camera as another character in the scene who must observe and understand your body language, then you'll always be real. Thus, if the camera is shooting in long shot, you are going to need more energy to connect up with that distant friend (while still interacting honestly with the other characters on set). If in close-up, then the camera is your closest lover or party to your most secret inner thought. The further the distance your thoughts have to cross, the more physical energy you will need. If your whole body is in shot, the thoughts will have to enter your whole body; if only your face is in shot, we have to read them in your eyes.

Sometimes a director will use more than one camera at different distances or use a moving as well as a fixed camera. If so, then do it as for the one taking the closest shot. On *Gosford Park*, Robert Altman used several cameras, moving them all the time. The actors wore radio microphones, so that he could cut in and out of dialogue as he wished, and they never knew when they were in close-up. This takes the heat off the 'close-up' moment but means the actors have to be on the ball the entire time!

The amount of body movement you use is dependent upon the actual situation as well as where your fellow actor is. Imagine telling someone to follow you into another room. You simply say quietly, 'Follow me,' and go towards it. Now you are at a party. It is noisy and you want to talk to your friend privately. So you need to make a small gesture to accompany your line to make your friend understand, and you have to say your words louder. Next, imagine your friend is not beside you, but across the room at that noisy party. You may shout, 'Follow me,' or, more likely, you will just use gestures – making them bigger and bigger until your friend understands. Now change the party to the wilds of Scotland – you are lost on the side of a boggy mountain. Suddenly you see a path, but your friend is a hundred yards ahead, lost waist high in the heather. 'Foll...o...w... me...e...e,' you call, using great waving arm movements to draw his attention to the path you've found.

Never be afraid to be as big as reality. Sometimes actors are so frightened of seeming untruthful that they are smaller than life. And that's just as untruthful. A good director will be choosing shots to suit the action. If a close-up were needed in that scene in Scotland, it would simply be the look in your eyes as you saw the path through the heather.

If you have to hit a mark for a close-up, pace out how many steps you will need in rehearsal by walking backwards from your mark to the point where you begin your shot. Back this up with some sight-line point of reference that will help you find where you need to get to without looking down (in shots where the floor is seen, the marks will have to come up anyway). Hitting your mark is not only crucial for focus, but it can also be important for lighting. And if you are off your mark, you may be blocking some important background action. You can choose whether you have just a visual mark done with tape (the most common), a wooden one you can feel with your toes or even a sand-filled 'sausage' to stop you in your tracks.

Talking of tracks, the camera may follow your movements by

'tracking' – gliding along rails or on a 'dolly' with wheels. Sometimes the camera operator follows you with a hand-held camera that gives a slightly shaky documentary effect (much used by director John Cassavetes) or the more modern Steadicam. This is a lighter camera (though still very heavy) that is strapped on to the body and manoeuvred in and out of the action by an extremely strong camera operator. It gives a smooth interactive feel to the shot. (Kubrick was the first major director to explore the flexibility of this camera in *The Shining*.)

When you have to move, sit down or stand up, be kind and let the camera operator know what you're going to do. Then be consistent. Do the move smoothly so that the camera can keep up with you. You can practise first with the operator and maybe have some subtle prearranged signal before a really dramatic move. Sometimes you may need to slow the movement down – if you do, don't slow down your dialogue! When you stand up out of a chair, especially in close-up, try to do it in the way recommended by Alexander teachers. Take your weight with your legs and watch your head doesn't tilt back with the effort. Don't come up looking at the floor, either, or we'll lose your eyes.

Sometimes you might have to 'find your light'. You'll see it as a kind of halo around things or feel it as a warmth on your face. Move in and out of it until you can sense the difference. You may have a 'key light' that is crucial to light up your eyes (used to excess in 30s and 40s films) and if you miss it, the take will need to be redone. Be aware of other actors' key lights – don't let your shadow take the light off their faces.

Make sure we see your face and that you are open to the camera. Don't put up barriers unless it's really essential for the character. Barriers are comfort positions for the actor, an instinctive protection from the prying eye of the camera: folded arms, hands behind the back, hands in pockets, an unnecessary prop that's clutched, a gaze avoided, hair that falls across an eye and so on. Make sure it's the character that needs protecting and not the actor – that it's not you that's hiding.

The best acting in the world goes for nothing if it's behind a screen of hair or over your shoulder! So watch you don't upstage yourself or others by turning away from camera more than you need to or by forcing them to do so.

It is worth thinking about the body space your character needs – the distance between you and the other characters in long or wide shot. This varies in terms of status, country and period. For example, a king takes up more space in the world than a beggar and wide period skirts need far more room than modern clothing. Generally, on stage, an actor feels further apart from fellow actors than would be normal – and on film, you're too close for comfort! In close-up and mid-shot, positioning will usually be out of your hands.

You'll have worked closely with the make-up and costume departments to find the right look for your character and they will continue to support you on set. After the last rehearsal, the first assistant will say, 'Shooting next time. Last checks,' and these departments will run over to inspect you, powder you and add any last minute touches. The more you can look after their work between shots, the less time they'll need for these touch-ups.

When they leave you, breathe, moisten your lips and think where you've come from and what you want in the scene. Then you're ready for the camera.

You'll hear the camera and sound crews confirm that they are turning over and then the first assistant will say, 'Mark it,' and the clapper loader will name the shot, '36 take 1 – clap.' (If there are extras involved you might hear 'Background action' before you're cued.) The director (occasionally the First) calls 'Action' and you're away. Never cut until the director does. Even if a take goes wrong, there may be parts of the scene he or she can use. And take a breath after 'Cut' before you stop acting or wait until you see the camera operator has stopped shooting. The director might see something wonderful in that last second.

Now it's time to do it again. Breathe and remember where you've come from, why you're there and what you want. 'Going again ... first positions ... turn over ...' – you're not off the hook till you hear, 'Moving on.' Remember, a big feature is only looking to make between one and two minutes of eventual screen time a day. So you're in for a lot of takes and a lot of set-ups.

There is a general move towards more freedom for the actor in the filming process, but it does give the editor more choice if you can use consistent energy from take to take. The director may print a few or all the shots, depending on the budget and whether the rushes will be on film or video. If you have done different things in different takes of the master shot, you need to know which prints the director has chosen so you can match your moves in later set-ups.

Sometimes you'll be called on to work with imaginary creatures that are going to be conjured on to the screen later by computer-generated imaging – CGI. You will usually do this in front of an enormous blue or green screen. Blue screen means that the camera won't see anything blue (bad news for blue-eyed actors), green screen means that it won't see anything green. You will often see small 'tracking markers' on blue or green screens – white crosses, red discs or lights. These tiny details, which the camera sees in frame, are read later by the computer to work out the original camera move.

Incidentally, these tiny tracking marks can also be put on to your face so that the visual effects department can animate your eyebrows or grow your nose longer. Visual effects supervisor, Stefan Lange, tells me that in a recent big-budget TV Hans Christian Andersen fairytale involving a mermaid, the actor had her hair tied back and a ring of tracking markers was fitted round her head. She later grew computer-generated tresses that floated and drifted gently in the water!

You will need to know exactly what you are seeing in your blue or green screen world and imagine it there in all its detail. This can be particularly tiring as it gives you one extra dimension to believe in. Sometimes someone on set will stand in for the imaginary creature or an object will be put there to represent it. If this is offered, take it. Almost anything is better than nothing to act as a partner. If you and a fellow actor have to look at something that isn't there, make sure you agree a fixed point. You need the right distance to look at as well as the direction.

These days, editing is being done digitally (non-linear editing) more and more, rather than the old 'razor blade and sellotape' method. The film is transferred to video and edited digitally until it's right, then these final cuts are made on the actual film stock. It saves money but better than that, it gives the director more choice. Instead of ordering prints, the director is able to see, on a machine called an Avid, all the material that was shot, not just selected takes. So more of you will be on offer for the final version. The material can also be manipulated much faster and different versions of a cut can be easily assessed. The only minor problem is that little details of performance are harder to see.

Ideally, budget permitting, in order that the director, crew and actors can watch the performances more clearly and in viewing-theatre comfort, the rushes will be shown on film and then transferred to video for editing.

Which brings us to the question of rushes or dailies (the shots of the day's filming that are shown to key crew members the following day) – should you go or shouldn't you? Unless you've got a major role, you probably won't be asked. If you are, well, it's up to you. Lots of really established film actors choose not to see themselves in rushes as it puts them 'outside' their role. Both Lauren Bacall and Judi Dench say they can't bear to watch themselves; some actors find it useful. You won't be able to judge anything about the film from rushes but you might pinpoint a personal problem if the director points it out to you.

Actors are usually too self-critical. If you're a beginner and you have the choice, I'd advise you not to go as it will never be as it was in your head. If you've become really objective about watching yourself or you're trying to solve something in particular, then it might be right for you.

Film cameras these days have small video cameras attached, which means directors can see instant playback during shooting. When this system first arrived, some directors felt it would make everyone play safe and leave no room for magic mistakes or inspired guesses, but since it also stops costly and uninspired mistakes, studio executives will never do without them now. It certainly helps the crew to be able to check continuity, to see whether the stunt worked and what footage they have. And the magic happens anyway. As Denis Crossan, DOP on *The Hole*, says, 'When something inspired or just simply exciting happens, watching playback can be a buzz.'

There is a temptation to watch yourself on this playback and many experienced actors do just that. Again, I wouldn't recommend it unless it's a really difficult shot technically and watching will help you solve logistical problems. I think it takes you out of character (at an even more crucial time than when rushes are shown) and makes you too judgemental.

Also yours, of necessity, is the subjective eye of the actor who sees the script in terms of your own character, rather than the objective eye of the director who sees the shot in the context of the film as a whole. So the shot might not make sense to you. And it wastes time.

It is very difficult for actors who direct themselves to jump in and out of these two roles and it's arguably not a good idea. But many do it and Orson Welles did create a masterpiece with *Citizen Kane*. So luckily some people break all the rules.

Film editor, Scott Thomas, whose credits include *The Final Curtain* and *The Lawless Heart*, has this advice for actors and directors from an editor's point of view:

> I always ask artistes to enter frame if possible for tighter shots. If they are standing up into frame, or walking into mid-shot or close-up, or turning around – all these moves are useful to me because the movement in the frame helps the cutting. If an actor is static, the cut is less fluid and more obvious. Movement in static dialogue sequences is useful too. Eating, smoking, walking, gestures – all of these things are good if they are natural and if they are in continuity with the master shot.

The editing process makes the film more intense, building on the work of the actor by cutting out the weaker moments and tightening the action to expose the core of the drama.

As said before – get a camcorder. Film yourself from every angle and in lots of situations. Get used to seeing yourself on screen. Know what looks right and what doesn't. Find and eliminate habitual movements and facial tics that don't serve you. Old actors always knew which was their 'good' side and how they wanted to be lit. When you are in a film, you will rely on your DOP, but for your home movies, developing an awareness of how you look on camera can be really useful. You don't want this awareness to block your truthful responses or to make you precious, but you can use it to take out the things that get in the way and to make interesting choices.

You will sometimes see directors holding up a viewfinder or put their hands together to frame a shot during set-up. They are trying to see what the camera will see. (They do this less now that film cameras have instant video feedback.) It's useful to develop a feeling for framing and how it affects what an audience understands. Try this for camcorder homework:

- Set up an improvised scene with a friend, say, telling each other what you did that day or find a suitable scene from a script.
- Film it sitting together talking in profile.
- Film yourselves talking straight to camera.
- Now film it as before but looking close to the lens, not *into* the lens, re-seeing the events you're explaining.
- Try it with one person standing behind the other who is seated (you may have to cheat a bit to stay in frame). This will alter the status. First do it with both of you looking ahead, just to one side of the lens. Then look at each other when you want to.
- Now swap positions and do the last exercise again.

Play it back and you will see that with each staging, you are learning something new about the characters and the film is telling another story.

If you are alone, you can try it yourself with a monologue:

- Sit looking straight ahead just to the side of the camera, then stand.
- Film it letting an object distract you while you talk.
- Tell it straight to the lens.
- Now tell it to a photograph of someone you love.

Each time, even if you play with the same objectives and energy, the result will be different. Every picture tells a *different* story.

THE FOURTH WALL

Generally speaking, film is shot in naturalistic style or what would be called in theatre, 'fourth wall'. That means, as far as the actor is concerned, there is no audience and when you look in the direction of the camera you see the 'fourth wall' of the set. So it is important not to look into the lens of the camera or the viewers will feel that you are interacting directly with them, and that will break this illusion. For close-ups, you may need to look very close to the lens indeed, but not directly into it. The closer to the lens you gaze, the more we'll see into your eyes and so into your thoughts. The camera is a voyeur. You never play to the camera; you let it observe you and read your mind.

There are rare, specific instances when you might be asked to look directly into the camera lens, like presenting a television programme or doing a publicity shot within a film. Perhaps, as when Michael Caine looked directly at us in *Alfie* or Ian Richardson in the television series, *House of Cards*, the hero is talking to us – making 'asides' to the audience. A character might look directly into the lens if he has become the observed within the film, for example in the sight of a gun or at the end of binoculars as in Hitchcock's *Rear Window*. In these instances, the camera has become another character's POV (point of view).

By giving an audience the POV of the protagonist, they take on his persona. If a victim looked at the lens while being tortured, it would cast us, the viewer, as the torturer.

Theatre only started to adopt a fourth wall approach around the 1880s. With the advent of film, it became the norm. Now theatre has begun to enjoy a direct interaction between players and audience again. So who knows where film or new media will lead us.

For the moment, though, *the rule is never to look into the camera lens unless directed otherwise.*

THE CLOSE-UP

On a big screen – and there are still a few about – a close-up could blow you up to around 50 times your real size. So you can see what I mean when I said cinema is like a microscope. You have to be sure that the audience will read only what is true for your character, and not pick up any of those extra tension signals that come from the adrenalin racing through your veins.

Remember, don't try to show us what you are feeling or tell us what we should understand. This is called 'signalling' or 'mugging' because the face works too hard, adding extra facial expressions and movements. So your eyebrows go up or your mouth twitches. And in close-up, these little movements look enormous. Watch others and observe yourself. When you are really emotionally involved, you'll see how little movement there is in the face.

If you consciously release your facial tension when you are acting, you will actually feel more. And remembering to breathe will keep the tension away from your face. There is a direct link between breathing and emotion. Remember that where the main muscles that power your breathing are located is also where your sympathetic and para-sympathetic nerve endings meet and you feel a physical manifestation of your emotions – people clutch their stomachs or clasp their arms around themselves when they are in emotional pain. The stronger your feelings are, the more you will connect up with this area around your solar plexus.

It has often been said that to work in close-up, you need stillness. But it cannot be empty stillness. It has to be filled with thoughts and needs. Great screen actors can appear to be doing nothing on set, but when you watch the rushes, the camera has caught their internal life. It has gone, like laser surgery, beneath the skin. They are alive with thoughts and feelings. This 'stillness' is about having a hidden maelstrom at the centre.

Gabriel Byrne says, and I agree with him, that in some mysterious way, the camera photographs thought. Many famous actors have talked about the telepathic properties of the lens in close-up. Shirley MacLaine said, 'In front of a camera, I have to be careful what I think – it all shows.' Katharine Hepburn advised a young actor to 'let the camera do the work'. Liv Ullmann, whose thoughts become so transparent in close-up, confided, 'Bergman taught me how little you can do, rather than how much,' and Joan Crawford remarked that a movie actor has to paint with the tiniest brush.

The great film director, Friedrich Murnau, way back in the era of silent films, didn't tell actors what to do – he told them what to think. And Elia Kazan, who pioneered a new realism in film acting, said that when actors were under the microscope of the camera, they revealed things they didn't know they were revealing.

Being 'still' is about being focused on the moment, harnessing breath to thought and opening the channel to the emotional life through the breath. So, really breathe – don't hold your breath (we often think we're breathing when we're not). You can put your hand on to your stomach – out of camera view – and check that it really releases with the incoming breath. Send your thoughts, feelings and reactions from that hand. This can work like magic. The tension comes off your face, your eyes are alive and your voice has the ring of emotional truth. (Incidentally, this also helps if your head has a tendency to 'wobble'.)

In close-up, you may not be able to see your fellow actor but have to make do with being given an 'eye line'. Be really focused on where that is and know if you are looking near, middle or long distance. We will be able to tell if you cheat on this. If you are supposed to be seeing something close to you, it is no good looking at the far studio wall. Ask for a flag or a runner's hand to be held at the right distance. Then see in your mind's eye what is there – your partner's face, the burning car, the vase of flowers – whatever was in the master shot.

The eyes become all important in close-up. They really are 'the windows to the soul'. John Ford once said, 'The main thing about directing is to photograph the person's eyes.' Be careful about blinking too much, as you'll lose power. You will find most experienced screen actors blink very little. Anthony Hopkins, as Hannibal Lecter, doesn't blink at all! Obviously not blinking until your eyes run is carrying it too far – unless the resultant tears can be your 'trigger' into an emotional scene!

Be careful that nothing inadvertently breaks your attention in a shot so that you flick a glance to the lens. If you do, your character will be lost. Really watch your fellow actor. Watch like a hawk for the reaction to what you're saying. Really drive your need.

Even which of your partner's eyes you choose to look at can become important and change the effect we read on the screen. James Cagney said that all you had to do was look at the other actor's camera eye (that is – the one closest to the camera) and tell the truth.

Add these eye exercises to your warm-up so that they don't get 'sleepy':

- Blink your eyes a few times then shut them.
- Open them really wide. (If you want to go the whole hog, you can do the full yoga 'lion' exercise and open your mouth wide, stretch out your tongue and let your breath out on 'Hah' at the same time!)
- Repeat, shutting your eyes and then opening them wide three more times.
- Look straight ahead with your eyes open. Now turn your head to the left, leaving your eyes looking ahead centre as long as you can. Then turn your eyes to the left.
- Leaving your eyes looking left, turn your head back to centre, letting your eyes follow last.
- Repeat to the right.
- Now back at centre – let your eyes look to the left but leave your head where it is. Then turn your head left too. Be sure to keep the same point of focus.
- Take your eyes back to the centre, then follow with your head.

- Repeat to the right.
- Facing centre hold up your middle finger about six inches in front of your nose. Alternate focusing between your finger and the far distance about six times.
- Now look up left, then down right, then down left and up to the right a few times.
- Finish by following an imaginary figure of eight with your eyes, twice, starting it at top left, and twice more starting it at bottom right.

In conversation, eye contact will be maintained or broken depending on status and what you want from the other person. When you are remembering an incident from your past, you will flick between 'seeing' the past again and reliving it, and sharing that internal vision with the listener. If you're reacting instinctively to your thoughts and needs, this eye contact will happen naturally.

You can choose to 'see' things in the direction of the camera. This will open up your thoughts to us. You sometimes need to open out to the camera a little in a two-shot, so that both people's thoughts can be read through their eyes, instead of being in profile. (This is even more crucial for TV as there is less time for single shots.) For this reason, you may be asked to play a scene with both of you very close together, looking out front. As long as you keep seeing these internal pictures and thinking the character's thoughts, it will look natural, even though it sometimes feels odd.

Observe yourself in life and you'll find you hardly ever look at someone all the time you talk. In fact, the longer two people have been together, the more this is true. If you look round a restaurant, you can tell the old married couples from the first dates by the amount of eye contact. In a really long relationship, the most important things end up being shouted from one room to another!

But if you look down or away from the camera's eye, it must be the needs of the character that drive these looks, not your desire to buy private space for yourself. When you look away, we will be cut off from you, so choose and justify these moves with care, making sure it is the character who needs to avoid the other's gaze.

In really intense scenes, when you, as the character, are trying hard to communicate or listen, completely lock in to your partner's eyes. If your partner is not there, imagine them. Feel you are sending your energy through your gaze.

On the practical side, get your weight evenly distributed when doing a close-up. You will be in such tight frame that even a fractional move will take you out of focus. The focus puller and camera operator will guide you as to how much freedom you have to move. Watch you don't shuffle, sway or change weight from one foot to another. If you are in very tight frame, be careful that you don't bring your hands in and out of shot – they will look very strange. As the frame will generally be tight to the top of your head, don't bring your hands higher than your head.

You will often see the DOP or an assistant holding up a light meter to check the light level. (The famous lighting cameraman, Douglas Slocombe, was so experienced that he would just draw his thumb across the palm of his hand and know from the shadow it cast which f-stop to choose.) If the light is low, then the camera's aperture will be more open and focus will be even more crucial.

And think about where you hold props – if you want them to be seen and they are important to the plot, they must be in frame. If you are bringing them in and out of shot, do it swiftly. If the gun or the knife disappears out of frame for too long we won't remember it's still there. Playing with a prop out of sight, drumming your fingers or flapping your feet will make little tremors and wobbles that will show in extreme close-up. These displacement activities will also weaken your acting. If you allow yourself to become really still, you will find your thoughts come sharply into focus and you will feel more.

Think about how you sit so that you don't get strangely hunched shoulders. Even crossing your legs can affect your upper body and because we can't see the rest of you, it will look odd. Align your head and neck – if you tilt your head back there will be a lot of chin in shot and very little of your eyes.

The more you can experiment the better. Keep using that camcorder and film yourself in close-up. Get really familiar with seeing your thoughts on your own face – in your own eyes. What reads and what doesn't. Learn to distance yourself from your first reaction to seeing yourself on film, and be objective. Do all kinds of characters and scripts in close-up and review the results. Don't forget reaction shots.

Observe any little facial habits, tics or tensions. You might have a habit of raising an eyebrow, for example (like a certain James Bond!). You need to be able to choose when to use that movement and when not to. Looking in a mirror is not as good as using the camcorder as it reverses your face and can make your performance too objective. But it can be useful for eliminating habitual grimaces.

One technical note: when you're in single tight close-up, don't overlap dialogue with the actor doing lines off-camera, so the film can be edited later. More on this in the section on sound.

REACTION SHOTS

Reaction shots, done in close-up, are where the character is reacting, without dialogue, to another character's lines or to what is happening in the scene. To react honestly, all you can do is to really listen and watch the other character or the action – and to think.

You should be doing this anyway in the master shot and every other shot and you can increase your eventual screen time this way. The director will often decide on a reaction shot just because you did something interesting in the master, in rehearsal or even the read-through.

In a reaction shot, you will usually have something or someone to look at. The other actor will invariably be kind and give you the lines you are responding to. Because you are in close-up, you will usually have to look very close to the camera lens. This will mean your partner getting into some very strange positions indeed in order to give you an eye line. Don't giggle!

Sometimes it won't be possible to look at them at all and they will feed you the lines while you have to look at the camera operator's hand or the side of the camera. Try to keep the vision, in your mind's eye, of the other actor's face as she or he was saying it in your two-shot. Keep listening. Keep thinking. If you don't speak, why don't you speak – what stops you? Keep breathing!

QUICK TIPS FOR CAMERA

- **Home camcorder practice** is invaluable! Try focusing on a strong thought without adding anything else. See something and react. Listen to someone.
- **Use your scene cards** before going on to set.
- **Accept you will often stand closer** than feels natural. Sometimes you'll be asked to work in uncomfortable positions that feel weird – trust the director and the camera department.
- **Check the size of the shot** so you can focus your energy accordingly.
- **Pace out your move backwards** from your mark to the starting place during rehearsal. Find a visual clue for extra reference.
- **Make movements** smooth if in tight shot. Rehearse them with the camera operator. Don't do surprise moves.
- **Keep breathing** and your emotional channels will stay free.
- **In close-up, put your hand on your abdominal area** in an emotional scene to feel 'centred', keep breath flowing, minimise 'wobbles' and take tension off the face.
- **Think really hard!** Have a clear strong thought. That's all you need to do – don't add any extra facial expressions to 'signal' what you're feeling.

- **There is no audience** – only the private world of the other actors and the imaginary environment. The camera is a secret observer.
- **In close-up** be still but alive in every second.
- **Watch your hands** in a tight frame – don't let them come in and out of shot. Know what needs to be seen in the shot and only show what's essential so we can concentrate on your face. If a prop is important make sure it's in frame.
- **Keep your weight evenly distributed** in close-up. Watch your posture so your upper body looks normal. Keep grounded – don't shuffle or shift weight: the focus may be fractional.
- **Your eyes** really are the windows to your inner world.
- **Try not to blink** too much. The eyes shutting off breaks the thought process for the audience. It is also distracting and has the effect of making you lose status.
- **Really look** – watch your fellow actors like a hawk. Watch for reactions to what you're saying. Make those reactions important to you.
- **Really listen** – check that you're not holding your breath – this will stop you listening.
- **Go back** to your original impulse for each take.
- **Don't miss the moment** – go with the impulse.
- **Never 'cut'** before the director. Follow through: keep thinking, acting and reacting till director says 'cut' and then for a moment longer.
- **Seeing 'memory pictures'** in the camera's direction can look real, but keep aware of your relationship and status to other characters. In close-ups, the director will direct your gaze.
- **Be sure of what you want**. Don't drive the words – let them just happen in pursuit of your need or fall out as you think the subtext.
- **Don't hide** – e.g. looking down when the character doesn't need to, turning away. Always separate the character's needs and yours.
- **Finally – never show on your face any distaste** or embarrassment for your own performance. It takes you out of character and it lets everyone see your vulnerability. If you let it happen in rehearsal, it might happen during a take or just at the end of it when the director wanted to use the last moment.

KEEPING CONTINUITY

Continuity is important to you as an actor. If you keep changing it, the editor will have fewer choices of your scenes to use, because they won't match. So lots of wonderful work will end up on the cutting-room floor.

Continuity is about matching – not just what you do and when you do it, but the tempo of movements and feelings. It is important to know what exact state you were in the last time we saw you. Although weeks may have elapsed between scene 102 and 103, you need to know that you were anxious, crying, running, out of breath and wet in scene 102 so that you will enter scene 103 the same way.

Script supervisor, Brigitte Schmouker, whose credits include *Secret Passage* and *Seven Years in Tibet* says that emotional and speed memory (happy or anxious, fast or slow, calm or out of breath) is the most important part of continuity. She adds, 'A trick I have about memorising the matching of feelings or speed is to think (and note down on my script) about a piece of music or a song – this gives me the rhythm and mood for the character, and so for the actor.'

Choose your props carefully and keep the action simple. Cigarettes and drinks can be particular nightmares. You need to keep changing them between takes so that they're the same size and you have to remember when you put them down and which hand you used and all those fiddly details. Avoid them as much as you can. The script supervisor will help but it's a good discipline to be in charge of your own continuity.

Eating with dialogue isn't easy but you might be forced into it. You'll have to eat great quantities if you do lots of set-ups. You can ask for a bowl and spit the food out between takes. Choose a food that's easy to swallow and try not to talk and eat at the same time unless you're sure it makes a character statement – and you can still be understood.

If you have to use noisy props, like cutlery or keys, put them down before or after your line. If you do it on important dialogue, you'll be doing retakes later.

Although wardrobe will be watching too, take the responsibility for your costume yourself. Are you wearing the same shoes you wore in this scene last time, was your shirt buttoned right up? Whole scenes have had to be discarded because a hot actor undid a couple of buttons between takes and nobody noticed until rushes!

Sometimes actors get too complicated. A naughty old trick when you wear glasses is to take them off to speak and then put them back. This makes it hard to cut away – they have to see you put them back. You have to be very clever and experienced to play games like this and it might take away from the depth of your performance.

Make your life easier. Choose minimal props with care and stick to simple 'business'. Try to be good about noting your own choices of movement, which way you turned, which hand you used and so on. But don't be shy about asking for help when you need it. It'll always be there.

BUSINESS AND BLOCKING

'Business' is what you do with props, 'blocking' is where you move. Although the director will guide a lot of the business and blocking, it is your job to make it feel right for the character. In rehearsals and line-up, follow your impulses to move – don't censor them through shyness. There's a good chance that they'll seem so natural that the director will keep most of them.

In life, we very rarely speak standing still. As we discussed before, we are usually carrying out some secondary activity – packing a suitcase, laying the table, sorting the files. When we get really involved with what we are saying, this secondary activity stops and we give the other person our full attention. Being still can be very important in film especially in close-up, but a lot of the time you will be using 'business'. Make it important and real. If you are carrying out another activity then it needs to get done. Imagine packing for your lover to leave quickly to escape capture, yet you want to tell each other you care. The packing has to be done – the escape has to be made. So the moment of stopping and hugging will be the eye of the storm – the moment of stillness where the emotional need has overwhelmed the practical need. Then it will be back to business.

If you move all the time and never have any stillness for your dialogue or other people's – if there is never any eye of the storm – then the scene won't have any emotional centre and there will be no character revelations. Also you won't get any close-ups, as the editor won't be able to cut any in if you're always in motion. Obviously if the purpose of the scene is all about the activity, like a chase, then you won't be able to stop and it will probably be filmed in a wide shot anyway.

PROPS

Props can be very useful to an actor. They can also get in the way. The best props are those that show the emotional subtext of a scene. For example a mother holding a lost baby's jumper or picking up a beloved object damaged after a burglary and holding it during the police interview. Look at how Marlon Brando uses Eva Marie Saint's gloves to show how he feels about her, but can't admit, in *On the Waterfront*. In the silent movie by DW Griffith, *Intolerance*, a single mother has her baby taken from her by do-gooding matrons. The scene closes on a tight close-up in an 'iris' (an aperture that opens or closes, mimicking a camera lens) of the mother's hand clutching the baby's bootee. These are 'emotional objects' as discussed in 'The Art' section.

But you can have a very real relationship with everyday objects. I heard the expression, used of the comedian Lucille Ball, that she 'treated her props like treasures'. We all have objects that we carry round, dust or wear that are precious to us. They have a history. They carry deep associations or we are drawn to their beauty, the smoothness of their texture or derive a comfort from them. It might be the leather cigar case that you inherited from your grandfather, your birthday watch, your new silk scarf. If you are going to use a personal prop, develop a relationship with it. Know where you got it, how long you've had it, how you feel about it. Handle it enough to become familiar with the feel of it so it seems like yours. Then bury all that, trust you've done the work and use the object just as you would in life.

Sometimes actors use simple tricks like putting away a handkerchief as they enter the room to show a life outside the scene. But be careful not to overdo this. You can also use props during preparation to find your way into the character. Rehearsing with the kind of props your character might use can give the character an inner life – then you can discard most of them for the performance.

Too much 'business' or prop use can be distracting and take the edge off your emotional intensity. As mentioned above, they can also present extra continuity hazards, especially cigarettes, drinks and food. Always try out any props you are going to use as early as possible so that you don't waste shooting time. This is particularly true for doors, technology and fiddly props. Make your hands dextrous and supple so you don't keep having to retake because you drop or break the prop!

Here's a magic exercise shown to me by a Russian theatre director. It keeps your hands dextrous and it increases co-ordination. It might be good for left–right brain connections too:

- Put the thumb and little finger of your left hand together, and the thumb and forefinger together on your right hand.
- Now walk your fingers, one at a time in opposite directions, so that

your left thumb ends up touching your left forefinger and your right thumb ends up touching your right little finger.

- Now go back the other way, ending as you started.
- Work to get up speed without looking at your hands, so that your fingers can keep travelling back and forth in opposite directions.

It's strangely hard to do. Your fingers keep magically ending up copying each other instead of going in opposition. You can while away idle moments on set practising this exercise!

Don't use props on important lines unless you're using them to reveal your subtext. Check what shot you're in and how much of you is seen when deciding how to use a prop. If it's half out of picture it may look odd, and if we need to see it for the plot, then you'll have to have it high enough to be seen when the camera comes in close. Once you've committed to a prop in the master shot, you're stuck with it in every take, so know exactly when and how you use it and choose it with care.

Finally, if small mistakes happen in spite of all your good intentions, script supervisor Jean Bourne, whose credits include *The Madness of King George* and *The Count of Monte Cristo*, has a word of comfort: 'If a performance is riveting, the director will usually say, "Forget it: we'll go with it – if the audience are looking at an open button, we may as well all go home."' Although someone in an anorak will write in!

QUICK TIPS FOR CONTINUITY

- **Keep the emotional energy** the same between takes. Know which scene you have come from and what energy you used in the previous scene.
- **Choose props** with care. Only use ones that assist the characterisation, action or are really necessary to the scene.
- **Remember all your moves**, when you do them and the tempo and energy.
- **Remember where you use props** in the scene and which hand you use.
- **Bring props** quickly up into frame in close-up if it's important that they are seen. If it is not, keep them well out of sight. If you have to look at a prop, holding it with the hand closest to camera will show more of your face.
- **Check your clothing** – don't adjust clothing between takes.
- **Tell the script supervisor** if you change action or dialogue.
- **When in doubt** ask the script supervisor.

SOUND ADVICE

Sound conveys a large part of the film narrative: the music track, the sound effects and, most of all, the dialogue. The advent of 'talking pictures' fundamentally changed the nature of film acting from the pantomimic style of most silent films to the naturalistic approach we take for granted today. At first, it changed the nature of camera work too, as actors had to be static to send the sound towards the fixed microphones. (Think of the hilarious scene in *Singin' in the Rain* where the heroine, in her high-pitched squeak, keeps fading out mid-sentence as she turns her head away from the mic hidden in the flowers.) But, gradually, boom operators became more adept at following the action and pictures moved again. The talkies placed a value on actors with good voices and theatre actors started to work on film and learnt to master the techniques needed for that medium.

Unlike theatre, the voice you use for film should be at the sound level you use in life. If the situation calls for you to be very quiet then the level will be low.

Having said that, it is important that it is your 'whole' voice at a low level, rather than an unsupported 'half-voice' that carries no overtones to give emotional depth. Nowadays, radio mics can be used, in conjunction with boom and fixed mics, to pick up virtually anything. And that includes clothing rustles, sibilance and intakes of breath. Although these microphones are very sensitive, they can pick up only the quality of voice that you are using. No amount of technical boost can change a thin breathy tone into a positive, confident, resonant sound. If you have to whisper, find that small secret voice that still carries a little tone rather than just breath.

Incidentally, sound mixer Jeff Wexler (whose countless credits include *Nine to Five*, *The War of the Roses* and *Vanilla Sky*), working with Peter O'Toole, once asked him if it was true that he could whisper and be heard round the block. Peter walked 50 feet away and whispered, 'It is true' – and it was!

When sound recordist Phil Smith worked with Laurence Olivier on *Brideshead Revisited*, Olivier asked him to sit where he could see him and to wave his hand up if he needed more volume and down if he needed less. Phil never needed to wave, though, as the needle never wavered from a hundred per cent even though it *sounded* as if Olivier was whispering!

Sometimes the sound department will tell you they can't hear you. It's better to avoid replacing your dialogue in post-production as much as you can. It's so much harder doing scenes afterwards without the input from the other actors and the set and in tiny chunks out of context. So many actors complain later, 'If only someone had told me at the time ...'

Here are some reasons why you might be asked for more volume:

- Booms often can't get close to you in wide shots as they will be seen by the camera or create shadows, so they can't pick you up if you're very quiet. Sometimes a radio mic can't be used as it makes you sound too 'intimate' for the scene.
- The other actors in the scene might be much louder than you. This is particularly true if you're a woman playing against hearty men. If you're too quiet, the sound will be unbalanced, so you'll be asked for a little more volume.
- There might be a sound track laid underneath the scene later, like a train or rain or dance music. If you're very quiet, not only will it be hard for them to get the level up technically, but it will also sound false. In life you'd use a different quality of voice to compensate for the background noise.

I've often been on set where the director has had the sound department put on loud dance music for the actors to speak over, so that they get an idea of the level needed. As soon as the director calls 'action', the music has to cut to allow for editing later, and within a few moments the actors have forgotten about the music and have all come down in volume. You need to imagine the background noise playing in your head right through the scene.

Of course, you don't want to be too loud either. The general rule is just to talk as you would in that situation. Remember there's no audience to hear you, only the people sharing the scene. This is really important to you if you've worked a lot in theatre.

So if you need to talk intimately, you can. But be sure it's the level the character would use in life and you're not being smaller than life in a mistaken search for 'truthfulness'. If you need to shout, shout – but warn the sound department first! If you yell suddenly, you can cause them serious ear problems.

If you are asked for extra volume, then check that your voice is 'centred' and you don't 'push' the sound:

- Clasp your hands together in front of you and shake out a sound.
- If you've gone shrill, open your mouth and tip your head back gently and swallow on the way back down. This will relax your larynx and bring your voice down to a comfortable pitch.
- Make sure you're releasing your stomach to breathe.
- Then address the reality of the scene and try to find the right impulses for the extra level so that you feel real.

If, however, it would really spoil the scene for you and it isn't right for your character to talk more loudly in those specific circumstances, then you will have to sacrifice technical requirements to acting needs. There are some occasions when the amount of volume needed to get over the hazard, be it waterfall or car engine, is impossible. In life the conversation just couldn't be held in that situation. And I have seen it happen where extra volume has changed the focus of the performance and the actor has lost the sense of the scene. In the end it is your acting that matters most and you'll have the knowledge that post-production can save the day.

Unless the scene really calls for a change of mood or there are reasons for different intensity levels, try not to vary the volume too much as the sound mixer will have trouble balancing your levels. (Nigel Hawthorne would give a different choice to the director with each take, but always within the same parameters.) And in rehearsal always use the actual volume you will use in performance so everyone knows what you're going to do.

There are actors, like John Malkovich, who never do a take the same way twice. If they're asked whether they're going to be loud or soft on the next take, they won't know. They need to be free to react in the moment. You do run the risk of having to re-record your dialogue in post-production, but in the end it's the performance that's the most important thing.

Some actors do work so instinctively that they find it constrains them too much to 'plan' their performances and they need to use different levels every take, but it's awfully hard on the sound department if they don't know it's coming. Advances in new digital technology cope with this better than the old systems, so if you warn the boom operator that you might yell, they can reduce your recorded level. Sound mixer, Chris Munro, who won an Oscar in 2002 for *Black Hawk Down*, says, 'Our role is to allow people to be free.' He says that within a few days he has built up a mental 'dynamic sound picture' of each actor in the film.

Incidentally, it is rumoured that Alec Guinness used to speak very quietly in his early films so that the microphone would have to come in closer. That meant the camera had to come in closer too in order not to see the boom: an extra close-up! Alas, those days are gone. Now they'll either give you a radio mic or loop you afterwards!

Remember not to clatter with props during dialogue – your own or other people's – or you'll be bound to end up replacing it in post-production. This is not just because it might cover your lines but also because sounds need to be separated from dialogue for editing reasons. Films are dubbed into many languages, so the dialogue needs to be 'clean'.

Also, a sound like, say, coins jangling in your pocket could seem to come from many directions in a surround-sound auditorium if it can't be isolated and set up properly on the final mix. If you feel it's necessary for your performance, you can always ask the sound mixer to record it separately. For the same reasons, make sure you separate your dialogue from big noisy actions. So close the car door or pick up the drum kit before you speak – not at the same time!

Be kind about feeding lines to your partner when they are in single shot and you are off camera – don't go home early and leave them to play against someone reading in unless there are exceptional circumstances. Even top stars are generally good about this. Give a strong performance for the other actor to play against. Script supervisor, Annie Penn, with whom I worked on *102 Dalmatians*, says that the reactions from the other actors will change according to your performance level, so give them good off-screen lines to work with. But when doing off-lines with someone else, don't speak at the same time as them, leave a tiny gap before you say your dialogue.

If the actors speak too close together, it is called 'overlapping the dialogue'. (This only applies to single close-ups – in the master or two-shots you can overlap each other as much as you like.) If the sound mixer can't 'get the [virtual] scissors in', it will be hard to edit and post-production dialogue replacement can't always completely solve the problem. Sound and vision are shot separately and married at a later date, but if you can't be separated from your partner's dialogue, some of your off-camera line will be on your partner's close-up, but off-mic, so the quality won't be right. When your close-up is done, you want to be able to say your whole line in full vision. (And remember not to overlap on your close-up with the person feeding you off-lines, for the same reason.)

Sometimes the sound mixer will ask for quiet on set so that he or she can record the atmospheric background noise of the environment. All spaces have their own unique sound, even when all seems to be silent. This extra ambient sound is used in editing to smooth out any gaps and fill in empty spaces when sections of the original track are taken out or replaced. Sometimes you will be asked to go to the sound booth or to stand by the mixing desk to record some wild track. This will be dialogue that is either off-camera or that wasn't audible in the original take or had some technical problem. It can sometimes be used on the final film and it helps the editors assemble a rough-cut. If you do it straight away, you'll find it easier to keep your performance quality, so never treat it as a chore and put it off.

Airline versions are always censored and so a looped version is made for this market. If you've got some heavy swearing, ask the director if a toned-down version would be worth doing at the time rather than in post-production.

If you or the wardrobe department inadvertently move your radio mic at all, do tell the sound assistant as the position of it may be crucial: it's their department's responsibility to keep it out of shot.

Microphones are switched off at the sound desk when actors are off set or between set-ups so you won't be heard in too private a mode. You can also ask the boom operator to turn you off (if you do it yourself, you carry an enormous responsibility to turn it on again when you return to set). Radio mics have a short range anyway and don't pick you up much beyond the set.

If you are in tricky clothing, however, it is wise to be disentangled from the transmitter before it meets a watery end. I never confessed this to the sound mixer at the time, but I did have an accident once with the transmitter connected to my headset. Fortunately, after a wash and brush up and help from a sympathetic assistant, it obediently went on working for the rest of the film!

All mics are left on between takes, so beware of making comments on set you wouldn't like overheard. Sound mixers, producers, directors, script supervisors and coaches all make up your audience whenever you talk to anyone on set. Most directors hear someone swearing about them in the course of the film. Unless you're sure you'll never want to work with them again, don't let it be you!

THE MICROPHONE

Generally, a microphone will be held over you by an operator with a boom who will watch the rehearsal to see where you move and when you speak. If you do something too erratic in performance, the boom may not get to you in time.

Sometimes you'll have a microphone attached to your clothing around your neck or chest area or even occasionally in your hair. The transmitter will be strapped to some secret place – under your costume, in your petticoats or on your leg. If you rest your chin on your hands during dialogue, check it isn't muffling the sound. Be careful that you don't thump your chest (or your partner's) or bang your mic inadvertently while you're speaking. Especially when you say 'I' or 'me'!

We've talked about obvious prop noise but think about subtler sounds like the noise of your clothes, rustling chains, earrings and bangles, etc. during dialogue. And work for a clean intake of breath. Choose cotton underwear rather than silk (which rustles). Shoe noise can be a problem. The sound assistant may rush up with tessa tape or adhesive sponge for your heels or even a piece of carpet for you to stand on. Stage actors have been known to fix tacks to their shoes to give them atmosphere, but you can't wear taps on a film set! All footsteps are put on later to keep a consistency of level and rhythm from scene to scene. The cleaner you keep your lines, the less dialogue replacement you'll do later.

If you are part of background action, don't wait for someone to come up and tell you that your clothes are rustling or your shoes are making a noise. If you can hear the noise, so can the microphone. So pay attention to extraneous noise and ask the costume department to fix the problem.

Sometimes a microphone will be 'planted' near you as well. Although it will not be as directional as that one in *Singin' in the Rain*, best be aware of where it is so that you don't turn too far away from it – and don't hit it. Sound mixer Mike Westgate told me about setting up a restaurant scene for a television production involving Robert Mitchum. Not knowing what level the actor would use, he had secretly planted a microphone in a table napkin. Mitchum spotted it and spent the first rehearsal tapping it gently with his fork – just to let the sound department know a boom would be quite sufficient!

If you're using a fixed microphone as the character (if, for example, you're playing a DJ or a public speaker) or later when you do post-production, make sure it's at the right height and distance so that you're not straining to reach it. Jutting your chin forward will affect your voice quality.

Sound mixer John Rodda, whose credits include *Ripley's Game* and *28 Days Later*, says his department '. . . can seem a bit of a "black art". Everyone else you can usually see what they're doing and why, but sound can seem rather esoteric.' He adds that the boom operator or sound mixer will gladly explain their arcane secrets if you're interested.

POST-PRODUCTION – ADR

Replacing dialogue after shooting is expensive and it is hard to achieve the same quality of sound as the original. Ideally every film would have all the original synchronised sound (from the actual shoot). There is a move towards a more documentary style of film-making, with all the verisimilitude of the original sound track. But some shots will have sound problems that are not of your making.

Background noise or echoing environments, wind and weather conditions and aeroplanes all play havoc with the sound track. Noise from generators, cameras, lights, clashing swords and leather jackets all conspire against you. Or maybe another actor needs to be dubbed in a scene that involves you and the change involved unbalances your performance; the improvised dialogue has been censored for the American or airline release; or your lines overlapped in close-up. Maybe the director just thinks you can improve on what you did at the time. Whatever the reason, all is not lost.

Because sound and picture are laid on separate tracks, extra sound can be put on later. This includes your redone dialogue, sound effects and music. These are mixed at the very end when the final cut has been completed. At this point, sound and picture are married into the completed film.

When I first started in film, this dialogue replacement was called post-synchronisation or post-syncing for short. A term that is fairly self-explanatory – syncing sound and vision after the event. Sometimes it was called dubbing although more properly this is when another language is dubbed on top of the original actor's own voice or sound effects are added.

Nowadays it is called ADR, which is short for automatic (or automated) dialogue replacement and properly refers to how much quicker the process has become. In earlier days, the film clip you were matching to went round and round on a loop until you got it right, so American actors call it looping. Now it is computerised and more likely to be on videotape or hard disk.

You can do it by picture cue, sound cue or both together. You are generally standing up on your own in a studio, staring at the screen, while the director and sound engineer are at the desk behind you, either in a booth or in the same room. You can choose to hear your own voice, your fellow actor or none of the above. The scene is shown for you first. Listen to your line of dialogue carefully to pick up the rhythm.

Three beeps sound in your ear and a white line travels across the screen from the left (sometimes right) and hits the marker at the side of the screen at the moment your dialogue has to begin. You need to have prepared your breath so you can start instantly as if on the fourth beat. Once you get used to the timing of these beats, finding the start position is quite easy.

ADR is usually done months after shooting and you may be on to your next project. So it's hard to get the same intensity that you had in the original scene. You have to work very hard to remember the exact circumstances. What will make it even stranger is the absence of any background noise on the sound track. The engineer will tell you what will be laid behind your voice and if it's going to be noisy like a party, traffic or the sound of the sea, you may need to be louder than you were originally. Don't pull back. Use the whole voice that you would need in the real situation.

A sound mixer friend tells me of an American actor who always whispers her lines during filming: she knows she'll end up doing a lot of ADR. Now she's learnt not to move her mouth much, in order to make the looping easier! If she used more volume during shooting, she'd be freed of this worry – and look more expressive! Not only that, but even in ADR, whispering will never communicate expressively.

True sound has to have the source seated in the whole body. By that I mean that you can't separate sound and body. Look around you next time you are in a restaurant or a tube train. You can probably guess what kind of conversations people are having by the way they hold their bodies. They are tensed or relaxed, leaning towards or away from their companions, looking at each other or out of the window. If they get very angry, they stand up. If you were to hear them, you would find the energy and tone of their voices matching their body movements. We are very sensitised to people's voices and if body and voice do not match, we immediately pick up on the lack of truth in the sound.

So, if you're supposed to run or make a movement then I suggest you do so if you can (but be careful not to hit the microphone on the line); it will make the dialogue more natural. At least feel the echoes of the movement in your body. If you have to call someone, remember where they are and call over the same distance or it will never sound the same. The engineer can always get you to stand back from the microphone or use a baffle to adjust the level. If you have to sound intimate, then get closer to the mic. Be careful not to pop your plosive consonants if you get very close. The engineers will work around your requirements and move the microphone to match the mood.

You will need your original script or cards to remember the details of the scene, the relationships and what you wanted. If it is emotional stuff, you may need to use your triggers again. The voice is such a sensitive carrier of emotion that we will know if you are not driving from the same thoughts and needs as when you were shooting. The more you can visualise the scene, the better. You can re-create or even improve the performance, but you must go back to the original impulses. The director or the dialogue coach is usually there to help.

ADR is often done purely as a safety measure and the sound editor may end up being able to use the original track. When films are edited on video, it is sometimes harder to tell how the sound will finally turn out. With only a few weeks to do the expensive mixing of the film, everyone has to be sure they've got everything standing by that might be needed. One famous actor had, reluctantly, to re-record all his lines because the original track was suspect. When he came to make the sequel, he refused to give any extra volume, 'because,' he said, 'you'll loop it all anyway.' What he didn't know was that the first film had actually used all the original dialogue after all!

So enjoy doing your ADR, don't take it as a criticism, and who knows – they may not even need it.

VOICE-OVERS

You may have a voice-over to do after the film has finished shooting and the final cut has been produced. This is different from ADR as it is not lip-synced, but it may have to be done over particular shots. You will be in a studio, either standing by a microphone as in ADR or in a booth with a headset on, watching the screen through the glass. The technician will give you visual or audio clues as to when and where to start talking and it may be within a very tight time scale. But you won't have to match any mouth movements.

Decide with the director on the style of the voice-over. Is it the character speaking or a detached outside observer? Is the observer emotionally involved or objective? If it is your character speaking, is it factual, truthful or is there subtext? Do you want a conversational or confidential tone? Are you taking the audience into the interior of your head or acting as a travel guide to the film?

The narration in *A.I. Artificial Intelligence* is compassionate but viewed from a distance; in *The Royal Tenenbaums* it is factual, objective. In *American Beauty*, Kevin Spacey looked back at his own life with tenderness and wonder and in *The Shipping News* he is downbeat and confidential. In *Bridget Jones's Diary*, we eavesdrop on her private musings. If the voice-over is the voice of the character you played, you may have to go back to your original preparation, as some time will have elapsed. Ask to hear some of the original dialogue or to watch a few minutes of the film. Remember the relationships with other characters in the film – visualise the other actors' faces and the environments.

Think of one person that you're telling the story to and why. Think of your relationship with that person and what you want them to understand. Consider your distance to the microphone: the closer you are, the more confidential it will feel. If you are very close, you may have to watch your 'p's popping. Watch the placing of the microphone – don't crane your neck forwards or you'll change your voice.

Spoken English uses both 'major' tones, where we fully complete the cadences of our speech pattern, and 'minor' tones, where we seem to leave the tune hanging and incomplete – somewhat like the major and minor keys in music. (These tones are also known as 'high rise' – 'high fall', and 'low rise' – 'low fall'.) Major tones are associated with politicians, factual narration, sales pitches or telling children's stories. Minor tones are heard in the 'poetry' voice, indecision, questioning, musing or being unsure. You will need a mix of both but, generally, a voice that uses predominantly major tones is easier to listen to in storytelling. (If your voice has a predominantly minor tone, practise reading children's stories aloud.) Your mix of tones will be governed by whom you are talking to and why.

Here are some little tips and reminders:

- Check you're really breathing – with your stomach releasing on the incoming breath.
- Mark your script for new thoughts and stresses.
- Hit the key words and let the rest go.
- If the director asks you to change inflection and you find it difficult, tap your finger on your other hand, or in the air, on the word you want to stress. (Don't use the table or the microphone!)
- To get an intimate sound, put your hand on your stomach and 'send' the sound there.
- Whisper your lines slowly to yourself to refresh your thoughts.
- Swallow to bring down your pitch to its relaxed level.
- Gently release your tongue from the roof of your mouth before you speak to give a 'warmer' sound.
- Eliminate little glottal pops on your vowels. To smooth them out, run the vowels of the line together or think the line as you say a gentle 'Aah,' then go back to the words. It works like magic to get more flow to the words.

Because we only hear you and don't pick up any visual clues, we will be very aware of the quality of your voice. We need all the information that you would normally send with your face and body language.

DUBBING FOREIGN FILMS

Most foreign films are shown with subtitles in Britain, although sometimes you may be asked to dub a German film or a particular character whose dialogue needs to be changed. If English is not your first language and you work in Europe, then there will be plenty of opportunities for you. American and British films are dubbed into the national language of most major European countries.

The difference between dubbing and ADR – unless you are bilingual and dubbing yourself – is that you will have hardly any time to get to grips with the character. Usually, with a little guidance from a technician, you have to approach it like a cold reading at a casting. Obviously the more you can glean the better. Ask to have the scene run first and see what you can learn from the original actor. Even if you don't speak the language, you can learn a lot from tone of voice and body language.

The lip movements can't be exactly matched but your business is to make them as close as possible. Someone else will have translated, although occasionally you may have to make up dialogue if it's general exclamations or crowd scenes. Try to match the original tone and volume so that it blends with the other speakers. Work from objectives and actions even if you have to guess a bit. You have to find a way to bring back the original life. If the actor is doing lots of movement, then try to echo it to some extent so that your voice carries the same physical energy. A lot of dubbed films carry the information but not much of the life of the character.

Dubbing can be fun and can fit into the rest of your career as it only takes a few hours to do.

ANIMATION

Supplying voices for animated characters requires distinctive vocal characterisation and lots of technical ability. Animated movies often use well-known actors with recognisable voices whose names will help to sell the film. You'll find it a challenging but liberating acting experience.

You need to go about building the character in the same way as any other role while being aware of the style. It is bound to be more heightened or even surreal. Because the final image won't show as much information as your own face (though animation gets more sophisticated every year), your voice needs to convey your thoughts really clearly. Find a good variety of tone, pace and rhythm.

The most disconcerting thing is that you will always be alone to create your character in what John Lithgow, who worked on *Shrek*, called 'an isolation bubble'. You'll work to a storyboard, which will show you shot by shot how the character will behave. The director will use a pointer to take you 'frame by frame' through the dialogue, giving you the timing and the character's intentions. Then the animators will work their artistic and computerised magic to bring the creation to life.

As computer-animated films become more and more sophisticated, each muscle of the character's face will so closely resemble your own muscle action, as you did the dialogue, that the final image can bear a startling resemblance to your own expressions and speech movements!

QUICK TIPS FOR SOUND

- **Use the sound level** you would in life. There is no audience.
- **Use your whole voice.**
- **Keep your own truthful level** – don't drop to match your partner or in close-up.
- **Imagine** the background noise of the scene.
- **Don't clatter props** or bang doors during dialogue.
- **Watch out** for your radio mic – no bangs and rustles.
- **Rehearse** with the level you will use in the scene.
- **Tell the sound assistant** if you are going to yell or fire a gun!
- **In ADR** remind yourself of the original scene.
- **Use echo movements** in ADR.
- **For voice-overs,** know who you are, who you're talking to and why.
- **For dubbing,** pick up all the clues and go for a performance.
- **For animation,** find the style and use strong imagination to work from the storyboard!

SPECIAL SOUND NEEDS

ACCENTS AND DIALECTS

Sometimes a part calls for a change of accent or dialect. This can liberate you from your own quirks and inhibitions. But sometimes an accent may carry its own baggage and change parts of you that you may not want changed.

An obvious example of this is Southern British Standard or RP (for 'received pronunciation'), as it is sometimes called. RP is constantly changing and is no more the 'correct' way to speak than any other accent. The problem is that it is not really a regional accent and is often perceived as a class accent because of its roots. RP began in the universities and was originally used only by those with power and influence. This perception lingers today and means that, when many actors attempt RP, they slip into a 'hyper-RP' or a 'county' sound that enables them to play only certain parts like guards officers, landed gentry or period roles. They find it hard to feel truthful or to play against their preconceived ideas. A character who speaks RP may be raunchy and wild, a drug-addict or an alcoholic, homeless, a prostitute, illiterate or do menial work.

Different accents carry different status and character preconceptions. For example, we can perceive Yorkshire as an earthy, grounded, practical accent because it has full vocal closure (not breathy) and a strong positive tune. Can you be a poet with a Yorkshire accent? Well, Ted Hughes managed all right! Can you be a banker from Birmingham, a petty thief with a Morningside lilt or a man of few words in a Southern Irish brogue? Of course you can – but you have to put aside stereotypical generalisations. Some associated ideas about accents can be useful, but beware they don't get in the way of the specificity of your character.

If you are choosing a character's background, it can be worth considering that accents with 'twang' – like upper-class English, Glaswegian or Essex – would suit a character who didn't mind being overheard and liked taking centre stage. A softly spoken accent like Southern Irish or Scottish Highlands will seem more thoughtful and introspective. But having said that, working with opposites can be very exciting if there is time to undo the audience's assumptions and the character is written with enough depth.

Some American film actors who have to do English accents carry preconceived ideas about what it's like to be English. There's a 'niceness' evident in the tones that they adopt, which can be at odds with the character. The director who chose them for their strength and fire is not too thrilled when the English accent puts out that fire and leaves them a meek shadow of their former selves. So it's really important to be able to hang on to your natural pitch and drive and ensure that the accent doesn't make your voice quality less interesting.

Of course, there is a different placement for Southern Standard English from Standard American – it feels further forward in the mouth with more oral resonance. The tune is different too and there are generally fewer stresses. Nevertheless, within these new patterns, you have to feel that it is *you* talking. And you have to feel capable of any emotion within any accent.

When doing an accent, it is ideal to have a long preparation period to make it feel organic. But sometimes this can't happen and, in the end, you need to feel free as an actor, even if the accent isn't perfect. You can keep on refining it, right through to ADR.

Often a dialogue/dialect coach will be provided for work out of hours and will be on set. She or he wears headphones to monitor the dialogue and will make notes of inaccurate sounds to be redone later in ADR. But, together, you can fix things as you go along so you do as little ADR as possible.

Find a catch phrase in your new accent to bring you back to it if you find it slipping. And use an exercise that reminds you of the new 'placing' if you've been talking in your own accent between takes. Whispering the words slowly just before you speak can also help.

Accents are as much about cadences and rhythms as they are about individual words. Try to tape authentic speakers to use as models and listen to their whole tune as well as the pronunciation. You can buy excellent teaching tapes for particular accents from specialist bookshops.

CRYING AND LAUGHING

In the section on emotional triggers, we looked at how you might stimulate real emotion. You can also go from the outside in. When you chop an onion and it makes tears spring to your eyes, the body can respond to the external stimulus by providing the emotion. It is very easy to let the shallots in the kitchen start you really crying about the injustices of life. In the same way, the make-up department can provide a kit of similar tricks. As well as glycerine to make you look as if you're crying, they can also give you some drops or ointment to put on the edge of your eyes. This irritant makes them sting, redden and weep, and in no time at all, the real tears are running. You can make yourself cry by simply not blinking for too long!

Crying and laughing both start at the diaphragm. You can technically 'pulse' from there, rhythmically letting out little sounds on 'huh', and move from that into the real thing. If your character needs to sob uncontrollably, just keep bouncing the stomach in rhythmically as you let out the air in little gasps and you will find it easy to release into real sobbing.

Equally, you can use these exercises to go into laughter. You feel so silly doing them that it is easy to go from technically going 'huh' over and over again into really laughing. As long as the energy originates from the abdominal–diaphragmatic region, it will sound real. If it's made in your throat, it will sound false. Another way to produce laughter is to let all the air out and try to laugh with no air left. This will contract your stomach muscles and get the laugh started. You know how, if you want to laugh but shouldn't – in church or in a serious scene – you feel your stomach start to heave? Well, all you'll need is the beginning of this movement.

Obviously, you'll feel pretty daft doing these exercises on set. Use them at home until you find a way of being able to trigger a laugh from the right place. Crying and laughing both come from this contraction of the abdominal muscles. That's why it's so easy to flip from one to the other.

If you have to have real enormity of grief, this can help you find your way into it without having to rack yourself with terrible memories:

- Sit on the floor with your legs in front of you and shut your eyes.
- Rock forwards letting the breath fall out of an open mouth.
- Continue to rock back and forth letting out deeper breaths.
- Change the breath into sound so that you rock forwards and let the breath out on 'Huh'.
- Keep going, rhythmically letting the sound fall out every time you rock forwards.
- Let the sounds become louder and longer – 'Haaah'.
- Make them really long. If you go into wailing, that's fine, but keep a 'rooted' sound. (Don't let yourself go into hysterics.)
- Gradually let the sound become less, then return to just breath.
- Let the breathing become relaxed again.
- Become aware of the room and open your eyes.

This is a very powerful exercise. It is as if you open yourself up to a universal, rather than a personal, grief – all the sorrows of the world. You don't need to have real tears or know why you are making these sounds. Keening or wailing at funerals is usual in many parts of the world and, often, paid mourners wail for days to release the pain of the bereaved. It produces a cathartic release in both the keener and the listener. Because the grief wasn't about you, you should feel fine after doing this exercise. But some channel will have opened up that you will be able to find again, without trying, when you come to do the scene.

These tips will help you when you need to cry but remember, sorrow is the given condition – you fight through it to achieve the objective. I can't say it too often – if you feel sorry for yourself, we will pull back from you. We're moved if you're brave enough to overcome your emotion.

YELLING AND SCREAMING

If you have to yell or scream, take after take, you can find your voice going. It needs to feel real, but here are a few tips to protect your voice.

As you yell, really impel the sound from the abdominal-dia-phragmatic area. Pull in from your stomach as you start the sound and then release it afterwards for the incoming breath. Avoid 'pushing down' so that your stomach muscles distend as you yell – this will put enormous pressure on the larynx. Keep your throat open as you yell – feel as if you're about to sing loudly just before you yell. Try to avoid 'growling' on the sound and don't use a breathy voice.

Really anchor your body. Use a firm stance, stand against a wall or hold on to a piece of furniture. Think of sending the sound to the sounding board of your back. For screaming, keep the sound forward and use plenty of 'twang'. Try this exercise:

- Put your knuckle into your mouth so that it presses into the ridge of gum just above your top teeth (where you make your 't' and 'd') and count up to five (or say a line from the script) with your knuckle in place.
- Take out your knuckle and count again 'bouncing' the sound off the 'buzz' on your hard palate where your knuckle has been.

Your voice should have acquired an extra 'twangy' resonance and a 'forward' placement – this is where you want your scream to be placed.

If your throat does feel scratchy afterwards, rest your voice as much as you can between set-ups and at home. When you do speak, use your whole voice. Don't try to protect it with a half-whisper as this will cause constriction.

Use steam to soothe your larynx. You can do this by putting a towel over a basin of hot – not boiling – water, having a hot bath, using a steam room or buying an electric steamer designed for this use. You can buy these in specialist chemists.

Drink lots of water throughout the day to keep hydrated. Hum or 'siren' up and down your range on an 'ng' between takes to give your vocal folds a stretch. Stay away from anaesthetic sprays and lozenges, as you won't feel the damage you are doing and may compound the problem.

QUICK TIPS FOR SPECIAL SOUND NEEDS

- **Question your 'baggage'** about an accent. Make interesting choices.
- **An accent has to feel organic.** You must drive the accent – it mustn't drive you. Don't let it take you away from being grounded in the truth of your character's needs or to change the parts of you that you don't want changed.
- **Record authentic speakers** – check the tune not just pronunciation.
- **External help** like glycerine or eye drops can start real emotion.
- **Laughing and sobbing** start from abdominal contractions.
- **For yelling,** be anchored, throat open, use strong abdominal–diaphragmatic support, mentally sending it to your back.
- **For screaming**, be anchored, throat open, use lots of 'twang'.
- **Afterwards** – rest your voice, use steam, hum up and down your range.

PLAYING IN PERIOD FILMS

People in the past felt as we feel, wanted, more or less, what we want, cried as we cry. Be careful in a period movie that you don't confuse what you feel with what the social conventions of the period allow you to show you feel. What drives human beings has always been the same. Continue to make your 'brave choices' – you may simply need to cover them up more. In other words don't lose power.

Not all period films use period language. Some may be updated to be spare and colloquial, others will be contemporary except perhaps for using the long form of verbs – so 'I would have' instead of 'I would've', 'I am coming' rather than 'I'm coming' or 'we will be there' rather than 'we'll be there'. Often I've found that the writer isn't even aware they've written these in – they just hear more formality in their heads as they write. They're surprised when I've pointed it out and asked if the actors should stick to it. Sometimes these long forms, like the dress code, the accent or your physicality, can help you form a clearer picture of your character. But sometimes you may want to use a contraction if it is (it's) holding up your impulse. You can certainly discuss this with the director. Again though, make sure you are (you're) not just doing it because it's easier.

Sometimes the script will use the language form of the period. If it's an adaptation of Shakespeare or an existing stage play, the script will have been shortened or reshaped – Branagh's full length *Hamlet* excepted – because film primarily uses pictures to tell the story. But it may still contain more rich language than is usual in film – Baz Luhrmann's *Romeo and Juliet* completely updated the context but kept much of the original language. Shakespeare is very popular at present and you will benefit from knowing how the metre works and how to find the clues buried in the text. I suggest you do some workshops if you have never worked with Shakespeare before. I say workshops, because using Shakespeare in performance is completely different from studying it in an academic way.

There is less subtext in classical plays. People say what they mean, if not to the other characters, then in their soliloquies. Language reveals more than it conceals. People voice what they feel *through* words not *in spite* of words. Having said that, wherever there are human beings, there is subtext. But it is not the total mask of feelings that it is so often in modern drama. Although contemporary movies do have highly emotional scenes, where the mask drops, these are not usually language-driven.

Say the phrase 'I love you'. Now sing it. You had to elongate the vowel in order to sing and thus you expressed what you felt – without subtext. Do your lines on vowels only, then put back the consonants.

Classical language is rich, descriptive and emotional. It is physical, vital and full of energy. When you first approach the script, whisper it to feel it actually travelling over your lips but without being cut off from it by hearing your own voice. Review the work on 'physicalising' ('Seeing Is Believing', pages 100–101). This will also uncover any cheating on meanings!

Review the punctuation exercises from the 'The Character's Voice' section, pages 108–110, to uncover the strong argument of language. Both for verse and prose, this work will make the structure of the text clearer. Getting to grips with the syntax is the most important element to understanding.

Restoration and eighteenth-century drama revel in language. Words are used as weapons. Repartee and wit were social requisites. The film *Ridicule* offers a marvellous insight into this world and I really recommend you try to find it – also *Dangerous Liaisons*, *Tous les Matins du Monde*, *Barry Lyndon* and *Restoration* give a flavour of these times.

If you are dealing with a particular playwright or period, try to see the original stage work or read the plays. Whatever period your film is based on, find the pictures, explore the houses, furniture and objects, sing the songs, dance the dances, wear the clothes and research the politics and way of life of the times. Status between servant and master and different classes will be more heightened, as will class differences and the way of life between urban and rural dwellers.

People's relationships can be different. For example, a nurse working for an upper-class family prior to the late nineteenth century would have been a wet nurse – that is, she would have breastfed the baby of the family. This applies from Shakespeare's nurses right up to the ones in Chekhov, and even as late as the First World War. So the bond between nurse and child, right into adulthood and old age, would be very close. The parents, on the other hand, might have a more distant relationship, particularly the father.

Period films bring with them the hazards of swords and cloaks, large hats and dresses with trains. You may have to adjust your body space to cope without treading on someone's dress or stabbing them unintentionally. I worked on a film recently where the leading lady's dress had to be stitched up every night where too eager gallants had pinned her to the floor with their boots. Obviously, the more time you have to practise in clothing or to learn horse-riding and sword-fighting, the better.

The use of fans is best thought of as a way of signalling subtext. They are not about keeping yourself cool. They are for flirting, teasing or for being coy behind. You can use them in the way you would use 'emotional objects'. You may be saying one thing but be revealing your true thoughts by your conscious or unconscious use of your fan.

Different social greetings and the style of bowing and curtsying will depend on the exact period and status of your character. If you haven't got an expert to help, you may have to rehearse them yourself. The social pecking order, the seating arrangements, the niceties of sexual advances and how you eat asparagus all need research.

A useful book, although primarily addressed to amateurs, is Lyn Oxenford's *Playing Period Plays*. It covers English manners, costumes and dances from medieval times to the Edwardian period. It has a good contents section that divides everything up into periods and categories so you can easily check out an Elizabethan curtsy or an Edwardian bow.

But once you've done all this homework, remember that you are a real live human being who just happens to live in that period.

ACTING IN CORSETS

If you're required to work in a corset, here are some hard-won tips. Really make yourself as fat as possible at the fitting, by breathing in and allowing your abdomen to swell and your ribs to expand – then ask for it to be a little looser. Also ask if the front portion, over your stomach, can be flexible. When you are being laced in, do the 'fat trick' again. If the corset holds your stomach in too tightly, you are going to have breathing problems, your voice quality might change and you'll get dizzy and tired.

Once you've made your corset bearable, then start to enjoy it. Use rib expansion when breathing in and work against it to move it outwards (not upwards). It will change your posture and your body language. You can't easily cross your legs in a corset and it's harder to slump, so you will naturally start to sit and move more like women of the period. Buy a light one and wear it at home while rehearsing to see how it affects the way you move and even think.

HURRY UP AND WAIT

A film actor's life vacillates between terror and tedium. Every lost minute on a film costs a fortune and the second assistant is always anxious that the director doesn't have to wait for the actors. For the actor in a smaller role, the whole of filming seems to be summed up by the old adage, 'hurry up and wait'!

It's really important to be able to conserve your energy in the long wait from set-up to set-up. Do a short warm-up when you arrive and after lunch. Between set-ups, try to sleep, read and relax. When you get called for make-up, check your card and your script, remind yourself where you've come from, what you feel about the other characters and what you want.

Refind your focus to feel that you're entering the moment freshly but with an energy as if you'd never been away.

LAST-MINUTE NERVES
- Lie on the floor if possible (if not, lean back comfortably in a chair). Tense and relax through your body. Imagine you're a great sea sponge at the water's edge and let the breath, like the tide, come over your toes, up through your legs and into your belly, making you heavy. Let it drain away, slowly, out through your toes. Find a deep breathing rhythm.
- Stand up slowly (bringing your head up last) and feel your feet firmly rooted to the floor; relax your knees slightly.
- Feel your spine lengthening and your neck free and lengthening. Stand on tiptoe – the crown of your head pulled gently by an invisible sky-hook. Gently lower your heels, still feeling that gentle pull to the sky and really root your feet in the earth.
- Give yourself an oxygen 'high' – it's free and legal! Let out your breath slowly on 'Shh' and just before you run out, concave your chest slightly, bending over as you do so. *Now hold your breath* till you are standing fully straight again (this is important). Now breathe in – wow!
- Pant very lightly for a few seconds with no sound of breath – silently.
- 'The Seasons' (from chi gung): Spring: bend your knees slightly, lightly clench your fists and lift your arms to chest height in front as you

release the breath on 'Shh' (the sap rises). Summer: straighten up, draw your arms back, elbows bent as you breathe in (the living is easy ...). Autumn: let the breath out on 'Shh' as you bend your knees and press your hands down gently, straightening your arms (the leaves fall). Winter: straighten the knees, let your hands drop to your sides and draw the breath in quietly through the nose (gathering in). Do four more cycles.

- Rub your hands together hard until they're warm. Put them across your sternum – upper chest. Take in the warmth and allow yourself to release any tension in that area.
- Rub your hands together again and put them on your lower belly. Relax into the warmth and feel the breath dropping into that area, the stomach releasing outwards as you breathe in and inwards as you breathe out. Sigh out on a long 'Aaah'. Feel the stomach release back out for the next breath in.
- Rub your hands together once more. Put one hand on your stomach and the other on your lower back. Feel the warmth and your own inner strength. Say one word that stems from the forthcoming scene, sending the sound to the warmth at your back.
- Think clearly what your character wants at this moment. See your partner in the scene in your mind. Whisper what you say before the scene or what you think as you enter. Or tell the story of the film. (Only whisper the real script slowly once.)

SUMMING UP FILM TECHNIQUE

Film technique is about knowing exactly where to send your energy: what the framing of the shot is, where you are looking and how much leeway for movement you have. It is about understanding the importance of continuity, sound levels and how to use props.

It is also about accepting the presence of a large film crew. Key crew like boom operators, camera operators and grips can't 'clear your eyeline' except under very special circumstances like nudity shots or extreme emotional moments. They need to be there to ensure you look and sound your best on screen.

You need to be ready to enter the moment and to go on being in the moment to the end of the scene and beyond. Start the thought before 'Action' and carry on acting till after you hear 'Cut'. Never stop in the middle of a scene without hearing 'Cut'. (Or a similar order – Clint Eastwood is reputed to say, 'That's enough of that shit,' when he directs – particularly if he's in the shot!)

Stanislavski wrote, 'Professionalism is a very necessary and healthy basis to begin any work, in any field of art ...' Professionalism means attention to preparation detail, to time keeping, to the specifics of the scene. It means being able to repeat the scene any number of times under any conditions without losing energy. And without losing your cool. Film crews admire professional actors. Professional actors keep working.

Your technique is important to you because the director can't use takes where the continuity doesn't match or you went out of focus because you didn't hit your mark or where the close-up didn't match the master, no matter how brilliant the performance. But at the same time you need to forget everything but the needs of your character.

When I identified the four kinds of thinking in an earlier section, I decided not to confuse you with a fifth. But, of course, there is another level on which you will operate. You will develop a little monitor that checks that the technical side of your work is in order. To use the car-driving analogy again, your technical skills will go on working subliminally while you pursue your objectives, and only jump into focus when you are faced with an unexpected problem. Maximilian Schell summed up this dual reality: 'There are two souls in every actor. One watches another. When both are content at the same time, you have a good moment.'

On a film you are never working alone; you are a team player. By respecting what everyone else does, you can make the whole set-up work for you to give your best performance. Most of what happens in the final film will be out of your control, so make sure you take all the control of your own role that you can.

Know what you want, from whom and why, then screw all your energy into that moment of being and try to get it. Keep thinking the whole time – never go dead. Know all the rules – and sometimes dare to break them!

William Hurt once said, 'You work hard for many years to learn a technique which you then have the audacity to forget.'

PART FOUR
THE WORKING ENVIRONMENT

MAKE-UP OF CREW

When you arrive on the set for the first time, the amount of people can be overwhelming but, like you, they all want to make a good film. So it's reassuring to remember that they're all on your side. They appreciate you knowing what they do and you can make their enormous expertise work for you. And it is an enormous expertise!

Because film pays well and offers a modicum of excitement in terms of travel and life-style (although the hours can be long and tedious), the last master-craftsmen and women left are all working in film studios. Film gathers together the best in every field: camera technicians, sound engineers, artists, designers, builders, restorers, prop-makers, make-up artists, hair stylists, animal trainers, computer wizards, gun experts and fight directors. It searches out the most capable and amenable nurses, caterers, security guards and drivers, the most eagle-eyed script supervisors, eagle-eared dialect coaches, knowledgeable casting directors, toughest producers – and prays for good writers, directors and actors.

This disparate group of people get together for a couple of months and expend enormous energy and commitment working as a team to make the film happen. Of course they grumble and scandal and quarrel and are quick to predict a bleak outlook for the film if they start to sense weakness at the helm, but they also become the most tightly knit group of people you'll find almost anywhere. They have no time for their private lives, they work twelve- to fourteen-hour days (and that's not including travelling) and their lives are a mixture of expensive cars, rich food, business class travel, grand hotels, physical discomfort and extreme sleep deprivation.

You'll find them, and the long-suffering actors, in the middle of glaciers, desert sandstorms, driving rain, humid jungles full of biting insects and the unheated 007 stage at Pinewood in the middle of winter, surrounded by water and smoke machines. They'll sleep four or five hours a night – less if they're in the make-up department (it's an irony that the most beautiful women in the world are filmed after five hours' sleep and need teams of make-up artists to repair the damage). They work a six-day week and sometimes travel on the seventh. They'll go down with tick fever, beriberi stomach, get drenched, need rehydration drinks to keep them going, spend all their money on the local jewellery and carpets and in the hotel bar and come back for more.

It's worth understanding and respecting this team – and knowing how they can help you. Film is quite hierarchical and it pays to understand film etiquette – like not walking in front of the camera when a shot's being lined up. On my inaugural film performance, the first thing I heard the director, Ken Hughes, say was, 'Who's that damn girl walking across my shot?' Unless you're being shepherded by an assistant, try to get a sense of your surroundings before you march off across the set. And you can always ask a runner or an assistant director for help. If you have a sizeable role, you'll be taken to a comfortable canvas chair with your name on the back!

Even now, as an acting or dialogue coach, when I arrive on the first day, I take it carefully. I check there's no red light showing (if there is, it means filming is in progress), open the door gently, then pause to let my eyes adjust and see which way the camera's pointing. Then I head for the script supervisor's desk or the sound mixer's trolley – I know I'll be safe there. Locations are a little trickier as the take might be in long shot. But if you stand near the food table, a light, a camera box or the make-up department, you know they can't be filming those!

So here's a brief run-down of what this bewildering array of people can do for you.

THE PRODUCERS

The title 'producer' covers a variety of positions. There will be an executive producer who is in charge of the whole project and funding (and probably many others in different stages of development). This executive may not ever turn up on the film set and may be based in a different country or work for a parent company. There will be a few producers directly in charge of the film, some of whom may have nursed the idea from birth. There will be a line-producer, brought on board more recently, who oversees production matters but who is not creatively involved. Then there may be an assortment of people who have had some part in putting the scheme together (or supplying the money) and who, for want of a better term, are called associate producers. They will all be caught in a balancing act between 'the bottom line' (money) and the desire to make a good film (art). Most of them live precariously job-wise and have learned to play good politics. Rest assured, whatever happens behind closed doors, they will be charming and kind to *you*. Producers respect good actors – your performance ultimately helps to sell the film.

* * *

THE PRODUCTION OFFICE AND ACCOUNTS DEPARTMENT

You'll only really deal with the production office or the hard-working accounts department if you haven't got an agent or you have queries about airline tickets or per diem (your daily expenses allowance on location). The production office will give out updates on the schedule and arrange call-sheets to be faxed to you.

The production assistant or producer's assistant (PA) does personal co-ordinating and secretarial duties for the producers.

THE DIRECTOR

Every director is unique. Most are men – a few (too few) are women. Some have been theatre directors; some actors; and a few have been editors, writers or cinematographers. Many have been none of these things. They can be great company or preoccupied and distant. They may or may not have written the script and can be wonderful or difficult with actors. Their direction can be illuminating or muddy.

But they are all carrying an enormous responsibility. This may be their own project or they may have been hired by the producers. And they may not have been first choice. Sometimes they are replaced if the film isn't coming in on budget or if there's a major disagreement with the big star. It's a lonely job. Hundreds of crew members ask questions every day, producers breathe down the back of their necks, the weather turns against them, the leading man gets ill, life is taken up with rushes, meetings, script changes and worry. The buck stops here.

Some directors will rehearse and share their ideas at length. At the very least they should be happy to answer any questions and to discuss your character. If you have a tiny role, this will still be true but remember how busy they are, so unless they approach you, wait until you are rehearsing the scene. If your director doesn't say much, don't worry. Directors often don't have time to reassure you, but the project is far too important to let problems go. If they say nothing – you're fine.

Since you're in their hands and have no control over the final product, the best policy is to trust, and work with, your director. The film is going to be their vision. Offer your own thoughts: most directors want your input. But if they are rejected, the film will be no better if you fight. So take their direction on board and make it work for you.

THE ASSISTANT DIRECTORS

Assistant directors take the heat off the director and liaise between him or her, the actors and the crew. Unlike assistant directors in theatre, they don't work on the creative aspects of a film at all.

The first assistant (known as the first or the first AD) is a kind of lynchpin for the movie. He – usually a 'he' – makes sure all is ready for shooting, calls for quiet and checks everything is in place for a take. It's also up to the first assistant to keep an eye on the schedule and hurry the director along a bit if things are running behind. You'll only have any dealings with the first assistant when you are actually on the set. You can ask any practical questions but keep artistic ones for the director.

The second assistant is the one looking directly after your interests. Here you'll find a good mix of genders and he or she will give you your calls, script changes, shepherd you to and from set and arrange your transport home. Never leave the studio or location without checking with the second assistant. Seconds often arrange the casting of extras and walk-ons.

The friendly third assistants are usually early on in their careers. They will be really helpful: bring you food when elaborate hairstyles won't allow you out in the rain, offer you water on set, tell you who people are and generally sort you out. Never leave the set without telling a third assistant. You can ask the third any question you like and they'll try to find you an answer.

Runners are like thirds but are paid a pittance or even work unpaid. They've usually just left film college and want to be directors. They run errands, turn the red light on and off, ring the bells between takes and guard the doors – duties they take very seriously. Be nice to them – they may be employing you in future years!

The director's assistant is the director's personal assistant.

THE CONTINUITY DEPARTMENT
'Continuity girls' – they are almost always women – are now more properly called script supervisors. This is a much fairer description of what they do, as they have to work through the script in detail in pre-production, sorting out the timescale of the story, the logic and the fine details of the script.

During shooting, they work closely with the director and have to watch everything. They note the camera set-up, the lens used and the camera speed, the timing of the shot, the dialogue changes, where everyone is standing and when they move. They check whether the weather matches, your clothes are the same as in the last take and how long your cigarette should be. They also liaise with the editor and provide the final shooting script with additions for the editor to work from. British and American script supervisors usually position themselves by the monitor so they can see what the camera sees.

Continental ones often prefer to be on set with the actors watching the action 'live'.

They are invaluable for checking which hand you used when, who kissed first and whether it's day or night. They are always helpful and you can and must ask what you need to know. But it is also *your* responsibility and with so much else to do, the script supervisor will be extremely grateful if you can take care of most of your own continuity.

They will prompt you if necessary and tell you of any script changes or additions to new pages. Let the script supervisor know if you have arranged to change the script and any ad-libs you use during the take. At the end of a scene, the script supervisor may take a photographic record.

Script supervisors develop a keen eye and ear for performances and often whisper advice into the director's ear.

THE CAMERA DEPARTMENT

Heading up the camera department is the director of photography – again usually a male preserve, although more women are entering the camera department. The DOP used to be called the lighting cameraman in Britain and is also known as the cinematographer. The DOP doesn't usually operate the camera. He liaises with the 'sparks' to set up and adjust his lighting and is responsible for making you look wonderful.

The camera operator – of which there may be more than one – looks through the lens and keeps you in frame even while the camera may be twisting and turning. You can help by letting him or her see the moves you are going to make in rehearsal and by not making surprise moves in close-up.

The focus puller or operator does just that – keeps you in focus. He or she measures up for the focus and gives you your marks. The shot is often lined up on a stand-in (if you have a major role) but you will need to be patient too for a while so that you'll stay a clear-cut image. The focus puller will be only too happy to give you invaluable advice as to what lens is being used and where you'll go out of frame.

The clapper loader sets your adrenalin racing by announcing the shot and clapping the board to give the editor a start point for the take. After the first assistant director calls for quiet, and the camera, sound and video (for playback) departments confirm they are rolling, you'll hear the shot number and then the take number. For example: 133 – Take 7 – Clap. (American style, it is the scene number followed by a letter denoting the shot, then the take number.) Then the director will say, 'Action.' If it's a mute shot (MOS – without sound), there'll be no clap,

Very occasionally, the board is held upside down at the end instead. For example, if you were working with an animal or a baby, a board at the beginning might give them a shock. Or if you were in a hurry to keep the light, the board might be left till the end. (The production company sometimes supplies champagne at shot 500!)

There are other members of the camera team as well, like grips who pull the camera along on tracks or wheel it on a dolly or operate cranes, etc.

The Steadicam operator has real muscle. The Steadicam is strapped to his body and its steadying apparatus absorbs shocks to gives a smooth fluid shot. It is often used in action shots or at the same time as fixed cameras to give extra footage without losing shooting time for another set-up.

THE ELECTRICS DEPARTMENT

Electricians are commonly known as 'the sparks' and have the bluest humour on the set. The gaffer (probably called after the hook for overhanging lamps rather than chief – a gaff was an iron hook) is the boss of the best boy (his first assistant), charge hands and electricians and assists the DOP with the lights for the shot and is responsible for all the electrics on the film.

THE SOUND DEPARTMENT

This is headed up on set by the sound mixer who sets levels and mixes all the sound sources for the sound track. His or her sound desk is often hidden away from the main crew so that the desk doesn't have to be moved every time the shot reverses. (The rest of the crew have to keep moving camp.) He keeps an eye on the proceedings via a monitor and by radio to his assistants.

The boom operator (there may be more than one) is with you on set. Depending on the shot, the boom may be close to you or way up in space. Boom operators adopt all sorts of weird and dangerous positions to catch your voice without being seen by the camera.

Boom operators also fumble amongst your undies to fit you with radio transmitters and mics. Bear this with understanding and patience. You can be kind to sound by watching your voice level within reason, avoiding silk underwear, not thumping your radio mic and trying to say your dialogue in between clattering props.

If you need to check some dialogue (and the director doesn't mind you listening to yourself), the sound mixer will be glad to play something back to you, as long as it's not just before he or she is getting ready for the next shot and you don't ask too often.

Sound departments know all the gossip – but they're very discreet!

THE DIALOGUE, DIALECT AND ACTING COACHES

Coaches will not be needed on every film but there are different reasons why you might be assigned one.

An acting coach might be there for pre-production and/or for filming. This might be because you are a newcomer, someone from a different field of performance, tackling a difficult kind of role, or just because the director likes the actors warmed up before filming. Or the director may not speak the actor's language well enough. (One director's acting instructions to a nine-year-old: 'Now you sit; now you cry.')

Occasionally, the executive producer or director watches the rushes, sees the actor in trouble, and decides to send in some help mid-shoot. This might be a temporary blow, but probably all that is needed is some confidence-building, a new strategy and a shoulder to lean on.

A dialogue coach can be an acting coach but is more often a voice coach concerned with a particular aspect of the text or style – with Shakespeare or classical oratory, for example. Occasionally they may assist with improvised text, especially if a foreign director can't understand all the nuances.

A dialogue coach may be a dialect coach and help with an accent or dialect. For example, an English actor might be doing an American accent or a Hollywood actor working in a British accent, or it might be a regional or foreign accent – or even Elvish.

The coach is there in the best interest of the director and the film and, most of all, is there as an ally to help *you* be at your best – which, after all, is the same thing.

Coaches are sensitive to your needs during filming, but if the accent slips too much, you'll have to redo the take in ADR, which is hard. So let your coach help you.

THE MAKE-UP AND HAIR DEPARTMENT

These departments work alongside each other or in adjoining rooms. Film, unlike television, has separate departments for hair and make-up. You can go to either make-up first or hair, depending on the circumstances. If you have an elaborate hairstyle or a wig you will usually go to hair first, then make-up, before returning to the hairdresser.

Hair and make-up artists are a great source of comfort, gossip and general sustenance. They always know the ins and outs of any film set-up, catering arrangements and who's sleeping with who! You'll have a close relationship with them and they'll make you feel and look good.

Together you can find the 'look' for your character that will assist you in the role. They'll come up between takes to adjust you and will often be under pressure from the director to leave you be. The director is worrying about time, but they carry the responsibility of how you'll look on screen. Always be still and patient for their attentions – they're on your side.

At the end of a scene, they will snap a picture so they can re-create the look later. Make-up artist Sarah Monzani says that she discusses what the character will look like with the director and then collaborates with the actor, who will already have a good idea of what they want.

Paul Engelen sent me these thoughts from the set of the latest Bond movie:

My main objective is to gain the confidence of the actor – to assist as much as possible in the quest to 'find the character'. Very often this requires the application of time-consuming prosthetics, and thus lengthy sessions in the chair, so it is essential to have a comfortable relationship with your actors. When the make-up has been established, the hardest part of my job is to maintain the continuity and, during the more lengthy make-ups, I find it quite difficult to prevent the actor from falling asleep!

THE COSTUME DEPARTMENT

Costume or wardrobe is headed up by the costume designer. Depending on the budget and the period, the costumes may be specially made for the film or bought under her or his supervision. You may have some say in the final choices and you can discuss your character's needs with the designer. If something is especially uncomfortable or a corset is too tight, then the wardrobe master may be able to adjust it. Designer Mel Corrie says that she works with the actor to choose the right clothes. Sometimes there's an element of wanting to look nice or feel comfortable – which she completely understands – that is at odds with the needs of the role: 'if it's right for the character – it's right'.

Your dresser who will see you at your most intimate and vulnerable moments and often act as the protector of your privacy, will become your friend and ally. Secret adjustments of underwear, urgent undoings and discreet alterations are all in the hands of your dresser, not to mention the washing of tights and the finding of lost belongings. You may even be brought the odd cup of tea if you're very good. Never take your dresser for granted.

Your dresser will also come up to you on set for last-minute nips and tucks and to hold or give you any small hand props you use. They will also take care of any personal items that you've had to bring on set, even your mobile or cigarettes. At the end of a scene, the dresser will want to take a picture for continuity records. The books that the costume department keeps of a film are works of art – and history.

THE STAND-IN
Your stand-in (who should become a friend) will stand in position while the DOP sets up camera and lights and for the camera moves and focus. This is to save your energy and allow you to change and get hair and make-up done. Ask the stand-in what moves they've been asked to do before you take over. It's not fair to expect them to run errands or get tea, although they often do offer all kinds of support.

THE DOUBLES
Lookalikes will sometimes be used by second unit in non-dialogue scenes where you won't be seen too clearly, like at the wheel of a car or in the distance. This is to save time.

THE STUNTS
These brave men and women do your dangerous escapades for you. If they're not in long shot, then they will look or be made to look like you and be called a stunt double.

Some actors like to do their own stunts. But remember, if anything happens after shooting starts, you can't easily be replaced. If you're injured, it could cost the production a fortune in lost time. Many stuntmen and actors, like Roy Kinnear who tragically fell from a horse, have been killed during filming. Only do what you know you can and check all safety procedures have been followed.

THE SPECIAL EFFECTS DEPARTMENT
The special effects department handle every aspect of magic that's shot during real-time production. If you have to work with fire, flood or battles, they will be there, keeping you safe and showing you how things work. Ask if you can watch them test any effects you're involved with and always listen to what the supervisor tells you to do. If you haven't met the special effects supervisor before and want to know if he's properly accredited, ask to see his special effects pyro and physical effects cards issued by the British Film Joint Industries Committee.

When special effects are being used, observe all precautions and turn off your mobile phone as it may cause radio frequency interference that could provoke untimely initiation of the explosives used on set! Better still, leave it in the dressing room.

Special effects may look terrifying, but everything is worked out with absolute precision. Special effects supervisor David Harris arranged for the actors on *London's Burning* to work amid flying gas bottles and in many simulated flashover situations. A flashover – as in the film *Backdraft* – is a potentially lethal situation where a fire has burnt all the available oxygen in a given area, like a room or corridor, and when a door is opened, it travels in a vast fireball to the new source of air. But because both actors and crew listened to David's safety advice, everyone was completely safe.

On *Legionnaire*, with Jean-Claude Van Damme, he arranged for walls around the actors and stuntmen to be dynamited to blow out to 60 or 70 feet. But all the special effects and stunts were so carefully planned that the actors could continue playing the scene in the foreground. David says that the aim is to put the actors in a 'completely safe but photographically extravagant position'.

THE ARMOURERS

This department is specifically in charge of all guns and armoury. Even blanks can be dangerous, and there have been deaths on sets, like Jon-Eric Hexum who killed himself in 1984 when, as a joke, he pretended to play Russian roulette. Armourers and weapons masters know all about guns. Follow their instructions precisely. Most seem to be ex-SAS!

THE FIGHT DIRECTOR AND STUNT CO-ORDINATOR

Fight directors and stunt co-ordinators arrange anything from sword fights to all-out warfare. They will expect you to train, rehearse and remember. You may have to learn new skills like diving, driving or playing golf as well as combat skills. (Angelina Jolie trained for hours each day for the part of Lara Croft.) When fighting, have an objective – know what you want from your opponent but keep your 'monitor' working.

Fight director William Hobbs, whose many credits include *The Count of Monte Cristo*, *The Man in the Iron Mask* and *Shakespeare in Love*, says in his book *Fight Direction for Stage and Screen* that the very nature of filming places greater stress on the actor as there is so little time to get it 'in the can', yet it has to seem real:

> No matter how cleverly a fight is arranged, nothing is as important as its acting. In the performance of a combat two contradictory things are happening. On the one hand, characters are seen to be working on a highly charged emotional level. On the other, the actors have to be

working mentally on a conscious level of coolness, with complete body relaxation and control, so that their acted aggression can be performed with conviction, and at the same time in absolute safety.

THE ANIMAL TRAINERS

Trainers, handlers or wranglers get the animals to act like veterans. You may have to do anything from handle snakes to learn to ride. These experts are the best you'll get. Animal use on films is overseen by several worthy organisations to ensure the animals aren't harmed. If you ever see cruel treatment abroad, which is rare on films, report it to the second assistant director. The film producers will not want bad treatment of animals on their production as it is terrible press!

THE ART DEPARTMENT

Heading up here is the production designer who, together with the director and DOP, is responsible for the look of the film. He or she liaises with the costume designer and props master. A good designer can have a tremendous influence on a film's style and success.

Working with the designer are gifted artists and sculptors, draughtsmen and decorators. Respect the set and don't put any cups down on it, sit on the chairs or sleep in the beds (however tempting) when not on camera.

Working with the director, the storyboard artist sets out the sequence of the film in pictures, shot by shot. Some directors rely enormously on the storyboard artist. If you have a chance to peek at it, do so. It will give you a sense of what the director's aiming for.

THE PROPS DEPARTMENT

The props department will arrange for any props needed on set and will guide you through any use of them. Don't touch or move anything on the props table. If something you use breaks or doesn't work, this is who will solve it for you. (I've even had my own wooden Victorian toilet seat mended by the props department . . .)

THE CONSTRUCTION DEPARTMENT

Getting the set made to the designer's vision is the business of the construction department. Sometimes working under dangerous conditions, this band of riggers, builders, carpenters, painters, plasterers and stagehands will construct virtually anything. The swing-gang will put up and take down the set while you're grabbing your short night's sleep. Don't offer to help with anything. Apart from stepping on their patch, you won't be insured if an accident happens.

* * *

THE GREENS DEPARTMENT

The greensmen and women take care of any planting or grass-laying involved in the construction. Be sure you only walk where they want you to – they're very protective of their lawns!

THE LOCATIONS DEPARTMENT

This department is in charge of choosing and running the locations. They will prepare useful maps and information sheets on foreign and home locations, which include restaurant guides and tips to stop you getting kidnapped or arrested.

THE MEDICAL DEPARTMENT

There is always a qualified nurse on set and on difficult locations there is sometimes a doctor too. The nurse on a film set is endlessly patient and resourceful and deals with everything from headaches and hangovers to the occasional serious accident.

Don't hesitate to see the nurse if you have any health worries that are affecting your work or worrying you when you're abroad. She will always have access to the best medical help available in the area.

She will oversee any vaccinations or tablets required for tropical areas. She will also carry sunscreens and insect repellents and provide rehydration drinks in dry or hot conditions – do use them.

THE SECURITY DEPARTMENT

You will notice security officers about, especially on location, and leading actors often have personal bodyguards as well. They are there to keep you secure and are not as forbidding as they look. (On one ten-week film shoot in the wilds of KwaZulu-Natal, the actors became such good friends with the security guards that the major star chose to go to their end-of-shoot party rather than to the posh one the producers had unwisely arranged for the same night!)

THE TRANSPORT DEPARTMENT

Because no one will trust you to arrive at a far-flung studio in time for your 5.30 a.m. make-up call, you will be ferried to and from set by a reliable, amiable driver. He won't expect a tip but might want to discuss the news. If you are too exhausted, choose the back seat and close your eyes – he'll understand.

In foreign climes you may have scary excursions in minibuses, jeeps and boats. Take your sea-bands and travel pills.

* * *

THE CATERING DEPARTMENT

This will be a very important department to you. Catering on film sets is excellent unless you are particularly unlucky in a far-flung land. Then you either get thin or ill until the company flies out a professional team.

It's hard to keep the weight off when there is food available at every moment: hot bacon butties at breakfast, school puddings with custard at lunch and sandwiches at tea.

If you're in a studio (unless you're on a special contract), you will have to buy your own lunch at the canteen but breakfast will be provided. On Saturdays, Sundays and on location, lunch will be served outside on a wagon. You collect your food and repair to a bus, dressing room or trailer.

If you are filming in France, you will have the luxury of an efficient waitress service and wine on the table. Sadly, unless you want to end up too relaxed, you might have to forgo that delight until you're back in your hotel!

If you're suffering from nerves, do try to eat as it will help to keep your blood sugars up. And drink lots of water.

THE PUBLICITY DEPARTMENT

If you are playing a major role, you will be asked to do interviews and have stills done throughout shooting. This can sometimes be wearing, but the better the film sells, the better for your career. So smile for the camera.

THE STILLS PHOTOGRAPHER

The elusive stills photographer lurks in the shadows snapping you at odd moments or in rehearsal. These pictures will be used by the publicity department. It is a difficult job because many directors don't want to hold up a shot for a quick snap, so stills photographers are practised at being invisible. Offer them a drink on location. They are well-travelled, urbane and witty – and they'll sometimes arrange a copy of a photo!

THE CHILD WRANGLERS AND TUTORS

If you are under sixteen (eighteen in America) you have to have a minder with you. (The age depends on the rules in each country.) On location this is often a parent but it can also be a professional chaperone. Children also have to have schooling during term time so there will be a schoolroom on set complete with qualified teacher and there are laws governing the amount of time they can work and how often.

* * *

THE EDITING DEPARTMENT

You will sometimes see the editors wandering on to the set to see what scenes are being shot. They liaise with the script supervisor and sometimes suggest a shot to the director that may help with the final editing. They are gentle souls who live like moles in their cutting rooms and blink a bit when they come out into the glaring lights of the set. But don't be deceived. Together with the director (and sometimes the producer) they will have the final say about how much of you appears on screen.

THE VISUAL EFFECTS DEPARTMENT

These are all the effects that are added in post-production – this department works to make possible the impossible. Because of them, you may be asked to work in front of a blue or green screen and to imagine what's going on. Then they will put in the missing links later. They are always delighted to explain the intricacies of what they do. Sometimes they can show you some of the forthcoming magic.

These computer whizz-kids scrub out booms, sheep or cars on the skyline, change a puddle into an ocean or create a solar system. Virtually anything can be done virtually, but it takes enormous time, money and skill. So it helps to have the original vista without too many items to be erased. In Morocco, filming a local reservoir that would become the Nile, I saw the visual effects supervisor morosely surveying the hills around. He turned to the local Mr Fix-it and said plaintively, 'I said *ships* – not *sheeps*!'

THE DAY AT WORK

Your day will start unbearably early. In fact so early that you might be able to kid yourself it's the middle of the night rather than just before dawn. Remember to pack your preparation cards, your script, a pencil with an eraser for last-minute additions and whatever you need to relax – music, a special pillow or a herbal balm – and be sure to bring a good book. You are probably going to have hours to kill today and although some of that time will be spent in preparation and some napping and conserving energy, a film studio dressing room or trailer can be a dull place.

You will be picked up at first light from home or your hotel by a friendly driver. He is part of the film crew and if you can eschew the fun of conversation about past stars he has escorted, you can sleep on until you reach the studio.

You'll be welcomed there by the second assistant and breakfast will be being served when you arrive. One of the joys and pitfalls of working on a film are the delicious high cholesterol breakfasts; there is nothing more appealing on a frosty morning as day breaks over the parking lot than a bacon and egg buttie. Anyway, some friendly runner will bring you black coffee and a slice of toast if that's more to your liking and you will be served it in the hair department.

Your session here could take up to an hour depending on the extent of the transformation and will be followed by a similar session with make-up. There is nothing more relaxing than shutting your eyes and leaning back into the comfy chair while an expert cleanses, massages and pampers you. This is also one of the best places to be consoled, counselled and given hot titbits of the latest gossip. If you are wearing prosthetics, this could be an even longer session. I remember arriving early into make-up on my first film, *Cromwell*, and being amazed to see Frank Finlay already there with his glasses perched on non-existent ears, blood pouring out of gaping holes in the side of his head, watching a small portable television set.

After make-up, wardrobe will take over and you will be kitted out from top to toe, with enormous attention to detail, in your character's clothes. From now on, with each move you make, you will feel the same freedom or constraints as your character. It will be high summer and you will be wearing a heavy Puritan costume in sets with roaring log fires, lights, smoke machines and no air conditioning or be on location by a lake in winter in the flimsiest evening gown.

During a long day of filming on *Secret Passage*, three of us had to assist the leading lady up the steps of a church in Venice in soaring summer temperature in the heaviest dress imaginable. And yet the dress was well researched and of original fabrics. Women like this really lived there, dressed like this and led active lives (though without having to repeat each climb through many takes!). So somehow they coped with these physical hardships. Try to fuse your feelings wearing the costume with your character's daily life.

At some point during these proceedings, you will be called into the studio, together with the other actors in the scene, for blocking and 'line-up'. This will start with a small, almost private, rehearsal with the director. The DOP, sound mixer and script supervisor may be present or it may be a completely closed set. Together you will work out the details of the scene, possibly make small alterations to the script and set the moves. It may be an in-depth rehearsal but often consists of just the physical aspects of the scene. If you have a small role, it may be the first time you've seen the director on the set and the first time you've met the other actors. Try to take in everything that's said and scribble any notes you need. If you can't remember the exact moves set, you can always check quietly with the script supervisor at the end of the rehearsal.

The director will then invite the key members of the crew to watch a rehearsal of the scene so that they know where to set the cameras and lights and then you will be sent back to continue getting ready or to wait in your dressing room.

Depending on the complexities of the shot and how much rearranging needs to be done, you've now got anything from forty minutes to three hours to make final preparations for your scene in light of the rehearsal. Look at your script, check out the changes to your lines, moves or fellow actors' responses. Do they affect your relationships or choices of action? If they do, then incorporate this new knowledge into your objectives and find the thought links in the new dialogue. Check out the card for this scene and make any changes. You may have been supplied with the 'sides' that you can carry around with the new words to learn. Now is a good time to do a short breathing and vocal warm-up and any physical memory work that you need.

When you've done all this, relax. Try to sleep a little without ruining your hair, make-up and clothes. At least shut your eyes for a moment. If you're lucky and in clothes that won't show creases, lie on the floor with your head on a book and your knees up, to allow your spine to relax. You have a long day ahead.

Eventually you'll get called back to the set and a third assistant or runner will escort you over. Your stand-in will have been there for you, allowing the focus puller to get the distance to the camera just right, the camera operator to sort out the right lens and the DOP to perfect the lighting. As you are welcomed into position, you can have a quick word with the stand-in to ask what they've been doing, and check the distance with the focus puller. Work out how to hit your mark, make sure that you're breathing, release any tensions and allow yourself to accept all the crew into your imaginary world. Remind yourself of your circumstances and objectives. Rehearse at the same vocal level as you will play the scene, and let the director see what he will get – but don't expend all your emotional energy before you get to a take.

The director will call another rehearsal. (Very occasionally, a director will rehearse on film, but this is unusual. Often a tricky shot might be rehearsed on video so that the director and DOP can watch a playback.) The director will call 'action' and 'cut' and you may rehearse several times to allow the actors and camera crew to perfect their moves. The director may rethink some of the blocking. When he or she is satisfied, the first AD will call for final checks. This means that the dresser, make-up and hair departments will come up to give you the final once-over; the sound assistant might give your microphone a tweak; continuity, dialogue and any other departments involved in your performance will come up with any last thoughts. The director might come too, for a final word. Then the first AD will call you back into position and say, 'Shooting next time.' The red light will be put on outside the studio to stop people from walking in and the bell will ring once.

You'll hear the words, 'Camera rolling' – 'Sound speed' – 'Mark it' and as the clapper assistant claps the board and announces the shot and take number, focus on where your character is coming from and on releasing any tensions. Take your mind to the story of the scene and to the situation your character has just left. As you hear 'Action', block out everything but the scene. Allow the breath to drop in and then just focus on your objective. On a parallel plane, your invisible technical guide makes sure you are in the right spot at the right time, using the correct hand for the action and remembering your moves while you never miss a heartbeat of the character. Soon you'll hear 'Cut'. Allow one more breath and complete your thought or action before you stop – try to sense when the camera stops rolling.

Sometimes the first take feels the best and it can be disheartening to go again. Directors very, very rarely rely on one take. There are so many other ingredients in the scene, such as background action, camera moves, sound quality and continuity details, that it is very unusual for them to all come together at once. Sometimes, in the final cut, they *will* use the first take – but be prepared to go again and again. To do twenty or thirty takes is not that unusual, especially in a complicated scene with a lot of extras or special effects. (It is rumoured that some directors buy drinks all round if it goes above fifty!) Don't try to reproduce your last performance but return to your original impulses each time. Each take has to feel like the first and have a fresh new energy and yet be done within the same parameters as the last. If you lose your lines, never 'cut' yourself – pick it up and continue. The director might be able to use part of the scene.

Lights may need resetting, the camera may need reloading or the sound department may have a problem. Try to keep your focus. If it's a long break, then drink some water and chat to the other actors if this doesn't distract you. If you need to pop out to the loo, remember to tell the third assistant where you're going. Never think problems are your fault. The director would speak to you if he/she wanted you to change anything.

Eventually you will hear the words, 'Check the gate'. This means that the camera operator checks that there was no hair (or fleck of emulsion) on the lens. When the lens has been checked – 'Gate clear' – that shot will have been completed. The red light will go off and the bell will sound twice. But don't run away: the continuity, hair, make-up, wardrobe and props departments all want to take pictures for their records.

And that's not the end of the scene, only of the wide shot or master shot. You will now repeat it in mid-shot and close-ups, or two-shots and singles and many other possible ways. If you have a major role, it may be worth finding out from the script supervisor which takes the director has chosen. It gives you a guide as to which one of your subtle variations to build on for the rest of the scene.

At last you will hear the first assistant say, 'Moving on,' and you will be on to the next scene or on your way home if the next scene doesn't involve you. (There is usually only time for a few scenes to be done in one day.)

At some point you will stop for lunch. Your dresser will try to make you a little more comfortable and protect your costume. If you are in the studio, you will be eating in the canteen. If you are on location, there will be an outside catering van and you'll line up to collect your food, which you will eat in a bus or in your trailer. Sometimes someone will offer to collect your food for you, depending on your status, hair and weather needs or state of undress. You will have to come back from lunch a little early to have hair and make-up repaired so that the film can start again on time.

After lunch, try to take a few moments to focus again, to look at the new scene coming up and to check your cards. Then relax and conserve that energy. Filming will continue all day and often into the evening. The crew will usually be working a twelve-hour day which means if you started filming at eight, you won't finish till eight! Unless you've got shorter hours built into your contract, you may well have come in earlier than that for make-up and have to travel at the end of the day. (Most studios are a good hour away from central London – more on a Friday night in rush hour.)

Finally you'll hear the magic words, 'It's a wrap.' But don't leave till you've seen the second assistant. He will arrange your journey home, give you a call sheet for the next day and see you off the premises. And then you're free to eat, drink and get as much sleep as you can until you're picked up again at 5.30 a.m.!

ON LOCATION

Location shooting is usually much more fun than the studio but can be harder physically. You'll be given a trailer to rest in, which is generally pretty comfortable and, if you're the lead, then it's very luxurious indeed, with television, music centre and fridge. On far-flung foreign locations, films usually bring a doctor as well as a nurse and great care is taken to give you all the right jabs and medical advice. When you arrive, you'll be given a folder with local information and tips. The location department is usually wonderful at this and it will even include recommended restaurants and details of where everyone is staying. Being on location is usually a pretty social affair and actors and crew are given to mass attendance at the local disco on a Saturday night.

One marvellous thing about being on location is that you see a part of the world in great depth. You may be in the same spot for days on end watching the light move, clouds form and the sky change colour. Even the wildlife starts to accept you. Often a film shoots in a hidden location, or in a city building that is shut to the public. So you might find yourself in the middle of a jungle in Cambodia or the desert in Morocco, on a hill in rainy Ireland or alone with high art in a church in Venice.

It's also a great extra boost to your character work as you'll probably be in a location that has some connection to your character, so it's worth trying to spend some time alone in the environment. For example, if it's a period film then try to walk the streets and go into the old buildings at night when there aren't many tourists (check it's safe first). Imagine yourself dressed as your character and give yourself a reason for being there – an errand, a visit, a liaison. Or do something physical that's right for the character – whittle a stick, run barefoot on the sand, swim in the sea or hunt rabbits. If you have no time off at all, then you can achieve a lot simply by walking a few feet away from your trailer dressed in your character's clothes, staring at the landscape and thinking the character's thoughts. Or writing the character's journal or painting a picture during the long breaks.

On long shoots, radios, portable music, kettles, books and a phone card for cheaper calls home make life easier. If it's going to be cold, add a pashmina for putting on the bed and maybe a hot-water bottle!

If you're shooting somewhere very hot, remember to keep drinking water. When it's very humid or very dry the nurse will make up rehydration drinks – these are well worth taking on a regular basis. Sometimes you don't realise how dehydrated you are until you start to feel headachy and dizzy. The nurse will also be carrying supplies of sunscreen and mosquito repellent if you've forgotten your own. Take a battery-operated fan. Wear sunglasses so that you don't get little lines round the eyes from squinting all day. Don't forget your swimsuit – though the make-up department won't thank you if you get a tan halfway through the film. Some actors carry an umbrella all day to stop themselves from changing colour!

NIGHT FILMING AND OTHER JOYS

Night filming really does mean that – usually from about 6 p.m. to 6 a.m. If you are on location it can get very cold. If you are the star, they will keep you as warm, fed and rested as they can. If, however, you're a mere mortal, you may be fending for yourself along with the rest of the crew. The make-up department often have jolly little disposable hand-warmers. But bring along lots of your own wraps. Eat when it is offered as you can find yourself very hungry at three in the morning, although you'll usually find hot soup available most of the night. Actually it can be rather wonderful out in a wilderness, having a barbecue, seeing the stars and the dawn.

HAZARDS

Filming can bring you close to all sorts of interesting hazards. Some of them can be more hazardous than you imagined. In Cambodia, on *Lara*

Croft: Tomb Raider we were in a wild area that had been cleared of bandits but not completely of landmines. We were on a riverbank that was safe but we were instructed to stay on the designated paths and clearings. But, like an idiot, I was constantly ploughing across muddy banks, keeping out of the camera's way. Later we were told that the area had been properly checked only where the main action was happening and that landmines can be so tiny these days that they are hard to find. That sobering thought prompted us to do fund-raising for the essential work of mine clearance.

In South Africa, for *I Dreamed of Africa*, we were filming scenes that involved snakes. As the actors had to handle them, these were the strictly non-venomous kind – no problem. What we didn't realise though, was that the snakes on these far-flung game reserves were coming out of hibernation. The props and greens departments were coming in early each morning and clearing twice as many fully poisonous snakes from the set as the ones on the pay roll.

More usually, you are coping with studios full of smoke or fields full of mosquitoes, ants and gnats. Expect rain, more rain and mud. Or a heatwave. Always pack a waterproof, a woolly, a sun-hat, and boots! You may be wet, cold or suffering from vertigo but your only defence in the end is to see it through the character's eyes. When you stop filming, you can be a wimp and run to your trailer!

HOME MOVIES

With the advent of digital cameras, you can make a film nowadays for not much more money than putting on a theatre show in the fringe – and like the fringe, you need to be prepared to lose it all. But if you can find a keen crew, it is possible to direct or act in your own movie.

The difficulty is distributing it later. There are many film festivals and organisations like the British Academy of Film and Television Arts and the European Film Academy who hold awards each year and some of these – like Sundance (www.sundance.org) and Moondance (www.moondancefilmfestival.com) in America and Raindance held every autumn in London (www.raindance.co.uk) – have helped to launch small budget movies successfully. But it's a continual struggle for independent film-makers to reach an audience. At worst, though, you'd at least have a show reel!

The Guerrilla Film-Makers Handbook has fascinating case studies of movies made on small amounts of cash and loads of energy and belief. *Rebel Without a Crew* by Robert Rodriguez is the story of the successful Hollywood director who made *El Mariachi* with one camera, no actors and around 7,000 dollars.

So if you're brave and passionate about film, go for it. Make your own!

PART FIVE
SUMMING IT ALL UP

Life in the film business happens at very short notice. One minute you're wondering whether you ought to take the dog for a walk or pay the bills, and the next minute the phone rings. You may be suddenly called for a casting, get your first few lines or be offered the leading role in the next Mike Leigh film. I once came home from South Africa rather thankfully after too long a shoot, picked up a phone message and found myself in North Africa for the following breakfast. As an actor, your life can change almost as instantaneously. So however long you've been out of work you need to stay prepared.

They say there are no small parts, just small paychecks! You can find something rewarding in everything you do. Work out how you slot into the film. Very small parts are usually more about *what* the character does than *why* they do it. That's fine – you just need to play your objective and actions really strongly. But it will still be worthwhile to research in depth – and good practice for your next, bigger role.

Filming can be a demanding business emotionally and physically. Work to your utmost ability but remember, there is a life outside as well. Tempers get frayed because everyone is tired, everyone has a job to do and everyone *cares*. There is never enough time and the director is always fighting the clock, so people can't always see your point of view or understand what's holding you up. Emotions can run high and yours are nearer the surface. Because actors spend their lives allowing themselves to be vulnerable, thin-skinned and aware of every nuance of subtext, they are bound to be hurt more easily. On a long film you'll probably want to cry at least once. Accept it as part of the process – the wrap party will always arrive.

Film is an unfathomable business. Orson Welles' all-time classic *Citizen Kane* – which came No.1 in *Time Out's* film centenary poll (1995) and was the top choice for critics and directors in the British Film Institute's *Sight and Sound* magazine's 2002 global poll (as it has been for the last five decades!) – nearly got destroyed by the studios under pressure from the newspaper magnate William Randolph Hearst, and failed miserably at the box office on its release. Ronald Reagan was originally going to play Humphrey Bogart's part in *Casablanca*. Would he have bothered with politics if he had, or would we have forgotten the film? Michael Cimino seemed to have everything going for him on *Heaven's Gate* – great cinematographer, great cast – but the budget crept up from $12 million to $36 million (a lot of money then). And the result led a New York Times critic to wonder whether Cimino had sold his soul to the devil to make *The Deer Hunter* and the devil had just come round to collect. Yet, who knows, one day the film may be re-evaluated.

The Blair Witch Project was made on an original budget of $22 thousand in an eight-day shoot and has made over $40 million to date. *Plan 9 from Outer Space* directed by Ed Wood, another low-budget movie, turned out so jaw-droppingly awful that it has become a cult film. It has no coherence, the special effects are risible, the script is excruciating and the lead actor died in the middle of shooting. These things are truly out of the actor's control!

You can never tell if a film will be successful. Sometimes the ones that you believed in most and had the best time making, turn out to be box-office failures and sometimes artistic failures too. Then a film that the crew predict will fail horribly, is hell to work on and stretches you to extremes, turns into a miraculous work of art that endures for decades. So just give of your best always – it's all you can do. And enjoy it.

Film is a powerful medium. At the moment it is being used primarily for entertainment but at other times in history it has been a strong political tool. Or the politicians have destroyed the films and silenced the film-makers. Film has been used for propaganda, for social messages and to provoke awareness of the horrors of the world we live in. It can show every aspect of the human spirit – good, evil, simple and at its most complex. John Boorman says, 'it is a quest for truths'.

The great thing about film, unlike ephemeral theatre, is its ability to survive into the future. Because of this, we can watch the art of Eleonora Duse, Buster Keaton, Jean-Louis Barrault and Louise Brooks. Many wonderful stage actors are never known outside their own country and are forgotten as their audiences move on. But the ones caught on film like Edith Evans, Noel Coward, John Gielgud, Alec Guinness, Ralph Richardson, Peggy Ashcroft, Richard Burton, John, Lionel and Ethel Barrymore will live on far into the future. This can also be an embarrassment if you are less than happy with your work as it can turn up to haunt you when you'd rather it didn't. Still, you can always hide behind the sofa!

To be a successful film actor, you need to combine the actor's awareness of techniques – your craft – with driving the needs of the character – the art.

Your craft will help you to assess the right energy for the framing and keep tensions away from your face, to remember your continuity, adjust your voice level and cope with ADR, and to find the same energy to repeat take after take and to give your character a coherent journey through a fragmented topsy-turvy course.

Your art consists in finding specific answers to those crucial questions – who am I, where am I, what do I want and how do I get it? In seeing the world through your character's eyes and thinking their thoughts, in knowing your objectives and driving your character's actions, so you stay alive in every second of screen time. By absorbing all you can about art, music and life, so that you give it all you are.

By using the improvisations, sense memory work and emergency triggers, you can make your inner life every bit as real as the world of the film set in which you can exist at one and the same time. In the words of Robert Donat, 'When that relentless eye goggles at us in close-up we may be sure of one thing – we must deliver up to it the finest work of which we are capable; nothing but the truth will do.'

Writing about acting is as slippery as quicksilver and sometimes I may have contradicted myself or missed the perfect words to describe the work. Acting, like life, is contradictory, elusive and personal. Different people in different films need different approaches at different times. This is what I believe at this moment – don't hold me to it, I may change my mind. All I can be sure of is this:

No word is ever spoken without the impulse to speak it. No movement is ever made without the need to make it.

PART SIX
RESOURCES

EXTRA EXERCISES

Exercises are very hard to follow from a book, so I suggest that you read the relaxation and breathing work into a tape-recorder and play it back while you do the exercises, pausing it when necessary. Eventually you will remember the ones that work best for you. (The rhythmic breathing exercises, which are drawn very loosely from the work of the Danish voice therapist, Svend Smith, can be enormously helpful in cases of vocal nodules and other functional voice disorders.)

A VOICE WORKOUT

This is not about voice projection but about giving you a natural relaxed sound that will carry your thoughts and feelings freely, find your normal pitch level and release tensions.

- Lie down in the 'Alexander' position.
- Tense and release muscles: toes, legs, stomach, hands, shoulders, neck, tongue.
- On the in-breath let your abdominal muscles relax and your stomach release out away from you, towards the ceiling, for a count of three. (Don't add any extra fill in the upper chest.)
- In three energetic pulses, with the middle beat the strongest, flatten your stomach towards the floor – 'Shh' – 'Shh' – 'Shh', trying to use up all your breath. (Don't breathe out at the end – it doesn't matter if you haven't used up all your spare breath. You can refill at any point.)
- Make sure your stomach is flattening towards your spine as you make the sound, not bulging outwards. (If you imagine your abdomen as a ball of air, you are starting from the bottom of the ball, scooping up, not at the top of the ball pushing down. The push down will put a lot of pressure on your larynx and collapse your upper chest.) If in doubt just go back to your relaxed, resting breath and your body will show you the natural breathing pattern.
- Fill – 2 – 3.
- 'Shh' – 'Shh' – 'Shh'.
- Repeat six times then do it on 'Zzz'.
- Now alternate between 'Shh' and 'Zzz'.

The exercise above encourages recoil and stops you taking a high locking breath. It soothes your larynx and makes your voice sound 'buzzier' and more resonant. You can do it on your side as well – some people find this more comfortable.

- Put a finger a few inches above your mouth.
- Imagine it is a birthday candle that keeps relighting.
- Blow it out with three little puffs (keep neck relaxed).
- Change breath completely to voice and 'bounce' the sound off the imaginary candle like little pebbles of sound – 'Mah' – 'Mah' – 'Mah'.
- Alternate between breath and sound – don't mix the two.
- Now roll on to all fours – hands and knees.
- Come to standing slowly uncurling your back as you go and bringing your head up last. If you feel dizzy, come up slower next time, you may have taken in more oxygen than you're used to. Don't worry, the feeling will pass.
- Now you are standing. Check your feet are taking your weight evenly and your neck is lengthening away from your back.
- Windmill your arms backwards, six times each, letting the weight of your arms take them round and allowing your shoulders to drop on the last swing.
- Lift your shoulders to your ears and let them drop.
- Put the palms of both hands on your cheekbones and gradually draw them down past your chin, releasing your jaw and allowing your mouth to open.
- Drop your head and gently roll it in a half-circle, just as far as your shoulder in each direction, then balance it upright again.
- Now gently stretch your neck, bringing your ear towards your shoulder for a few moments in each direction and then balance your head on top of your spine.
- Stand with one foot in front of the other. Put one hand on the stomach and one on the upper chest. Breathe in as you rock forward and feel the stomach release *out* for the incoming breath. Rock back on 'Shh' – 'Shh' – 'Shh' pulling the stomach *in*. Don't let your upper chest rise on the in-breath or collapse on the out-breath. Repeat 10 times.
- Gently massage your face, particularly the hinge muscles of your jaw and your mouth area.
- Blow out like a horse, making your lips vibrate loosely.
- If you have no back problems, hang over again, letting your neck go completely so that you are like a rag doll from the waist up.
- Shake your shoulders (not your head) as you come up, shaking out a sustained 'Maah', letting your head come up last.

- Hold your hands out in front of you and move them up and down vigorously, shaking out a sound on 'Maah'.
- Wiggle your hips and bum and shake out a sound on 'Maah'.
- Put your hand on your head and hum so you feel your lips vibrating and vibrations on your hand.
- Put your fingers on your mouth – feel the vibrations – thump your chest lightly like Tarzan on 'Maah' – wobble your belly with your hand on 'Maah'.
- Put your hands over your ears, breathe in and out through an open mouth, hearing the breath and then making it silent, feeling your throat open and the breath coming deeply into the abdomen.
- Go up and down your range gently on 'Ng' (as in ring).
- Chew vigorously for 10 seconds with mouth open. Chew vigorously for 10 seconds with mouth closed.
- Pin your top lip up with your fingers, like a rabbit – count aloud to 10. Hang your tongue out – count to 10. Count to 10 like a ventriloquist, trying not to move your lips. Now count normally – feel the freedom.
- Put the knuckle of your forefinger in your mouth pressing lightly into the ridge of gum above your top teeth (where you make your 't's and 'd's). Count aloud to 5. Take your knuckle out and count again – send the sound to where you feel your knuckle has been pressing, making it 'buzz'.
- With your mouth open, push your tongue gently against your bottom teeth and push the middle out. Touch the outsides of your top and bottom lips as fast as you can with your tongue. Say 'la la la' as fast as you can. (You can do this to a tune like the 'Can Can').
- Go through some unvoiced and voiced consonants as fast as you can (keeping your neck free and relaxed) p/b, t/d/, k/g, f/v, s/z. (Make 't' in the same place as 'd' – not against your front teeth – and don't slide the tongue forward, drop it down briskly, or your voice will acquire extra sibilance.)
- Put one hand on your lower abdomen. Count 'one' out loud, feeling stomach muscles contracting inwards.
- Release stomach back out into your hand letting breath come in through your open mouth without effort.
- 'One, two'.
- Breath dropping back in –
- 'One, two, three'.
- Continue, adding one number at a time to a count of 10, letting the breath drop back in each time before you speak.

- Physically throw some words like a ball. Release the word at the end of the throw.

After a long day's work do a cool down:

COOL DOWN
- Sip some lukewarm water.
- Yawn gently and sigh.
- Hum a tune gently.
- Go up and down your range quietly on 'Ng'.
- Imagine a basket of air on your head. Drop your head gently and let the air 'fall out' of your mouth. Repeat six times. (This will soothe any tiredness in your vocal folds.)

VOCAL HEALTH
- Drink at least six glasses of water or juice a day. Don't get dehydrated. Film sets are often very hot. You need the mucous membranes in the larynx working freely. Pee pale!
- Steam reaches the larynx and soothes tired muscles. Use steam rooms, hot baths, electric steamers, or a towel over a basin of hot water.
- Avoid late, spicy food: this can cause acid reflux in the night and you will wake with a sore throat. (If it gets better through the day, suspect acid reflux. If you wake fine and develop a sore throat later, suspect voice use. But if it continues, see a doctor.)
- Don't clear your throat as a habit. It will abrade your vocal folds and cause soreness.
- Watch hard vocal attack on vowels. Aim for a smooth, flowing delivery. Allow consonant endings to link into vowels.
- Avoid a breathy tone if you have to project – you will lose your voice.
- Warm up and cool down. Just like the gym, it's important to prepare the muscles before use and to allow them to stretch out afterwards to avoid trauma.
- Use large muscles to take strain. Don't push with your throat muscles to shout, use the strong support muscles of the body. Do your voice workout.
- If you have a sore throat, lose the upper range of your voice or sound husky for more than a month, see a specialist. You may have developed a soft nodule, like a corn, on one of your vocal folds. This is not dangerous and can be eradicated by voice therapy but it will get in your way as a performer.

* * *

SENSE MEMORIES

- Imagine a bowl in front of you. Put your fingers in it. They are in warm water.
- Wiggle your fingers in the clean water. Gradually it becomes thicker and stickier – it is treacle – molasses. It gets stickier and stickier until it's chewing gum that you have to keep pulling from one finger to another.
- Now it's drying out, falling off your fingers, turning into feathers – soft and warm. They get moister and send up the scent of summer – they've become rose petals that you're gently crushing with your fingers.
- These get colder and colder and you realise they're now snowflakes – your fingers are icy as you run them through the snow. Then just as it starts to feel unbearable, you realise the bowl is now full of silver sand. Fine, cool sand that trickles through your fingers reminding you of exotic beaches.
- Now it's cold seawater.
- Finally the bowl is full, once more, with clear warm water.
- You lift out your hands and dry them on a rough, white towel. The bowl and the towel disappear and you are back to the present.
- Take off your shoes and socks. Shut your eyes. Feel the surface under your feet. Is it soft? Hard? Cold? Warm? Smooth? Rough? Imagine your feet are on a soft sand beach. As you walk, feel the sand between your toes.
- Change the sand to layers of cool rose petals – smell the perfume as you bruise them. Tread grapes into wine, walk through snow, stand on warm tiles, splash in seawater – anything you can imagine.
- Change gravity: walk on the moon. Let your whole body become involved – feel yourself as weightless. Explore a planet where your legs turn to lead.
- Walk through water, through treacle or molasses, through thick fog, through mountain air.
- Try calling through all these different atmospheres.

CHARACTER

- Close your eyes and see yourself as your character standing in front of you – how you dress – how you stand. Take a large pace forwards and step into the character. Open your eyes and see the world from your character's POV.
- Lie on the floor and pretend you are asleep as in your own bed this morning. Act out the first five minutes of what you actually did, being

as accurate as you can and speaking aloud the thoughts that you had at the time.

- Now wake up in your character's bed. Get up and dress in the character's clothes. Plan the day – think what you want. Rehearse what you'll say to the other characters in your life. Think what stands in your way. How will you act to get what you want? Speak your thoughts out loud.

SECONDARY CENTRES

As well as your true centre, you may also find a secondary centre from where the character drives energy. Cyrano de Bergerac has an obvious secondary centre – his nose. Joan of Arc may have two – her feet (earth) and above her head (spirituality). A washerwoman could focus on her strong arms, a belly dancer on her hips. You may feel you have a secondary centre yourself. The actor, Burgess Meredith, said that he sent his energy from the centre of his forehead. You need only to throw a thought in the direction of your secondary centre to feel you are led by it in a deep hidden way. This work has to be immensely subtle for the camera.

CHANGING PATTERNS

The movement teacher Rudolph Laban categorised human activity into what he called the eight efforts of movement. These were *glide*, *float*, *dab*, *flick*, *wring*, *slash*, *thrust* and *press*. Each effort has three qualities. It is either *sustained* or *sudden*, *light* or *heavy* and *directional* or *non-directional*.

Sustained means that, until you decide to stop, the movement is continuous. *Sudden* means that the movement or series of movements are sharp and sudden, coming to an abrupt halt. *Light* movements feel 'weightless' and require little force. *Heavy* movements require stronger force and weight. You may be moving towards a fixed point – *directional* – or flexible and constantly moving direction – *non-directional*.

You can use this very simplified version of his system to explore different rhythms, both external and internal, and to increase your own range. These movements can be coupled with text to change vocal patterns as well. Let's take each effort in turn:

- *Gliding* is sustained, light and directional – skating is obviously gliding, so is ironing or walking with graceful flowing movements.
- *Floating* is sustained, light and non-directional – a feather blown by the wind has no control over which direction to go, it floats gently at the wind's will.

- *Dabbing* is sudden, light and directional – a chicken 'dabs' with its beak, a finger is 'dabbed' at someone in admonition, or tapped with boredom.
- *Flicking* is sudden, light and non-directional – a girl flicks her long hair, Parisians habitually shrug with a flicking gesture of their hands, you flick crumbs off the table.
- *Wringing* is sustained, heavy and non-directional – you wring out clothes or wring your hands in distress.
- *Slashing* is sudden, heavy and non-directional – you slash grass with a scythe, slash with a sword or with your hand to signal 'cut'.
- *Thrusting* is sudden, heavy and directional – you thrust when you throw a punch, attack with a fencing foil, kick or thump your hand on the table.
- *Pressing* is sustained, heavy and directional – a wrestler presses someone to the floor, you press your rolling pin on to the pastry, you press your hands together.

Efforts can be actual and physical, like those described above, or they can be psychological and internalised. They can also be reflected by our speech patterns. Blanche DuBois, from *A Streetcar Named Desire*, *floats* through life without direction, 'relying on the kindness of strangers'. A salesman will *press* you to buy a product; you yell, 'No!' on *thrust* when you really mean it or, 'No, No, No' on *slash* when you're out of control. Elegant socialites *glide* through the social ritual of a cocktail party and people full of guilt *wring* their way through self-recrimination. You can speak in a flowing, *gliding* way through the sentence, *dab* at the words in a more staccato rhythm or *flick* them away nonchalantly.

- Start by finding the physical movement at its most extreme. Then add text, letting your voice follow the patterns and energy of the movement. Now bury it – make it really subtle.

You may find some movements and vocal choices more comfortable than others and, through this work, you can start identifying your own patterns of effort. If you are a *dabber* and are playing in a period movie, then *gliding* can help you find the flow of the character. If you find it hard to get angry or have power, then using *thrust* or *press* can release a new more forceful energy.

THE ZOO
A time-honoured way of finding new energies and rhythms is through animal work.

- Lie on the floor, shut your eyes and clear your thoughts. Choose an animal, bird or reptile that you feel is a long way from your physical or psychological rhythms. In your own time, open your eyes and try to see the world through the eyes of your animal. Don't try to appear like the animal from the outside but decide what the animal wants.
- Now start to move around, pursuing that objective, finding sounds for your animal (these movements and sounds don't have to be ones that the animal would really use, but are governed by your needs as the animal).
- Gradually, you can learn to stand on your feet, becoming a little more human and burying the animal inside you.
- Now you can gradually acquire the use of speech. At this point, you are looking more and more human and I would think, if I met you at a cocktail party, that you were. But really it is your animal that still governs your objectives and actions and has influenced your body tempo and patterns. (These changes are now very subtle.)
- Now you are comfortable with your animal, find a way to distil the work into one big movement and one phrase that embody the essence of the animal (like the psychological gesture). Repeat these words and this movement together, over and over, till you feel you 'inhabit' your animal.
- Now revert to being completely human – with a little of the animal's essence buried deep inside you.
- Next, choose another creature that seems diametrically opposed to the one that you first worked on and do the exercise again.

Which one was actually harder for you and further from your own patterns? You might have been surprised to find that it was the second animal, even though you chose the creature you felt was furthest away from you the first time. Instinctively, we often make choices that are easy to us, even when we don't mean to or because we don't really understand our own habitual physicality.

Animals are a very good way to access a character that seems far from your own persona. If you need to find sexuality, be a cat or a tiger. If you have to play strong, try a mountain lion or a wolf. If clumsy, a bear or a puppy. If secret and unpredictable, a snake. If aloof and private, an eagle.

The possibilities are endless. Don't forget that by the time you come to film, your animal will have to be buried really deeply within you – we might just catch a glimmer from the depths of your eyes, the way you toss your hair or the set of your shoulders. The work is part of your character research rather than anything you overtly show us.

MAGIC

- Work with a partner. Take their arm closely and ask them to close their eyes. Secretly decide on a particular point in the room. Now 'think' them to it. Don't overtly guide them in any way. Allow them to stop, start and change direction. Magically they will eventually go to your chosen point or even pick an item up from a table (I did this work, as an actor, with a Russian theatre director, and eventually I even played the right note on a piano). It may be that there are subliminal signals coming from your body contact without you realising it. Even if it's not telepathy, this exercise is attuning and sensitising you to your partner and you are sending out strong objectives, so it's great preparation for a scene. Swap over and try again.

KAFKA LAND

This work stops you preparing and keeps you open to instant change:

- Go to sleep and wake up somewhere you're not expecting. You went to sleep in a hotel room and you wake in a cell. You went to bed at home and woke up on the edge of a cliff.
- Open the door to your flat and find yourself somewhere else – a desert, a night-club, a jungle, a mirrored cube. (Disasters, like earthquakes, fires or aeroplanes falling out of the sky, are the juxtaposition of normality and a terrible new reality that arrives instantly.)
- Look in the mirror and see someone you don't recognise. (Like the bathroom mirror when, in the middle of a heavy party, you peer into your own eyes and think 'who are you?') This can be disorienting, so end by seeing yourself again.

WORDS, WORDS, WORDS ...

- Take a line of text and do it as if you were ... at a football game, a musical instrument, a medieval monk in a monastery, a schoolchild having a midnight feast, incanting a spell, in a modern opera, doing mime, in a circus, in a horror film, an aviary of birds, a storm, etc., etc.
- Say your lines in mad gibberish allowing yourself to feel free and physical. Then go back to the real lines.
- Sing your text then go back to speaking.
- Paint a picture while you say your lines.
- Try some text against different kinds of music. Dance your lines.

- If you are using classic text or have a long speech, mark your script with breathing places (thought changes). Prop it where you can see it, and with a hand on your stomach to check, make sure you are really letting the breath drop in on the breathing marks, and only there – no snatched breaths.
- If the text feels 'flat', walk around touching the floor or a wall on each important word. Or pick up an object on each word that you need to stress.
- Lie on your back and just whisper your words really slowly, allowing the pictures to form in your head.
- Do some improvised scenes without subtext where speaking the words is difficult – like telling someone you're leaving them, that their illness is incurable, that you're pregnant, that you've got Aids. Don't dodge the truth.
- Pick a scene, like the one from *Victory*, and speak your chosen subtext aloud before you speak the written lines. Then speak the lines and think the subtext. Then do them off instinct, trusting the previous work.

A FINAL WORD FROM QUENTIN TARANTINO ...

In *Reservoir Dogs,* Tarantino has the cop Holdaway (Randy Brooks) tell his undercover colleague Freddy, aka Mr Orange (Tim Roth), that 'to do this job you got to be a great actor. You got to be naturalistic. You got to be naturalistic as hell. If you ain't a great actor you're a bad actor, and bad acting is bullshit in this job'. And then proceeds to give him the following acting lesson:

> *Now the things you hafta remember are the details. It's the details that sell your story. Now your story takes place in a men's room. So you gotta know the details about that men's room. You gotta know if they got paper towels or a blower to dry your hands. You gotta know if the stalls got doors or not. You gotta know if they got liquid soap or that pink granulated powder shit. If they got hot water or not. If it stinks. If some nasty motherfucker sprayed diarrhea all over one of the bowls. You gotta know every damn thing there is to know about that commode. And the people in your story, you gotta know the details about them, too. Anybody can tell who did what to whom. But in real life, when people tell a story, they try to recreate the event in the other person's mind. Now what you gotta do is take all them details and make 'em your own. This story's gotta be about you, and how you perceived the events that took place. And the way you make it your own is you just gotta keep sayin' it and sayin' it and sayin' it and sayin' it and sayin' it.*

HONEY WAGONS AND DOLLIES – USEFUL JARGON

- Abby Singer – penultimate shot of the day (so called after a first assistant who always called for last shot of the day, but never won).
- Above-the-line – all expenses film incurs before shooting starts: director's, producer's, star's salaries, etc.
- Aces and Deuces – 1000 and 2000 watt lights.
- Action – (1) director's command to start actors' action, (2) any activity in shot, (3) acting terminology – how you get what you want.
- Ad lib – words that aren't scripted.
- AD – assistant director.
- ADR – automatic (or automated) dialogue replacement (see lip-syncing, looping, post-syncing), replacing original dialogue in post-production.
- Aerial shot – very high-angle view from helicopter, plane, etc.
- Ambience – sound of atmospheric conditions of location or studio.
- AP – associate producer.
- Armourers – department handling all guns and firearms.
- Aspect ratio – the proportions of width to height of the finished film.
- Atmos – (1) atmosphere recorded to even out sound track, (2) smoke used as a lighting effect.
- Audition – meeting casting director and/or director for role in film.
- Avid – industry standard non-linear (digital) editing system.
- Background action – (1) command for extras to start prepared business, (2) action in background of shot.
- Back light – lights the back of the actor.
- Back lot – area with outdoor sets on studio premises.
- Barn doors – four metal flaps attached to front of light to cut out light spill.
- Beat – acting terminology for a change to an objective or action.
- Bell – sounds one long ring for silence on shooting and two short rings for all-clear.
- Below-the-line – all expenses incurred by the production during shooting.
- Best boy – one of the main electricians, first assistant to the gaffer.
- Bit-part – small role, usually one scene.
- BG – background.

- Blimp – soundproof cover fixed over camera to absorb running noise.
- Blocking – preparation of actors' moves and positions for scene to be shot, often done with director and key crew only.
- Blue screen – large blue screen that you act in front of. Anything blue disappears so that computer graphics or backgrounds can be added later.
- Body double – doubles up for part of actor's body when face is out of shot.
- Boom – telescopic pole to which microphone is attached.
- Breakaway – a prop specially designed to break or shatter.
- Breakdown – (1) pre-shooting script with everything needed for shooting, (2) detailed list and description of roles.
- Brutes – and blondes, redheads, inkydinks, HMIs, kinos – different lights some of which are now past history.
- Business – use of props and prepared reactions.
- Buzz track – sound recording of atmosphere.
- Call – time you are due on set or in make-up.
- Call back – follow-up audition.
- Call sheet – issued at the end of each day's shooting to give information on times, location and any other essential information to get artists and crew to set on time next day.
- Cameo role – closely resembles a bit-part but done by a famous actor (coined by producer Mike Todd on *Around the World in Eighty Days*).
- Camera angle – viewpoint chosen by director or DOP to photograph a subject.
- Camera reloading – camera needs to load more film to continue filming.
- Camera left – the actor must move to his/her right (stage right), left as seen by the camera.
- Camera right – the actor must move to his/her left (stage left), right as seen by the camera.
- Camera running/rolling – camera is filming.
- Camera tape – inch-wide tape used for actor's marks.
- Cans – headphones.
- CGI – computer-generated imaging – computer graphics used to add things, subtract things or magically change environments in post-production.
- Chaperones – all under 16s need chaperones on set (under 18 in USA).
- Character actor – ambiguous term (aren't all parts characters?) taken to mean an actor in a non-romantic supporting role.

- Cheat it – a direction to perform an action or take an eye-line that doesn't seem 'truthful' to the actor but looks fine on the camera.
- Check the gate – checking the section of camera where the film moves mechanically through the film aperture for hair or dust.
- Cherry picker – high crane used for high-level camera shots or holding lights.
- Chippie – a carpenter in England, but be careful in the USA as it means something different (a British producer who called for some chippies while shooting in the States was surprised to find some cheerful hookers who were none too hot at woodwork!).
- Clapperboard – (Clapstick: American) – square board with name of production, director and DOP's names, date, interior or exterior, scene (American), shot and take number. Top end, with diagonal black and white lines, lifts and comes down with a clap to mark start of scene to sync sound for editing. Can be digital with timecode. (*See* slate)
- Clapperloader – member of camera crew who loads camera and operates clapperboard.
- Clean – soundtrack with no sound problems and dialogue clear. 'Clean single': only one person on shot.
- Clear the eye-lines/Clear the sight lines – clear everything or everyone away from what the character or the camera will see.
- Closed set – only essential crew allowed, often used for sex scenes.
- Cold reading – reading from script without preparation time.
- Commission – (1) percentage an actor pays to agent, (2) arrangement to write a script.
- Cookie/(Gobo) – cut-out pattern placed in front of light to throw patterned shadow.
- Coming in tight – camera is close, subject fills frame.
- Composite – set of photographs for publicity on one sheet.
- Conditioning factor – acting terminology for emotional and physical conditions affecting the character.
- Continuity – the attention to details throughout the shooting that ensures linear continuity through the film.
- Corpse – to laugh while performing.
- Coverage – a variety of shots from different angles that 'cover' a scene – from wide angles to close-ups.
- Crab dolly – dolly with short crane incorporated that has tight enough turning circle to move sideways. (*See* dolly)
- Craft services – the running catering service available all day on set (American).

- Crane shot – shot taken from crane. These days cameras can be operated remotely.
- Crossing the line – this is to do with eye-lines. The director has to make sure the camera is placed so that the characters appear to be looking at each other. If the camera is set on the wrong side of the imaginary line of axis between them, the visual geography won't make sense.
- Crowd shot – shot of background artists.
- CU – close-up.
- Cue – signal, line or move that precedes your line or action.
- Cut – (1) director ends camera action, (2) film edit.
- Cutaway – intervening shot used in editing that cuts away from main action of scene.
- Cutting room – where the editors work.
- Cutting-room floor – as in 'ending up on the cutting-room floor'. When the film is edited, some of your precious screen moments are discarded and fall to the cutting-room floor. These days it's often a virtual floor as film is edited digitally.
- Cyclorama/(Cyc) – smooth curved screen at the back of the set, lit for daylight effect.
- Dailies – printed takes of yesterday's shoot (American). (*See* rushes)
- Day for night – film shot during daylight but adjusted later to look like night. (French – 'La Nuit Américaine', as in the wonderful film by Truffaut.)
- Deep focus – foreground and background in focus.
- Depth of field – distance between nearest thing in focus and furthest thing in focus.
- DFI – change of plan: 'different f***ing instruction', or as joked by the director, 'director's a f***ing idiot'.
- Diffusion – (1) filter on camera for soft focus, (2) material or mesh that softens light (also gauze, scrim, spun).
- Dirty single – will have small part of other actor in shot.
- Dolly – (1) cart or platform on wheels carrying the camera, (2) movement of camera on dolly. (*See* crab dolly)
- Dolly grip – grip who moves dolly.
- DOP (DP) – director of photography, cinematographer, lighting cameraman.
- Double – someone who takes the place of a main artist in long shot (usually works with second unit photography).
- Downstage – direction to move forwards towards the camera.
- Dresser – person who helps you dress and stands by on set to adjust your costume.

- Dry – to forget your lines.
- Dry ice – frozen carbon dioxide for low-lying white smoke or vapour effect. (Can suffocate in quantity and pellets extremely cold and can burn bare skin.)
- Dubbing – (1) adding sound effects, music and dialogue in post-production, (2) replacing sound in post-production for other people's original lines.
- Dutch tilt – to tilt camera so that horizon in picture is not parallel.
- ECU – extreme close-up.
- ELS – extreme long shot.
- End board/End slate/Tail slate – clapperboard used at end of take.
- Establishing shot – the first shot of the scene that shows the audience the location or situation, usually long or wide shot.
- EXT. – exterior.
- Extra – crowd artist, background artist.
- Eye-line – the imaginary line from the actor's eye to whoever or whatever he or she is looking at.
- f stops, f numbers – these denote the openness of the lens aperture. The higher the number, the more closed the aperture.
- Fade – gradual transition from normal image on film to complete white or blackout.
- FG – foreground.
- Field of vision – what the camera can see.
- Fill light – light filling in shadows created by the key light.
- Film noir – French term meaning 'dark film', used mainly for 40s American thrillers with contrastive lighting style (has links to German expressionism), e.g. *The Maltese Falcon, Double Indemnity.*
- Fine cut – final or near-final cut of film.
- First – first assistant director.
- First positions – take up your position at the start of the scene for another take.
- First unit – crew with director shooting main action.
- Fix it in post – sort it out during post-production.
- Flag – used to cut out unwanted light spill and to protect camera from light.
- Focus puller – first camera assistant who adjusts focus.
- Foley – additional live sound effects put on in post-production.
- Foley artist – person who puts on live sound effects in post-production.
- Foreground action – action happening in foreground of shot.
- Freeze frame – film edited to give effect of all action stopping.

- From the top – going from the beginning of the take or scene.
- FUCT – failed under constant testing!
- FX – (1) effects, (2) sound effects.
- Gaffer – head of electrics, sometimes called chief sparks.
- Gaffer tape – sticky cloth tape used to repair, hold or stick anything on set.
- Gate – metal channel on camera just behind lens through which single frame is exposed.
- Gate clear – no fleck of emulsion, hair or dust on the gate after the take.
- Gauge – size of film format, e.g. 16mm, 35 mm, 70mm.
- Gels – coloured transparent sheets put in front of lights to change colour.
- Given circumstances – acting terminology for plot and situation of scene.
- Given the green light – studio has approved finance, film is ready to cast and crew.
- Gofer – a runner who 'goes for' things.
- Going again – going for another take.
- Green screen – large green screen that you shoot in front of. Anything green in shot will disappear so that computer graphics or backgrounds can be added later.
- Greens – department in charge of plantings.
- Grips – people who set up and move cranes, dollies, tracks, etc.
- Hair in the gate – a hair, dust or a tiny piece of film emulsion gets caught in the metal channel the film runs through as it's exposed, which means a reshoot as it can scratch the film or show up like a wriggling worm at the edge of the frame. It can also be used as a euphemism for some other problem.
- Hand-held – camera not on dolly but carried by camera operator.
- Hand model – artiste whose hands will be used in shot.
- Hays Code – called after Will H. Hays (president of Motion Picture Producers and Distributors of America 1922–45) who imposed censorship control on the industry.
- Haze – light mist effect.
- Hitting your mark – being in the right position on the mark at the right time to be in focus for the shot, for lighting requirements and so not to block others.
- Honey wagons – mobile toilets used on location. (These are usually fairly civilised but on some locations, the name acquires a nice irony!)
- Idiot board – lines for forgetful actors, written on boards and held up by an assistant.

- In the can – take satisfactorily completed.
- Insert – close-up shot (often shot by second unit) inserted in editing.
- INT. – interior.
- Iris – (1) aperture of camera, (2) contracting or expanding cut-out circular shaped framing used in silent movies.
- Jump cut – cut in finished film that catapults you to an unexpected time or place.
- Key grip – head of camera grips.
- Key light – the brightest light casting main shadows and giving sense of directionality to the scene.
- Lavalier (American) – radio mic (so called after Madame Lavalier in the court of Louis XVIII, renowned for her similar shaped pendulous earrings).
- Lens sizes – the higher the focal length number of the lens, the smaller and more magnified the area photographed; the lower the focal length, the wider the area photographed.
- Light meter – DOP used to measure intensity of light.
- Lip-syncing (Lip-sync) – synchronising dialogue with lip movements in post-production. (See ADR, looping, post-syncing)
- Line of action – imaginary line drawn through the action of a scene allowing the audience to understand the 'geography' of the world they're watching (see crossing the line).
- Line up – getting everything ready for the shot: setting camera positions, focus, lights, etc.
- Location – shooting area away from studio.
- Locked-off camera – camera fixed in position.
- Looping – replacing original dialogue in post-production (American). (See ADR, post-syncing, lip-syncing)
- Loose – loose framing includes a lot of space around the subject.
- Losing the light – it is getting too dark to shoot.
- LS – long shot.
- Macguffin – coined by Hitchcock to mean a detail of plot that helps story action but isn't important in itself, e.g. the gismo that could destroy the world.
- Magic hour – dawn, sunset or on the brink of twilight when there is a particular silver or golden effect to the light.
- Mark – point for the actor to find for shot; can be tape, sandbag or piece of wood.
- Mark it – (1) use clapperboard to put a starting point for synchronising picture and sound in editing or mute board for MOS, (2) block scene without fully acting it.

- Married print – composite print of sound and picture.
- Martini shot – last shot of the day; glass in hand: the next 'shot' is alcoholic!
- Master shot – wide or long shot that sets the main action of a scene.
- MCU – mid-close-up, medium close-up.
- Mise en scène – how the shot is staged and framed.
- MOS – 'mit out sound' (or 'sprache') means to shoot without sound. Probably comes from Erich von Stroheim or Michael Curtiz, famous for fractured English.
- Monitor – television screen on set that shows what film camera sees.
- Motion control rig – computer-controlled equipment for accurate and repeatable camera moves (pan, tilt, track, etc.), used mainly for visual effects work.
- Moving on – going on to the next scene.
- MS – medium shot, mid-shot.
- Mute board – no clap used when marking take; no sound on take.
- Night shoot – usually from about 6 p.m. to 6 a.m.!
- Objective – acting terminology for what you want.
- Off-camera/Off-screen – not in shot.
- Off-lines – shorthand for off-camera lines when cue lines are read off-camera.
- Off-mic – microphone is not in correct position or the actor is not sending lines in the right direction.
- On-camera – subject in shot.
- One for Lloyd's – extra take for insurance in case there turns out to be problem with earlier shot.
- Optical soundtrack – sound exposed on the edge of the film photographically.
- OTS – over the shoulder shot; camera shoots close-up of one actor showing portion of another in shot.
- OTT – over the top: doing too much as in a performance or costume choice.
- Out-take – take not used in final movie.
- Overcranking – the film runs at a faster speed so that the action appears slower – slow-motion effect. (Hearkens back to when film was turned by hand: hand cranked.)
- Overlap – actors don't leave enough space between dialogue when in close-up so shot can't be edited.
- Over the top – acting is exaggerated.
- PA – producer's assistant or production assistant.
- Pan – camera pivots side to side (whip pan/zip pan/swish pan/flash pan: extremely fast pan).

- Per diem – daily allowance given to crew and actors on location.
- Pick up – to reshoot small part of scene.
- Playback – (1) playing back scene just shot, (2) music played during rehearsal or shooting.
- Post-production – everything that happens after the shooting is over.
- Post-syncing – post synchronisation: replacing original dialogue in post-production. (*See* ADR, looping, lip-syncing)
- POV – point of view as seen by a character.
- Practical – prop that actually functions, e.g. household light, telephone that rings, fire that lights.
- Preproduction – everything that happens during setting up the film.
- Print! – director's instruction to print up that take for viewing.
- Print it – order from the director to print a particular take.
- Property master – person in charge of props.
- Props – any items used in shot as decoration or by actors.
- Prosthetics – any artificial bits added to your body or face.
- Psychological gesture – (acting) term coined by Michael Chekhov for gesture that gives external form to inner emotional state.
- Pull-back – dolly shot or zoom that starts in close-up and slowly widens.
- Pyrotechnics – live fire and explosive effects.
- Quiet on set – self-explanatory! Called by first assistant for rehearsals or shooting.
- Radio mic – small wireless microphone hidden somewhere on you.
- Reaction shot – close-up of actor listening or reacting.
- Red – red light outside studio showing shooting in progress.
- Reflectors – polystyrene or shiny boards used to reflect back natural or artificial light.
- Rehearsal – final try-out for actors, camera and sound before the take.
- Rehearse on film – some directors like to shoot straight away rather than rehearsing first in case the action can't be repeated, e.g. working with children, animals or fading light.
- Residual – fee paid to actor for a rebroadcast of film, commercial or TV.
- Résumé – (American) CV (Curriculum vitae).
- Reverse shot – shooting the scene from the opposite angle of the one just done to see the other side of the action.
- Rhubarb – background conversation that will be heard only as murmur. (Careful – sometimes you can hear the words!)
- Rim – backlight giving halo effect.
- Roll camera – request from first assistant director to have camera running and ready.

- Rough cut – first assembled complete cut of film.
- Running order – order that scenes will be shot.
- Rushes – the printed takes of the previous day's shoot. (*See* dailies)
- Sausage – little sandbag used for actor to feel where to stand for shot.
- Save the red – turn off red light, shooting suspended.
- Screen test – audition on film.
- Script supervisor – head of continuity department. Works with the director and liaises with the editor, records all changes to script, everything camera does, set-up, prints and timings.
- Second – second assistant director.
- Second unit – crew with second unit director shooting exteriors, action or pick-up shots – usually without dialogue but occasionally on green screen work, etc.
- Set dresser – person who decorates the set.
- Set-up – (1) camera's position, lens info, f-stops, filters, etc., (2) composition of shot.
- The Seventh Art – cinema.
- SFX – (1) special effects, (2) sound effects (theatre).
- Shooting ratio – ratio of film shot to finished film appearing on screen.
- Shooting script – final approved script.
- Sides – script pages for work being covered each day, often printed in small format.
- Sight-line – imaginary line from actor to whatever or whoever is being looked at.
- Signalling – acting term for overtly showing what you feel.
- Single – one person in camera frame.
- Slate – clapperboard.
- SNAFU (American) – situation normal: all f***ed up: general chaos reigns.
- Soft focus – shot slightly out of focus, sometimes on purpose.
- Sound mixer – person in charge of all sound recording and mixing.
- Sound reloading – sound mixer needs to 'reload' to continue recording.
- Sound speed/running – sound mixer confirms sound is ready for shooting to commence.
- Sound stage – studio soundproofed enough to shoot sound. (Not always true!)
- Smoke – smoke used on sets is supposedly non-allergic.
- Sparks – electricians.
- Special effects – effects done during shooting, e.g. explosions.
- SpFx – special effects as written on call sheets.

- Spiking the lens (American) – looking straight into the lens.
- Stand by – get ready to shoot or to come to set.
- Stand-in – person who stands in for actor during set-up.
- Static shot – camera does not move.
- Steadicam – camera strapped to operator with steadying apparatus absorbing shocks and movements for a smooth hand-held shot.
- Stills – photographs taken by the stills photographer who records the making of the film mainly for publicity department.
- Storyboard – shot by shot cartoon-like pictures done by an artist to aid director.
- Strawberry filter – not a real take. Camera won't turn over.
- Stunt double – person who looks like actor from a distance and does the stunts.
- Subtext – thoughts running under the line of dialogue.
- Swing-gang – section of art department who put up and take down set.
- Take it down (acting) – make the reactions subtler.
- Takes – as many attempts as it takes to get the particular shot right.
- The talent (American) – the actors.
- Telephoto lens – allows you to shoot from a great distance.
- Ten by eight – a publicity photo (as in 10 inches by 8 inches), usually black and white.
- The money – bankable star who ensures funding for the film or the provider of the money!
- Third – third assistant director.
- Three-shot – shot of three people in frame.
- Three-way – actors' dressing room, one of three on a mobile trailer.
- Tight – a tight frame encloses the subject with very little extra space around it.
- Tilt – to pivot camera up or down.
- T mark – mark in shape of T for actor to stand on to be in focus.
- Tracking shot – (1) camera on dolly moves along a set of tracks, (2) lateral movement of camera.
- Tracks – like a railway track for camera to move along.
- Trailer – (1) Winnebago: luxurious caravan for leading actor parked near set (preferred by stars to dressing rooms) or used by all actors and departments on location, (2) selection of shots put together to advertise film.
- Transition – acting terminology for the movement from beat to beat.
- Travelling shot – any shot where camera is moving, like a crane or tracking shot.

- Treatment – abridged script used to sell the movie idea; longer than synopsis.
- Turn over – command from first assistant for camera and sound to run.
- Turnaround – a completed film moving from one production company to another.
- Turning over – rolling: response from camera or sound departments that they are ready for action.
- Two-shot – shot of two people in frame.
- Undercranking – the film runs at a slower speed so that action appears faster, e.g. chases. (Hearkens back to when film was turned (cranked) by hand.)
- Upstage – (1) direction to move back away from camera, (2) to pull the other actor's gaze away from the camera, your own face away from camera, or the eye of the audience away from the foreground action.
- VFX – visual effects.
- Visual effects – computer-generated effects put on the film in post-production.
- Voice-over – a dialogue track which runs over the visuals and is not spoken in vision.
- You're on the wrong set – moving on to the next location.
- Walk on – background artist given particular business to do. Actor with small non-speaking role.
- Wardrobe – costume department.
- Wardrobe mistress/master – person in charge of costume department.
- Wide shot – camera shot that takes in width of scene.
- Wild lines – dialogue, atmosphere or sounds recorded off-camera.
- Wrangler – animal handler. (Sometimes used of children's chaperones!)
- Wrap – the end, either of the day's filming or the whole shoot.
- WS – wide shot.
- Zoom – changing distance of field of vision with adjustable lens without changing camera position.

HELPFUL BOOKS ETC.

Aitken, Maria, *Style: Acting in High Comedy* 1996 (Applause) – terrific for this style.

Alexander, F. Matthias, *The Alexander Technique* 1969 (Thames and Hudson) – writings on his technique for eliminating unnecessary tensions.

Andrew, Geoff, *Directors A-Z* 1999 (Prion) – useful guide to 250 film directors.

Berry, Cicely, *The Actor and the Text* 1987 (Virgin Books) – classic work, invaluable for Shakespeare but also for acting with any text.

Boorman, John, *Money into Light* 1985 (Faber & Faber) – not an acting book but fascinating and gruelling account of raising money for *The Emerald Forest*.

Caine, Michael, *Acting in Film* 1990 (Applause) – highly personal but helpful book on his film acting techniques.

Chekhov, Michael, *To the Actor* 1953 (Harper & Row) – classic acting text, 'psychological gesture' work.

Contacts (The Spotlight) – an annual which lists everything and everyone for the British actor: agents, casting agents, photographic repro services, show reel services, etc.

Davy, Charles, *Footnotes to the Film* 1938 (Lovat Dickson) – out of print. Great essay by Robert Donat.

Dunmore, Simon, *An Actor's Guide to Getting Work* 2001 (Papermac) – auditioning hints.

Feldenkrais, Moshe, *Awareness Through Movement* 1972 (Arkana) – exercises for mind and body awareness.

Finburgh, Nina, *Some Do's and Don'ts of Sight Reading* 1992 (Maverick Press) – a slim but excellent tutorial.

Goldman, William, *Adventures in the Screen Trade* 1983 (Abacus) – acerbic insider's lowdown on Hollywood.

Gordon, Mel, *The Stanislavsky Technique: Russia* 1987 (Applause) – good overall view of all the variants of the exercises.

Hagen, Uta, *Respect for Acting* 1973 (Collier Macmillan) – classic acting text, excellent on emotional 'triggers'.

Halliwell's Film & Video Guide yearly (HarperCollins).

Halliwell's Who's Who in the Movies yearly (HarperCollins).

Hirsch, Foster, *Acting Hollywood Style* 1991 (Abrams/AFI Press) – overview critique of Hollywood acting – great pictures.

Hobbs, William, *Fight Direction for Stage and Screen* 1995 (A & C Black) – interesting practical book on fight scenes.

Horwitz, Betty, *Communication Apprehension* 2002 (Singular) – a highly technical/scientific look at stage fright. Can be helpful to pin down the beast.

Houseman, Barbara, *Finding Your Voice* 2002 (Nick Hern Books) – up-to-date, clear, practical help with voice work.

Jones, Chris, and Jolliffe, Genevieve, *The Guerilla Film Makers Handbook* 2000 (Continuum) – for small-budget movie makers, technical info. Gripping case studies of low-budget movies.

Lecoq, Jacques, *The Moving Body* 2000 (Methuen) – legendary French teacher working with masks and physical theatre.

McCallion, Michael, *The Voice Book* 1988 (Faber & Faber) – good sound voice book.

MacDonald, Glynn, *Alexander Technique* 2002 (Element) – book from a top practitioner.

Meisner, Sanford, *On Acting* 1987 (Vintage) – a little hard to follow, but stimulating. (The Actors Centre, London, offers excellent classes on the Meisner technique.)

Newlove, Jean, *Laban for Actors and Dancers* 1993 (Nick Hern Books) – thorough book on Rudolph Laban's work.

Oxenford, Lyn, *Playing Period Plays* 1957 (J Garnett Miller) – primarily directed at amateurs but excellent reference books for period manners.

Pinter, Harold, *Collected Screenplays* 2000 (Faber & Faber) – 3 volumes of source material.

Rodriguez, Robert, *Rebel without a Crew* 1996 (Faber & Faber) – making a movie with no money.

Salt, Chrys, *Make Acting Work* 2001 (Methuen) – informative work-getting guide.

Stanislavski, Constantin, *Creating a Role* 1961 (Eyre Methuen) – all Stanislavski's books are worth reading, but this is probably the most help to the screen actor.

Time Out Film Guide yearly (Penguin)

Young, Jeff, *Kazan on Kazan* 1999 (Faber & Faber) – interviews with the legendary film director. Perceptive about acting.

In The Actor's Studio Bravo TV, shown in UK on Performance channel. Elucidating interviews with film actors.

SOME USEFUL ADDRESSES

The Actors Centre (London) 1a Tower Street, London WC2H 9NP Tel. 020 7240 3940. Email: act@actorscentre.co.uk

The North-East Actors Centre 1st Floor, 1 Black Swan Court, Westgate Road, Newcastle-upon-Tyne NE1 1SG Tel. 0191 221 0158

The Northern Actors Centre 30 St Margaret's Chambers, 5 Newton Street, Manchester M1 1HL Tel. 0161 236 0041

Amazon Books www.amazon.co.uk (books and films for sale – quick arrival)

British Film Institute 21 Stephen Street, London W1T 1LN Tel. 020 7255 1444. Email: library@bfi.org.uk www.bfi.org.uk/nft

British Register for Alternative Practice (feldenkrais, t'ai chi, etc.) www.brap.co.uk

British Voice Association at the Institute of Laryngology and Otology, 330 Gray's Inn Road, London WC1X 8DA www.british-voice-association.com Email: bva@dircon.co.uk

Equity Guild House, Upper St Martin's Lane, London WC2H 9EG Tel. 0207 379 6000 www.equity.org.uk

Feldenkrais Guild UK www.feldenkrais.co.uk

Internet Movie Database www.IMDb.com

John Bell and Croyden (chemists) 50 Wigmore Street, London W1 (for steamers)

Offstage Theatre Bookshop (scripts and accent teaching tapes) 37 Chalk Farm Road, London NW1 8AJ Tel. 020 7485 4996. Email: offstage@btinternet.com

Samuel French Ltd (scripts & tapes) 52 Fitzroy Street, London W1T 5JR Tel. 020 7255 4300 www.samuel-french-london.co.uk Email: theatre@samuelfrench-london.co.uk

Screen Actors Guild (American) www.sag.org

The Society of Teachers of the Alexander Technique www.stat.org.uk

The Spotlight (publishes *Contacts*) 7 Leicester Place, London WC2H 7RJ Tel. 020 7437 7631. www.spotlightcd.com Email: info@spotlightcd.com

Women in Film & Television 6 Langley Street, London WC2H 9JA Tel. 0207 240 4875 www.wftv.org.uk

Paul J. Underwood (Traditional Chinese medicine, t'ai chi, etc.) Tel. 020 8341 2456 www.seven-stars.demon.co.uk

Finally, my own website can be found at www.melchurcher.com

FILMS LISTED AND GREAT PERFORMANCES

Here are all the films mentioned in the book. I also include a non-definitive personal list (marked with asterisks) of particularly great performances from different genres and periods. This started out three times this long! Details of all these films, cast and crew, can be checked out at www.IMDb.com – lots of them will turn up on television or at the National Film Theatre and many have been re-released.

A.I. Artificial Intelligence (2001) (d. Steven Spielberg)
Accident (1967) (d. Joseph Losey)
**The African Queen* (1951) (d. John Huston) – Humphrey Bogart, Katherine Hepburn
Alfie (1966) (d. Lewis Gilbert)
Ali (2001) (d. Michael Mann)
Alien (1979) (d. Ridley Scott)
**All About Eve* (1950) (d. Joseph L. Mankiewicz) – Bette Davis
**American Beauty* (1999) (d. Sam Mendes) – Kevin Spacey
American Pie (1999) (d. Paul Weitz)
Anna and the King (1999) (d. Andy Tennant)
Annie Hall (1977) (d. Woody Allen)
The Apartment (1960) (d. Billy Wilder)
Apocalypse Now (1979) (d. Francis Ford Coppola)
Around the World in Eighty Days (1956) (d. Michael Anderson, Kevin McClory)
**Babette's Feast* (1987) (d. Gabriel Axel) – Stéphane Audran
Backdraft (1991) (d. Ron Howard)
**Bad Day at Black Rock* (1955) (d. John Sturges) – Spencer Tracy, Robert Ryan, Ernest Borgnine
The Band Wagon (1953) (d.Vincente Minnelli)
Barbarella (1967) (d. Roger Vadim)
Barry Lyndon (1975) (d. Stanley Kubrick)
Batman (1989) (d. Tim Burton)
**A Beautiful Mind* (2001) (d. Ron Howard) – Russell Crowe
Betrayal (1982) (d. David Jones)
The Big Sleep (1946) (d. Howard Hawks)
Billy Elliot (2000) (d. Stephen Daldry)

Black Hawk Down (2001) (d. Ridley Scott)

The Blair Witch Project (1999) (d. Daniel Myrick, Eduardo Sánchez)

The Blue Angel (1930) (d. Josef von Sternberg) – Marlene Dietrich

Bonnie and Clyde (1967) (d. Arthur Penn)

Bridget Jones's Diary (2001) (d. Sharon Maguire)

Brief Encounter (1945) (d. David Lean) – Celia Johnson, Trevor Howard

Bringing Out the Dead (1999) (d. Martin Scorsese)

Broken Blossoms (1919) (d. DW Griffith) – Lillian Gish, Richard Barthelmess

Butch Cassidy and the Sundance Kid (1969) (d. George Roy Hill)

Casablanca (1942) (d. Michael Curtiz) – Humphrey Bogart, Ingrid Bergman, Peter Lorre, Claude Rains et al.

Cenere (1916) (d. Arturo Ambrosio)

The Chain (1984) (d. Jack Gold)

Charlotte Gray (2001) (d. Gillian Armstrong)

Citizen Kane (1941) (d. Orson Welles)

Cleopatra (1963) (d. Joseph L Mankiewicz)

Cool Hand Luke (1967) (d. Stuart Rosenberg) – Paul Newman, George Kennedy

The Count of Monte Cristo (2002) (d. Kevin Reynolds)

Crimes of the Heart (1986) (d. Bruce Beresford) – ensemble

Cromwell (1970) (d. Ken Hughes)

Crouching Tiger, Hidden Dragon (2000) (d. Ang Lee) – Chow Yun Fat, Michelle Yeoh, Zhang Ziyi et al.

Dangerous Liaisons (1988) (d. Stephen Frears)

Das Experiment (2001) (d. Oliver Hirschbiegel)

Day for Night (*La Nuit Américaine*) (1973) (d. François Truffaut)

Death in Venice (1971) (d. Luchino Visconti) – Dirk Bogarde

The Deer Hunter (1978) (d. Michael Cimino)

The Dish (2000) (d. Rob Sitch)

La Dolce Vita (1959) (d. Federico Fellini) – Marcello Mastroianni

Don't Look Now (1973) (d. Nicolas Roeg) – Donald Sutherland, Julie Christie

East of Eden (1955) (d. Elia Kazan) – Julie Harris, James Dean, Raymond Massey, Jo Van Fleet

Elizabeth (1998) (d. Shekhar Kapur) – Cate Blanchett

The Emerald Forest (1985) (d. John Boorman)

The English Patient (1996) (d. Anthony Minghella)

Enigma (2001) (d. Michael Apted)

The Fifth Element (1997) (d. Luc Besson)

The Final Curtain (2002) (d. Patrick Harkins)

First Wives Club (1996) (d. Hugh Wilson)

Four Weddings and a Funeral (1994) (d. Mike Newell)

*Frankenstein (1931) and *The Bride of Frankenstein* (1935) (d. James Whale) – Boris Karloff

The French Connection (1971) (d. William Friedkin)

*The Full Monty (1997) (d. Peter Cattaneo) – ensemble

*Glengarry Glen Ross (1992) (d. James Foley) – ensemble

The Go-Between (1970) (d. Joseph Losey)

*The Godfather (1972) (d. Francis Ford Coppola) – Marlon Brando

*The Godfather Part II (1974) (d. Francis Ford Coppola) – Al Pacino, Robert De Niro

*Goodbye Mr Chips (1939) (d. Sam Wood) – Robert Donat

*Gosford Park (2001) (d. Robert Altman) – ensemble

*La Grande Illusion (1937) (d. Jean Renoir) – Jean Gabin, Erich von Stroheim

Hamlet (1996) (d. Kenneth Branagh)

Heaven's Gate (1980) (d. Michael Cimino)

*High Noon (1952) (d. Fred Zinnemann) – Gary Cooper

*Hobson's Choice (1954) (d. David Lean) – Charles Laughton

The Hole (2001) (d. Nick Hamm)

The Hunt for Red October (1990) (d. John McTiernan)

*The Hustler (1961) (d. Robert Rossen) – Paul Newman, George C Scott

I Dreamed of Africa (1999) (d. Hugh Hudson)

Ice Cold in Alex (1958) (d. J Lee-Thompson)

If... (1968) (d. Lindsay Anderson)

The Importance of Being Earnest (2002) (d. Oliver Parker)

*In the Bedroom (2001) (d. Todd Field) – Sissy Spacek, Tom Wilkinson

Intolerance (1916) (d. DW Griffith)

*Iris (2001) (d. Richard Eyre) – Judi Dench, Jim Broadbent

*Ivan the Terrible (1942/6) (d. Sergei Eisenstein) – Nikolai Cherkassov

Jackie Brown (1997) (d. Quentin Tarantino)

*Je Rentre à la Maison (Vou Para Casa) (2001) (d. Manuel de Oliviera) – Michel Piccoli

*Jules et Jim (1961) (d. François Truffaut) – Jeanne Moreau

Kind Hearts and Coronets (1949) (d. Robert Hamer)

*Klute (1971) (d. Alan J Pakula) – Jane Fonda, Donald Sutherland

Lara Croft: Tomb Raider (2001) (d. Simon West)

*Last Orders (2001) (d. Fred Schepisi) – ensemble

The Lawless Heart (2001) (d. Tom Hunsinger and Neil Hunter)

*Lawrence of Arabia (1962) (d. David Lean) – Peter O'Toole

Legionnaire (1998) (d. Peter MacDonald)

*The Life and Death of Colonel Blimp (1943) (d. Michael Powell) – Roger Livesey, Anton Walbrook

The Loneliness of the Long Distance Runner (1962) (d. Tony Richardson)

Looking for Richard (1996) (d. Al Pacino)

The Madness of King George (1994) (d. Nicholas Hytner) – Nigel Hawthorne

The Man in the Iron Mask (1998) (d. Randall Wallace)

The Man Who Wasn't There (2001) (d. Joel Coen) – Billy Bob Thornton, Frances McDormand

Manhunter (1986) (d. Michael Mann)

El Mariachi (1992) (d. Robert Rodriguez)

*M*A*S*H* (1970) (d. Robert Altman) – Elliott Gould, Donald Sutherland, Robert Duvall

Midnight Cowboy (1969) (d. John Schlesinger) – John Voight, Dustin Hoffman

Miss Julie (1950) (d. Alf Sjöberg)/(1999) (d. Mike Figgis)

Monsoon Wedding (2001) (d. Mira Nair) – Naseeruddin Shah, Tilotama Shome et al.

Moulin Rouge (2001) (d. Baz Luhrmann)

Mrs Brown (1997) (d. John Madden)

Much Ado About Nothing (1993) (d. Kenneth Branagh)

Mulholland Dr. (2001) (d. David Lynch)

Network (1976) (d. Sidney Lumet) – Peter Finch, William Holden

Neverland (2003) (d. Marc Forster)

Nikita (1990) (d. Luc Besson)

Nine to Five (1980) (d. Colin Higgins)

No Man's Land (2001) (d. Danis Tanovic)

Nosferatu (1922) (d. FW Murnau) – Max Schreck

The Odd Couple (1968) (d. Gene Saks)

Odd Man Out (1947) (d. Carol Reed) – James Mason

On the Waterfront (1954) (d. Elia Kazan) – Marlon Brando, Eva Marie Saint, Rod Steiger, Karl Malden, Lee J Cobb

One Flew Over the Cuckoo's Nest (1975) (d. Milos Forman) – Jack Nicholson

102 Dalmatians (2000) (d. Kevin Lima)

Pandora's Box (1929) (d. GW Pabst) – Louise Brooks

Paris, Texas (1984) (d. Wim Wenders) – Harry Dean Stanton, Nastassja Kinski

Pauline and Paulette (2001) (d. Lieven Debrauwer) – Dora van Groen

Persona (1966) (d. Ingmar Bergman) – Liv Ullmann, Bibi Andersson

Le Petit Soldat (1968) (d. Jean-Luc Godard)

Philadelphia Story (1940) (d. George Cukor) – Katherine Hepburn, Cary Grant, James Stewart

La Pianiste (2001) (d. Michael Haneke)

Plan 9 from Outer Space (1958) (d. Edward D Wood Jnr)

Pleasantville (1998) (d. Gary Ross)

*The Producers (1968) (d. Mel Brooks) – Zero Mostel, Gene Wilder

Psycho (1960) (d. Alfred Hitchcock)

Pulp Fiction (1994) (d. Quentin Tarantino)

*Queen Christina (1933) (d. Rouben Mamoulian) – Greta Garbo

*Raging Bull (1980) (d. Martin Scorsese) – Robert De Niro

*Rashomon (1951) (d. Akira Kurosawa) – Toshiro Mifune

Rear Window (1954) (d. Alfred Hitchcock)

**The Remains of the Day* (1993) (d. James Ivory) – Anthony Hopkins,
    Emma Thompson

Reservoir Dogs (1991) (d. Quentin Tarantino)

Restoration (1996) (d. Michael Hoffman)

Richard III (1955) (d. Laurence Oliver)/(1995) (d. Richard Loncraine)

Ridicule (1996) (d. Patrice Leconte)

Ripley's Game (2002) (d. Liliana Cavani)

Robin Hood: Prince of Thieves (1991) (d. Kevin Reynolds)

Romeo & Juliet/William Shakespeare's Romeo & Juliet (1968) (d. Franco
    Zeffirelli)/(1996) (d. Baz Luhrmann)

The Royal Tenenbaums (2001) (d. Wes Anderson)

Run Lola Run/Lola Rennt (1998) (d. Tom Tykwer)

Saturday Night Fever (1977) (d. John Badham)

Secret Passage (2002) (d. Ademir Kenovic)

Serpico (1973) (d. Sidney Lumet)

*The Servant (1963) (d. Joseph Losey) – Dirk Bogarde, James Fox et
    al.

Seven Years in Tibet (1997) (d. Jean-Jacques Annaud)

**The Seventh Seal (Det Sjunde Inseglet)* (1957) (d. Ingmar Bergman) – Max
    von Sydow, Bengt Ekerot, Gunnar Bjornstrand

Shakespeare in Love (1998) (d. John Madden)

The Shining (1980) (d. Stanley Kubrick)

The Shipping News (2001) (d. Lasse Hallström)

Shrek (2001) (d. Andrew Adamson, Vicky Jenson)

The Silence of the Lambs (1990) (d. Jonathan Demme)

Singin' in the Rain (1953) (d. Gene Kelly)

Snatch (2000) (d. Guy Ritchie)

*Some Like it Hot (1959) (d. Billy Wilder) – Marilyn Monroe, Jack
    Lemmon, Tony Curtis

The Son's Room (2001) (d. Nanni Moretti)

*A Star is Born (1954) (d. George Cukor) – Judy Garland, James Mason

Star Trek: First Contact (1996) (d. Jonathan Frakes)

*A Streetcar Named Desire (1961) (d. Elia Kazan) – Marlon Brando, Vivien Leigh, Kim Hunter

Sunset Boulevard (1950) (d. Billy Wilder)

*Sweet Smell of Success (1957) (d. Alexander Mackendrick) – Tony Curtis, Burt Lancaster

The Talented Mr Ripley (1999) (d. Anthony Minghella)

The Tempest (1980) (d. Derek Jarman)/ *Prospero's Books* (1991) (d. Peter Greenaway)

Thelma & Louise (1991) (d. Ridley Scott)

*The Third Man (1949) (d. Carol Reed) – Orson Welles

The 39 Steps (1935) (d. Alfred Hitchcock)

Timecode (2000) (d. Mike Figgis)

Tous les Matins du Monde (1992) (d. Alain Corneau)

*Training Day (2001) (d. Antoine Fuqua) – Denzel Washington

Trapeze (1956) (d. Carol Reed)

*Truly, Madly, Deeply (1990) (Anthony Minghella) – Juliet Stevenson, Alan Rickman

*Tunes of Glory (1960) (d. Ronald Neame) – Alec Guinness, John Mills

*12 Angry Men (1957) (d. Sidney Lumet) – Henry Fonda et al.

28 Days Later (2002) (d. Danny Boyle)

*Under the Sand (Sous le Sable) (2000) (d. François Ozon) – Charlotte Rampling

*The Unforgiven (1992) (d. Clint Eastwood) – Clint Eastwood, Gene Hackman, Richard Harris

The Usual Suspects (1995) (d. Bryan Singer)

Vanilla Sky (2001) (d. Cameron Crowe)

Victory (1940) (d. John Cromwell)/ (1995) (d. Mark Peploe)

La Ville est Tranquille (2000) (d. Robert Guédiguian)

Wag the Dog (1997) (d. Barry Levinson)

The War of the Roses (1989) (d. Danny DeVito)

West Side Story (1961) (d. Robert Wise, Jerome Robbins)

*Who's Afraid of Virginia Woolf? (1966) (d. Mike Nichols) – Elizabeth Taylor, Richard Burton

The Wicker Man (1973) (d. Robin Hardy)

X-Men 2 (2003) (d. Bryan Singer)

INDEX